D1611954

Applied Law in the Behavioral Health Professions

PETER LANG
New York • Washington, D.C./Baltimore • Bern
Frankfurt am Main • Berlin • Brussels • Vienna • Oxford

Andrew B. Israel

Applied Law in the Behavioral Health Professions

A Textbook for Social Workers, Counselors, and Psychologists

PETER LANG
New York • Washington, D.C./Baltimore • Bern
Frankfurt am Main • Berlin • Brussels • Vienna • Oxford

Library of Congress Cataloging-in-Publication Data

Israel, Andrew B.
Applied law in the behavioral health professions: a textbook
for social workers, counselors, and psychologists / Andrew B. Israel.
p. cm.
Includes bibliographical references and index.
1. Mental health personnel—Legal status, laws, etc.—United States.
2. Mental health laws—United States—Decision making.
3. Law and ethics. I. Title.
KF2910.P75 I87 344.73'044—dc21 2002022498
ISBN 0-8204-5722-1

Die Deutsche Bibliothek-CIP-Einheitsaufnahme

Israel, Andrew B.:
Applied law in the behavioral health professions: a textbook
for social workers, counselors, and psychologists / Andrew B. Israel.
–New York; Washington, D.C./Baltimore; Bern;
Frankfurt am Main; Berlin; Brussels; Vienna; Oxford: Lang.
ISBN 0-8204-5722-1

Cover design by Joni Holst
Cover art, "Justice and Health," by Martín Montoya, Tecolote, New Mexico

The paper in this book meets the guidelines for permanence and durability
of the Committee on Production Guidelines for Book Longevity
of the Council of Library Resources.

Printed in the United States of America

For Joseph Y. Israel

Table of Contents

Preface

The behavioral health professions are more alike than they are different. Although distinguished by unique jargon, knowledge bases, and historical traditions, they are united in the aim of assisting clients with problems that often cannot be categorized within the confines of one professional discipline. The comparatively recent tendency to treat clients through multidisciplinary team approaches is one reflection of this fact.

These points notwithstanding, professional textbooks and treatises tend to be discipline specific. Moreover, practitioners searching through such tracts often have a hard time finding practical legal and ethical guidance that helps them to resolve practice dilemmas involving clients and co-workers. When such guidance is offered, it is often presented in the context of standards unique to one profession. As a result, common practice dilemmas that may be shared by social workers, counselors, psychologists, physicians, and nurses often appear to have different "answers," depending on which professional code of ethics or law treatise one consults. This approach is archaic and inefficient.

In response to a significant problem, this book approaches professional choices from a unified perspective that views decision making as an orderly process sharing essential characteristics in all of the behavioral health professions. More than that, it invites the reader to interpret professional issues from a communitarian, rather than individualistic perspective. With these issues in mind, the system for addressing professional dilemmas is useful for practitioners and students in the behavioral health professions. The book is intended as a textbook for law and ethics courses in multiple disciplines and a reference manual for practicing social workers, counselors, and psychologists; the vignettes and case examples included use scenarios culled from these professions. Additionally, ethical standards cited in the book emphasize the *National Association of Social Workers Code of Ethics* (the NASW Code), the *National Board for Certified Counselors, Inc. Code of Ethics* (the NBCC Code), and the *American Psychological Association Ethical Principles of Psychologists and Code of Conduct* (the APA Code). Provisions from the aforementioned professional codes are reprinted with the permission of each board.

Note About Terminology

The phrase *behavioral health professions* is meant generally to convey occupations whose primary aim is to enhance the mental health and social functioning of clients and patients through direct services; these professions include social work, counseling, and psychology, among others. Professionals trained in these disciplines often provide additional support services to their clients and to the public in general that advance basic survival needs. These include, among other things, welfare and public assistance, child welfare investigations, probation services, community organizing, and social program research, development, and administration. Where described here, these forms of support are referred to cumulatively as *human services*.

Note About Vignettes and Case Examples

This book includes three brief vignettes and 27 case examples that demonstrate application of a decision making system for behavioral health professionals. Although several of the scenarios are inspired by actual events of national significance, the characters described in them are entirely fictitious and not intended to portray any real person, alive or deceased.

1

Introduction to Law Based Decision Making in the Behavioral Health Professions

Tools Necessary for Effective Decision Making

Why present a book on *applied law* and *decision making*? Behavioral health professionals and students alike understand that making practice decisions involves a consideration of legal, ethical, moral, regional, cultural, and personal factors that influence practice. The decision maker consulting these various reference sources for guidance is faced with the problem of choosing an appropriate legal or ethical principle, or perhaps a more subjective consideration, based on its apparent applicability to the problem at hand. Even worse, the decision maker consulting law treatises is likely to find broad, technical surveys of legislation and court decisions that offer little help in the resolution of everyday practice problems.

Applied law means law that is usable and applicable to the solving of everyday practice problems in the behavioral health professions. Law that is simply explained and practical to apply is more likely to be used by the decision maker as a primary source of reference in addressing common practice dilemmas.

Consider, for example, the case of a child protective service worker investigating the possibility of medical neglect within a Hispanic family in northern New Mexico. The professional fears that a child is being denied appropriate conventional medical treatment for asthma in favor of a faith based remedy that employs the use of *curanderos* and herbal therapy (Applewhite, 1995; Harris, 1998; Keegan, 1996; Turner, 1996). Is this a ground for removing the child from the home? In order to address this question, the professional may consider legal principles (including the law governing the professional's responsibility to protect vulnerable children), ethical standards (the right of the family to make its own choices concerning health care), regional and cultural standards (the long-standing acceptability of traditional forms of medical treatment within some communities), and personal standards (for example, how the professional's own ideology views the treatment provided to this child).

The decision maker considering the preceding problem may look to a number of reference sources, including law and ethics textbooks, professional ethical codes, and agency policies, in order to make a choice about what action to take. The professional will quickly discover that a variety of scholarly textbooks and manuals exist on the market today, with each tending to focus singularly on the subjects of "law" and "ethics" as separate disciplines. Moreover, the professional may find a significant amount of overlap or even contradiction among each of the principles presented in these reference sources. At this point, the professional may be overwhelmed both by the contradictory answers sometimes suggested by these textbooks and by their failure to address the "big picture."

In reality, making a decision concerning the above dilemma depends on the professional's ability to integrate and apply legal, ethical, cultural, and regional considerations in a specific order that maximizes the likelihood that both the professional's and client's obligations and interests are addressed fully and simultaneously. This book presents a strategy for doing just that.

Organization of This Book

This book surveys basic legal principles governing practice decisions in the behavioral health professions. More than that, however, it presents the subjects of law and ethics not as separate disciplines, but rather as related and interdependent, with each one having a role in guiding professionals to make effective and sensitive practice decisions. Toward that end, this book invites practitioners and students to consider the legal and ethical aspects of professional practice in a ranked order, and introduces a *decision making framework* whose primary aim is to assist them to address practice dilemmas in a structured and unified way.

In addition to surveying legal principles that affect practice, the decision making framework and supporting materials teach a law based strategy for reaching informed practice decisions in a regional and cultural context. This diversity model uses illustrative practice examples highlighting work with the Hispanic and Native American populations of New Mexico. The reason for this emphasis lies in the special usefulness of New Mexico and its populations in illuminating the interplay between law, ethics, and cultural context. New Mexico, with its unique diversity of cultural traditions stemming from centuries-old Native American, Hispanic, and Anglo-American influences, represents an ideal model for the communitarian emphasis stressed here. New Mexico has become the first "minority-majority" state in the U.S., with the Hispanic population reaching approximately 42 percent of the total, and the combined minority population, including Hispanic, Native

American, and African American groups exceeding 50 percent (Bureau of the Census Staff, 2001). With cultural traditions predating Columbus, the state's 1912 constitution included protections, primarily to Spanish speakers, that have encouraged the preservation of some of these traditions. Indeed, New Mexico now leads the nation with the highest percentage—28 percent—of Spanish speakers (Bureau of the Census Staff, 2001). Moreover, New Mexico contains rural and urban centers whose diverse populations increasingly represent a microcosm of the U.S. in the twenty-first century.

With the preceding points in mind, the decision making framework presented is applicable for use in a variety of practice contexts and with a diversity of client populations. Additionally, although the readings emphasize social work, counseling, and psychology practice, the framework is easily adaptable for use in practice within any of the behavioral health professions. For this reason, appropriate provisions from the codes of ethics of several such professions are presented.

The materials and case examples included in this book are intended to assist practitioners and students to accomplish the four goals described below.

Goal 1: To Develop a Strategy for Making Effective Professional Practice Decisions. As noted, this book will introduce a decision making framework that invites practitioners and students to make practice decisions based on an ordered consideration of both legal and ethical standards. Construction of the framework is described in chapter 2, and a summary of the framework itself is provided in the appendix. The terms *law* and *ethics* will be defined and their interrelationship explained in more detail later. In the meantime, in order to make the most effective use of the framework, it is important for practitioners and students to realize from the outset that both legal principles (e.g., informed consent and confidentiality) and ethical standards (e.g., the social worker's responsibility to seek social justice or the counselor's duty to be aware of stereotyping and discrimination) may impact the resolution of a practice dilemma. Additionally, it is important to note that the order in which one considers these principles will influence the decision. Various practice dilemmas to which the framework will be applied will illustrate this concept.

Goal 2: To Gain a Knowledge of Basic Legal Principles Associated With Common Behavioral Health Practice Areas. As a primary step in making practice decisions, behavioral health professionals must have a sense of the more overarching legal standards governing the rights and obligations conferred upon members of our society. These principles, such as those bestowed by the U.S. Constitution (e.g., the right to due process and equal protection) and by the legislative and common law of our states (e.g., informed consent and confidentiality), govern professional practice and impose specific responsibilities upon all providers offering services to the public. Developing an understanding of these principles is perhaps the single most important step in constructing an overall strategy for addressing everyday practice dilemmas, as will be demonstrated when the decision making framework is introduced and applied to specific problems. Furthermore, an understanding of basic legal principles governing practice serves to make the behavioral health professional more effective as a fully informed agent for social change.

The overarching legal principles that will be discussed (chapters 3 through 8) include

- The duty to practice reasonably competently
- Informed consent
- Identifying the primary client
- Special legal responsibilities of public agency professionals
- Constitutional principles influencing practice
- Confidentiality
- Completing a legal inventory
- Staying abreast of state, local, and agency responsibilities governing practice

Goal 3: To Understand the Purposes and Limitations of Professional Codes of Ethics. Professional codes of ethics have both their purposes and their limitations, as will be more fully explored later. The interrelationship between "law" and "ethics" is an area of confusion for practitioners and students alike, and this differentiation will be described subsequently. One of the commonest pitfalls for decision makers facing practice dilemmas is their tendency to attempt to apply professional codes of ethics without considering the impact of legal standards governing the same dilemmas. The result may be that the decision maker makes an ethically "correct" decision that violates the law. The decision making framework introduced here presents a system for avoiding this problem. The appropriate use of professional codes of ethics and subjective considerations in decision making will subsequently be more thoroughly addressed. Although primary emphasis in this book is placed upon the NASW Code, the NBCC Code, and the APA Code, the strategy suggested by the framework has applicability for behavioral health professionals bound by alternate codes.

Goal 4: To Make Decisions in a Cultural and Regional Context. Legal principles are important but not exclusive sources of information in making professional decisions. Sometimes their explanation requires a consideration of regional and cultural norms used to interpret these standards. For example, taking the *curandero* example again, the law may permit the use of alternative healing methods if practiced according to recognized religious practices in a jurisdiction. Furthermore, there are occasions—perhaps many of them—when neither the law nor any professional code of ethics will address a specific practice dilemma. In these instances, cultural and regional norms may attain a dominant role in guiding the decision maker to the most effective practice decision. In this book, numerous examples of the use of cultural and regional context in decision making are included to demonstrate the manner in which the framework treats the consideration of cultural and regional issues. For the reasons previously addressed, the diverse communities of New Mexico offer rich practice examples illustrating the framework's use. Although the practice scenarios selected focus on situations characteristic of northern New Mexico, and highlight practice with Hispanic and Native American communities, the essential strategy suggested by this diversity inspired approach has almost universal applicability.

2

Constructing a Law Based Framework for Professional Decision Making

Sources of Information for Making Professional Decisions

What sources of information are ordinarily relied upon in order to make practice decisions? To answer this question, consider the situation of a mental health provider in private practice offering counseling services to a variety of walk-in clients. Suppose further that one particular client has come in to seek the therapist's assistance in treating his depression. During a counseling session, he tells the therapist that he feels guilty over his commission of a bank robbery some 15 years earlier, which the police have never solved. How should this client's revelation guide the therapist's conduct with the client? What decisions are to be made from a professional standpoint relative to this client's treatment? The therapist's personal sense or morality, professional ideology, or religious conviction may suggest instinctively that this person is to be condemned, and that one is obliged morally to take some action to ensure his prosecution. Clinical training, however, may compel the therapist to continue to counsel this individual in order to ascertain what mental health issues, if any, may be driving this person's revelation. Moreover, pragmatic considerations may lead the therapist to believe that there is little the therapist can do realistically in the way of informing any authority without the client's additional cooperation; for example, the savvy therapist may reasonably fear that this client is going to deny the story as soon as it is revealed to the authorities.

Finding that personal feelings regarding this client are somewhat conflicting, the therapist might then seek guidance from a more formal authority. A natural next step would be to seek out the professional code of ethics governing the therapist's behavioral health field. In the case of a social worker, this would mean the NASW Code; a certified counselor, including a marriage and family therapist or other licensed mental health therapist, would likely examine the NBCC Code; a clinical psychologist would consult the APA Code.

Reviewing any of the above-mentioned codes for guidance in addressing this dilemma, one might reasonably reach the conclusion that one should maintain the confidentiality of all of the client's statements, unless there are "compelling professional reasons" (NASW Code, Ethical Standard 1.07), a need to prevent "clear and imminent danger to the client or others" (NBCC Code, Section B4), or it is necessary to "protect the client or others from harm" (APA Code, Ethical Standard 5.05a) making it necessary to reveal them. Perhaps the present situation might constitute such a "compelling" reason. Delving further into any of these codes, one might discover the professional obligation to help clients set their own personal goals and identify their own paths in life (NASW Code, Ethical Standard 1.02, governing self-determination), or the professional's burden to respect the integrity of the client (NBCC Code, Section B1), or the requirement that the professional promote the client's autonomy and self-determination (APA Code, Principle D). Perhaps any of these duties would conflict with some of the other choices the therapist has already considered.

Delving still further into an appropriate code, the therapist might uncover even more ethical standards suggesting still broader societal aims that the professional is admonished to promote, such as the commitment to seek social justice (NASW Code, Ethical Standard 6.01), the prevention of exploitation of individuals and groups (NASW Code, Ethical Standard 6.04), the protection of public confidence in professional practice (NBCC Code, Section A13), and the advancement of human welfare and alleviation of human suffering (APA Code, Principle F). All of these responsibilities certainly might have some application in the present scenario.

How can the professional resolve all of these seemingly inconsistent obligations? Reviewing any of the aforementioned codes will quickly reveal that the ethical responsibilities outlined in them *are not rank ordered*, so not much guidance is provided in the way of establishing which standards may take precedence. It therefore may be perplexing trying to get clear direction from an ethical code on the issue of what to do in this scenario.

Bewildered by the array of possible issues to be considered, the therapist in this example might decide to contact a personal or agency attorney in order to learn more about applicable legal responsibilities in the state in which the therapist practices. The therapist might learn from the attorney that a relevant licensing law requires professionals, including psychotherapists, social workers, counselors, psychologists, and other mental health providers to keep all of their clients' communications confidential, except when they represent a threat of future criminal activity. The attorney could reasonably suggest that, based on this law, the therapist's client is entitled to keep his past conduct a secret if he so chooses, and to hold the therapist to his bond of confidentiality. In other words, the attorney might advise, the therapist is obliged to take no action concerning this client's statements.

This may be the technically correct *legal* answer, but is it also the right practice decision? Put differently, is the answer consistent with the therapist's professional and therapeutic goals? The therapist's attorney might suggest that it is, because if one violates the law, jail is the outcome. Not swayed by this pragmatic argument, the therapist might express a sense of idealistic frustration to the attorney. The attorney is likely to respond that the law is based on good public policy, which suggests that this client, like all clients who seek out the help of behavioral health professionals, would be far less likely to have done so without the implicit understanding that what is told to the professional is private and must not go beyond the consultation room. Thus, the attorney might suggest, one should probably be thankful that the client has felt secure enough to seek a consultation, where now at least the opportunity exists to help him work on all of the issues that have inspired him to seek assistance. Without this law, in all probability the unfortunate story the client has revealed would never have been brought to the surface in the first place. Perhaps, the attorney might counsel, continued work with this client is possible in a manner that upholds the law, but that also fulfills some of the objectives of applicable professional ethical standards.

Does the "right" legal answer inevitably point the way toward the best practice decision in all professional dilemmas? As the preceding scenario suggests, and for reasons that will be more fully explored in the next section, assessing the legal impact of a professional dilemma at the very least leads to a more effective and efficient consideration of the range of practice options available to the decision maker. Therefore, the legal assessment is an inseparable part of thorough professional decision making.

A Law Based Strategy

Law Defined

As noted, the foregoing scenario suggests that seeking out the "right" legal answer to a practice dilemma eliminates some of the confusing alternatives one may face in attempting to resolve a frustrating problem. This is not an accident. Much law, including law governing professional practice, such as the requirement to maintain client confidentiality, is based on at least some sound, rational basis, and presumptively reflects the most basic, shared values of society. For that reason, the operating definition of *law* applied here is that it is a binding set of shared values within a community; the community being a city, state, nation, or other politically organized jurisdiction that unites people by language, culture, religion, tribe, or custom.

Defining law as a "set of shared values" serves the purpose of emphasizing the communitarian function (and not simply the "binding" nature) of law and law-making (Etzioni, 1998; Tam, 1998; Watson, 1999). *Communitarianism* in the present context is intended to convey the idea that the most effective and socially just practice decisions are the result of cooperative inquiry, a search for common values, and the recognition that all people within a community share some mutual responsibility for their collective good (Tam, 1998; Watson, 1999). Viewed in this light, no practice choice can be solely personal because each decision inevitably has consequences that affect others. Unlike the values represented by individual preferences and political ideologies, or articulated within particular professional codes of ethics, the values advanced by law are shared by most members of a community and not merely those espoused by one individual or profession. Understood in this way, the law can be regarded as a means to attaining the greatest good for the most members of a community. Additionally, this *utilitarian* interpretation of law, when incorporated into an overall decision making scheme, requires that all practice decisions be made at least to some extent from a communitywide, regional, or even global perspective, and not simply from a personal or professional one (Conry & Beck-Dudley, 1996; Murphy, 2001; Shaw, 1998).

What about law that does not reflect shared community values? A prime example of this problem may exist today in the Indian country of the Southwest, where tribes that have traditionally defined their communal values through an unwritten religious and social tradition are increasingly finding this "law" displaced by federal and even state legislation (see, for example, the Indian Civil Rights Act of 1968 (ICRA)). The assimilationist aim of this lawmaking may be a symptom of the overall trend toward the definition and codification of increasing numbers of laws by Congress and state legislatures. This tendency may well reflect a growing willingness by legislators to use lawmaking as a means of social control in a society that feels ever more out of control. Under the definition of law used in this book, a credible argument can be made that such law is invalid, unconstitutional, or both.

What, then, can be done about law that fails to reflect the shared values of a community? Behavioral health professionals keenly interested in the pursuit of social justice are well aware of the myriad examples of oppressive, racist, sexist, and ageist law that has existed historically. Often these examples are cited in support of the premise that all law is invalid, to be mistrusted, and inherently antithetical to the values of social change. This political ideology, perhaps best described as the "rebel without a clue" syndrome, is not pragmatic because it tends to ignore the vast body of law that is both useful in everyday practice and representative of the shared values of a community. Much of this law is very helpful in the daily resolution of professional practice dilemmas. The decision making framework presented here summarizes these basic principles.

As to laws that are unjust and oppressive, the framework offers a strategy for identifying and correcting them in a way that reinforces the ideal that law should be presumed valid—a presumption that is necessary in order for participation in a collective society. It also underscores the point that, so far as decision making in the behavioral health professions is concerned, individual choices should be considered in the context of the shared values of a community.

Law as the *First* Step in Decision Making

As suggested by the bank robber dilemma discussed earlier, basic legal standards such as the principle of confidentiality are helpful in the resolution of behavioral health practice problems. At what stage in the decision making process should they be considered and applied? The answer becomes apparent if the definition and purposes of law are borne in mind. These can be summarized in a way that offers three arguments for the proposition that a thorough review of applicable law should be the first step in making any practice decision in the behavioral health professions. Each is considered individually.

Communitarian/Utilitarian. The "right" legal answer to a problem, when considered *first*, best leads the professional to consider possible answers to a practice dilemma in a manner that ensures consideration of those values most important to the professional's community. This strategy maximizes the likelihood that the decision maker will make a choice that seems "right," while also increasing the benefit and limiting the likelihood of risk to all those immediately affected by the problem.

Effectiveness/Efficiency. The "right" legal answer to a problem, when considered first, best ensures that the decision maker will consider a range of options in a more expeditious manner. When a professional dilemma has a specific legal impact, applying the applicable legal principle minimizes the need for investigating and ranking other sources of information and narrows the gamut of practice choices available.

Practical. Following the law first is the best strategy for staying out of trouble. This may seem merely a banal consideration to anyone who has not had to contemplate the consequences of a professional decision while sitting in a jail cell. Nevertheless, in order for law to be binding, as that word is used in the definition of law presented here, there must be consequences for its infraction. These consequences, including civil litigation and criminal prosecution, are the focus of later discussion.

Additional support for the idea that behavioral health professionals should first consider the applicability of legal principles in evaluating practice dilemmas comes from professional ethical codes themselves. All such codes admonish professionals about the primacy of the law, although they sometimes do so in an oblique manner. For example, the NASW Code, in Ethical Standard 1.01 ("Commitment to Clients"), advises social workers that "specific legal obligations may on limited occasions supersede the loyalty owed clients." The APA Code, Ethical Standard 1.02, rather fancifully advises psychologists to resolve conflicts with the law "in a responsible manner," although use of the law for guidance is more formally mandated with respect to the issues of confidentiality (Ethical Standard 5.02) and the conduct of research (Ethical Standard 6.08). Professional counselors are urged by NBCC Code, Section A13, to "avoid behavior that is clearly in violation of accepted moral and legal standards." The indirect language used within these codes may be a reflection mainly of each profession's primary emphasis on defining a unique set of core values. In any event, all professional organizations, including those governing the major behavioral health disciplines, regard their members as owing an obligation to their communities that supersedes any consideration applicable solely to one profession.

Promotion of Diversity. Among the essential legal principles that are the focus of this book are the concepts of due process and equal protection, both emanating from the U.S. Constitution and each having a specific impact on the way behavioral health professionals make practice decisions. These principles protect the right of diverse people to be treated fairly despite their racial, gender, or religious differences. By elevating the examination of these constitutional protections to a place of first importance in decision making, the professional ensures that diversity considerations are raised to a preeminent role in the resolution of practice dilemmas instead of remaining merely an aspirational ideal to be reviewed along with other ethical and ideological factors.

In light of the preceding arguments, the decision making framework requires the user to consider the applicability of some basic legal principles governing behavioral health professionals and their clients *first* in considering any practice decision. Toward that end, the book outlines a series of essential principles, including the *duty to practice reasonably competently* (chapter 3), the *duty to seek informed consent* (chapter 4), the *duty to identify the primary client* (chapter 5), the *duty to treat clients and co-workers with due process and equal protection* (chapter 6), the *duty to maintain confidentiality* (chapter 7), and the *legal inventory* (chapter 8) that summarize the most important legal standards impacting behavioral health professionals in practice. Note that these six essential principles describe the basic elements of all professional relationships, and are virtually universal in their application within the U.S. For this reason, court decisions and legislation from a number of jurisdictions are used in this book to explain the scope of these principles. Readers, though, are discouraged from allowing the book to serve as a substitute for a thorough review and the seeking of legal advice concerning applicable standards in the state and community where they practice.

Step 2: Using Professional Codes of Ethics

As the "bank robber" example suggests, the law is an appropriate starting point for making practice decisions. In is not, however, the end of the story. In many practice dilemmas, one may find after reviewing applicable law that there is simply no clearly defined legal principle governing the outcome. In those situations, behavioral health professionals need to look to more discipline-specific sources for guidance in making practice decisions. Of these, the most often used are professional codes of ethics, such as the NASW Code, NBCC Code, and APA Code. Indeed, codes of ethics are often the first sources of enlightenment sought by decision makers concerned with resolving problems consistent with the ethical principles advanced within their own profession. Why is this *not* the most effective strategy for making professional decisions? In order to answer this question, it is necessary to explore the nature and uses of ethical codes.

Codes of ethics present sets of practice standards that direct the professional as to what is the "correct" thing to do in an area of practice. Here, the concept of professional ethics must be distinguished from the term *ethics* as it is used in common parlance: It frequently describes moral values or ideals that all members of society subscribe to in their personal lives. Unlike this general meaning, *professional ethics* describes a set of enforceable practice standards that support the values and aspirations existing within a profession. Just as the law binds the members of an entire community and enforces the shared values of that community, ethical codes are intended to promote the ideals of a single professional discipline. The law is enforceable against members of a community through civil or criminal remedies, and similarly ethical standards are enforceable through disciplinary action against the professional who has violated them.

To demonstrate the relationship between professional ethics and values, consider the APA Code's Principle C, which advocates "Professional and Scientific Responsibility." Among other things, this principle asserts the value that psychologists should "uphold professional standards of conduct." This ideal is enforced through a variety of binding guidelines, including Ethical Standard 1.04, which requires psychologists to practice "only within the boundaries of their competence." Similarly, promoting the "dignity and worth of the person" is an oft-stated social work value expressed in the NASW Code. Ethical Standards 1.09 and 2.07 support this goal by mandating that social workers refrain from sexual relationships with clients and employees under their supervision.

In contrast to legal standards, ethical principles vary from profession to profession because different disciplines advance differing internal goals. As an example, all attorneys share the professional value that authorizes them to take "whatever lawful and ethical measures are required to vindicate a client's cause," and to act "with zeal in advocacy upon the client's behalf" (American Bar Association Model Rules of Professional Conduct, 1983/2001, Rule 1.3, Comment 1). This value is enforced by an ethical standard requiring lawyers to represent their clients "with reasonable diligence and promptness" (American Bar Association Model Rules of Professional Conduct, 1983/2001, Rule 1.3). Correspondingly, social work values, as expressed in the NASW Code, Ethical Standard 6.01, articulate the somewhat broader aspiration that social workers have a duty to represent not only their clients' interests, but also the "general welfare of society." Does this difference in the expression of professional values between two disciplines mean, for example, that a public defender who defends a murder suspect vigorously and aggressively—knowing that the client is guilty—might be upholding legal values while contradicting the values of social workers? Can the practice decision to advocate strenuously for a client be the "right" practice decision for the lawyer but the "wrong" one for a social worker?

The answer to both of the above questions is possibly yes, and this point underscores one of the reasons why codes of ethics are not always helpful as the first step in a decision making strategy: Codes of ethics advance the interests of a particular profession without necessarily promoting all of the shared values of a community. Moreover, professional codes of ethics ordinarily are only enforceable through disciplinary action by an individual licensing body against one of its own members. In an age in which multidisciplinary practice strategies have been adopted for the provision of behavioral health and human services, including medical, psychological, child welfare, and even legal services, approaching a practice decision by primary reference to a professional code of ethics may work contrary to the interests both of the client and the professional.

One general weakness of ethical codes is that they often are better at articulating overarching and general aspirational ideals, i.e., values, than they are at setting standards that prescribe or proscribe particular behavior, i.e., ethics. Thus, the NASW Code broadly espouses the promotion of client well-being (Ethical Standard 1.01), the development of people, communities, and environments (Ethical Standard 6.01), and the advancement of client self-determination (Ethical Standard 1.02) as social work aspirations, but offers only a handful of enforceable standards in the pursuit of these ideals. For example, as already noted, the NASW Code proscribes conduct specifically in the case of social worker–client sexual relationships.

The reason for the limited number of enforceable standards may well be that the framers of the NASW Code have remained somewhat ambivalent about how they have envisioned the Code's purpose; they may have regarded the imposition of stricter standards as an undesirable substitute for flexibility. In the NASW Code, Ethical Standards 1.06 and 3.01, social workers are cautioned to avoid social relationships and conflicts of interest with clients and colleagues, but only where there is a "risk of harm or exploitation." The ambiguity inherent in this standard may serve the purpose of ensuring flexibility in its interpretation, but it also unfortunately makes it virtually meaningless in the absence of a situational, regional, cultural, or some other subjective context unique to every practice situation.

Another weakness of ethical codes in the analysis of practice decisions is that they often fail to rank order the standards contained in them. In other words, they identify specific duties, such as, in the case of the APA Code, guidelines relating to professional competence (Ethical Standard 1.04), informed consent (Ethical Standard 1.03), and confidentiality (Ethical Standard 5.02), and then offer little or no guidance as to which responsibility takes precedence. This tends to render codes of ethics problematic when they are used initially in the assessment of practice dilemmas. Instead, their usefulness is more evident as interpretive devices in the evaluation of professional responsibility. Specifically, they tend to advise the professional what to do to stay out of trouble.

A final general weakness of ethical codes is that they tend to emphasize practice goals all too often from a national, urban perspective, with precious little attention paid to regional variations and cultural issues in practice. For example, the NBCC Code, Section A2, cautions professional counselors that, when they accept employment with an agency or other employer, this acceptance implies agreement with institutional policies and principles. In the case of a counselor's employment with a national system of mental health providers, this would appear to encourage allegiance to professional practices that may not represent the best interests of persons within a particular community. Interestingly, the sole reference to diversity within the NBCC Code, contained in Section A12, advises counselors rather vaguely to have "awareness of the impact of stereotyping and unwarranted discrimination."

In light of the foregoing, what role should codes of ethics play in decision making by behavioral health professionals? To answer that question, it is appropriate to consider the relationship between the law and ethical codes. As already noted, the law represents a strategy to enforce the shared values of a community. Law governing the rights and responsibilities of behavioral health professionals often relies upon standards enunciated in professional ethical codes to describe the parameters of practice. Thus, legislatures enacting licensing statutes and courts interpreting the legal duties to be imposed on social workers, counselors, and psychologists, among other professionals, often rely upon ethical codes in performing these functions. Additionally, principles described in ethical codes occasionally themselves become law when they the public embraces them. Consider, for example, the ethical prohibition against sexual relationships between psychotherapists and their clients. In fact, in a number of states this practice has been criminalized.

The preceding discussion should make it evident that law and ethics are interrelated, with each having a role in the interpretation of the other. Therefore, ethics textbooks that treat this subject as a discipline discrete from the law do a disservice to the reader. This is especially true when such textbooks offer "ethical dilemmas" and an accompanying analysis based solely upon applicable ethical standards. In reality, most practice dilemmas have both legal and ethical aspects, and both must be evaluated in order to address these problems competently.

To reiterate, ethical codes are useful in evaluating practice decisions in the context of overriding legal burdens that the decision maker should first seek to satisfy. They offer guidance by articulating values and imparting ethical standards relevant to professionals within an area of practice. Moreover, they are enforceable in the sense that professionals subject to them face disciplinary sanctions for their infraction. For all of the reasons discussed in this section, they are most appropriately considered only after a consideration of applicable law has been completed. For that reason, the decision making framework introduced in this book urges that ethical principles be applied as a *second step* in the analysis of any practice decision. Two brief vignettes follow; these scenarios demonstrate typical ways in which an ordered consideration of law and ethics in decision making can be conducted.

Vignette 1: The Bigoted Client. Paula Mackey is a clinical social worker providing mental health services at a public clinic in a small, rural community in northern New Mexico. At the beginning of a counseling session, a Hispanic client makes disparaging remarks about Anglo clients, suggesting also that he believes they receive preferential treatment at the clinic and that this fact has influenced the amount of his progress with Paula, an Anglo therapist. Upset about the tenor of this discussion, Paula elects to review it with her supervisor, who suggests that Paula discuss it openly with her client at the next session, attempt to correct his mistaken impression, address directly his racism, and if all else fails, consider transferring the client to another therapist. The practice decisions Paula must make include the manner in which she discusses this issue with her client and his course of action at the next therapy session.

Consulting her code of ethics (in this case, the NASW Code), Paula ascertains that social workers have a responsibility to promote social justice (Ethical Standard 6.01), a guideline that might inspire Paula to take the stance that racism in all its forms must here, as everywhere, be confronted as it arises. Additionally, Paula uncovers Ethical Standard 1.02, which suggests social workers have a responsibility to honor their clients' right to self-determination, a rule suggesting Paula should ascertain the client's expectations concerning therapy and then attempt to honor them.

Consulting relevant law, Paula believes that constitutional principles, including *equal protection* and *due process*, may have application in this dilemma, specifically insofar as they suggest that neither the client's ethnicity nor the content of the client's speech should be used by a public employee as the basis for any official action involving the client.

Following the decision making framework, Paula elects to apply these general legal principles first, which leads her to choose not to modify the general course of her work with the client; instead of confronting the client with his racism, Paula elects to continue to explore the mental health aspects of the client's statements, consistent with those legal and ethical standards that may offer additional guidance in this area.

Vignette 2: The Coffee Shop. A licensed professional counselor observes a client in a local coffee shop in a small, rural town in which both the counselor and the client live and work. The client invites the counselor to have a cup of coffee with him at the small restaurant that serves as the "watering hole" for the town's population. What should the counselor do?

The counselor recognizes no law that specifically forbids this type of socializing. Indeed, several legal principles, including one governing conflicts of interest, seem to support it. Persuaded that a review of applicable ethical standards would help interpret the law, the counselor uncovers NBCC Code Sections A8, A9, B9, which warn licensees to avoid dual relationships that may harm or impair professional judgment. Whether there is actually such a risk in this scenario may depend in some measure on the cultural and regional traditions of the people in the town in which the counselor lives and works. Therefore, the counselor in this scenario would be wise to consider the application of this ethical standard in the cultural context of the community in which the counselor resides. (It is interesting to note that a psychologist facing the same situation as this counselor would get a bit more ethical latitude from the APA Code, Ethical Standard 1.17, which openly invites psychologists to recognize that in many communities, "it may not be feasible or reasonable . . . to avoid social . . . contacts with . . . clients.")

Step 3: Investigating Regional and Cultural Context and Personal and Ideological Beliefs

Vignette 2 suggests plainly that some legal and ethical standards are sufficiently general as to require some degree of subjective interpretation. Thus, a review of contextual issues, including regional and cultural factors, personal ideological considerations, and other subjective factors that assist in the interpretation of ethical standards, needs to be included during the consideration of practice dilemmas. This third step in decision making is an important component of the framework presented here. Another vignette underscores the importance of this step.

Vignette 3: The Dream Catcher. Fred Darrow, an Anglo clinical psychologist, is engaged in therapy with a Navajo client in Farmington, New Mexico. Upon the completion of services, the client offers Fred a *dream catcher* made of bird feathers as a symbol of the mutual shared association that the two have enjoyed. He makes an additional gift to Fred of artwork he has completed that arguably has at least some monetary value. Fred's practice decisions involve his handling of the gifts and his communications to the client regarding the gifts.

Following the framework, Fred explores the law applicable in this scenario, examining regional interpretations of the basic principles that apply both in his and his client's communities. Fred concludes that the law requires that he avoid conflicts of interest that threaten the integrity of the professional relationship. This principle also suggests that Fred is obliged to use independent judgment to support the client's therapeutic progress both before and after services have been formally completed.

Fred is inspired to review the APA Code in order to evaluate whether its principles support his initial legal analysis. Reviewing applicable ethical standards, Fred is particularly interested in determining whether it is ethical in any circumstance to accept gifts from a client. During this review, he encounters APA Ethical Standard 1.17, which sets forth guidelines concerning multiple relationships. Specifically, the standard suggests that social entanglements that might impair independent judgment are to be avoided, but also seems to offer some leeway to psychologists practicing in rural areas. As was the situation in case example 2, this ethical standard's ambiguity renders it virtually meaningless without a thorough review of community and cultural norms governing the scenario. This point is further supported by the APA's Ethical Standard 1.08, which requires psychologists to respect human differences and engage in culturally competent practice.

Consistent with the framework, Fred next proceeds to review the cultural context of the gifts conferred by his client, with a specific emphasis on evaluating the risk of harm or exploitation inherent in this interaction. Such a review naturally requires that Fred be versed in the cultural meaning of the transaction, including both before and after the initiation of services. The review might acquaint Fred with the cultural and spiritual meanings conferred by gift-giving and sharing in general within American Indian communities, and might further suggest to him that it might be more harmful to the client to reject these gifts than to accept them (Brucker & Perry, 1998). The framework's cultural component assists in the interpretation of legal and ethical standards that impact the dilemma. The answer suggested by this approach, namely that the therapist acts appropriately if he accepts the gifts, is consistent both with cultural competence and clinically advisable practice (Brucker & Perry, 1998).

In addition to considering cultural and regional norms, Fred might be likely to integrate his own clinical training and ideological perspectives in his resolution of the practice dilemma. Consistent with the communitarian stance, this consideration is most usefully undertaken only after the decision maker has objectively explored the cultural context of the client's gifts. This strategy is appropriate in the resolution of other practice dilemmas that require the decision maker to interpret legal and ethical standards.

Step Four: Doing What Is Possible to Do

A final concept incorporated within the framework is the issue of practicality, or *pragmatism*. To demonstrate how this principle applies in the resolution of practice dilemmas, reconsider vignette 2, "The Coffee Shop." As already noted, applicable legal and ethical standards require at least some subjective assessment of whether there is a risk of harm or exploitation to the client, or the further danger that the professional's judgment will be impaired if the professional has coffee with him. As previously discussed, this assessment requires some consideration of cultural expectations.

Missing from the above analysis is the point that, especially in a small town, it may simply be impractical to avoid patronizing a business establishment (including, for example, a coffee shop that is frequented by almost all of the town's residents) when the price of such avoidance is the forgoing of one's morning coffee. Aside from this somewhat frivolous example of pragmatism in decision making, the consideration of practicality is of more pressing importance to behavioral health and human service administrators acutely concerned with the daily economic, social, and administrative impact of their decisions. In other words, the "right" decision in practice may realistically hinge on how much money there is in an agency's budget.

In the final analysis, the "correct" professional practice decision may rest not just on the legal, ethical, cultural, regional, and personal considerations specifically governing a situation, but also on a consideration of what is doable or attainable in the real world. Unfortunately for decision makers looking for practical guidance, pragmatism as an ideal is not ordinarily addressed within professional codes of ethics. Nor, for that matter, is the concept generally embraced by professions expressly concerned with the advancement of social justice, such as social work, even though its unspoken role in the everyday consideration of practice dilemmas is undeniable.

Is pragmatism consistent with the ideals of the behavioral health professions? Does it comply with the framework's consideration of cultural context? The answer to both questions is yes (Joas, 1993; Shalin, 1986; Tamanaha, 1999; Topper, 2000). First, pragmatism aids in the evaluation of legal and ethical standards that require some subjective interpretation; additionally, it assists in the identification of laws and ethical standards that are overarching or unfair. Second, pragmatism and the promotion of cultural diversity are interrelated in the sense that it is eminently practical to serve clients and design behavioral health and human services that meet the needs and expectations of most members of a community. For these reasons, a consideration of pragmatic concerns is a specific part of the framework presented here. It represents the fourth and last component of this framework.

The Decision Making Framework Summarized

The decision making framework can be summarized in four essential steps:

- Step One: All behavioral health and human service practice dilemmas should be presumed to have potential legal and ethical implications. Attempt to address a practice dilemma by considering—with the assistance of agency or personal counsel, if possible—the potential legal implications first. If there is a clear answer based on an applicable legal principle, apply the principle.
- Step Two: If no clear legal answer is generated, or if multiple answers are generated, apply an appropriate professional code governing the behavioral health practice discipline.
- Step Three: If the ethical code suggests several possible answers, attempt to resolve the dilemma by applying cultural, regional, and ideological considerations.
- Step Four: If all preceding steps fail to identify a clear answer, apply pragmatic considerations.

These steps represent an overall strategy for making practice decisions in the behavioral health professions. Because this framework relies upon a review of essential legal principles as the first and most important step, these principles will be discussed individually. The complete framework, together with a summary of legal principles, ethical standards, and interpretive notes, is included in the appendix.

3

The Duty to Practice Reasonably Competently

Overview of the Duty

Several essential legal principles govern the behavioral health professions. The duty to practice reasonably competently is to be discussed first. As with all of the legal principles discussed here, the duty to practice reasonably competently states a responsibility that lies at the heart of the relationship between all professionals and their clients. As the case examples will show, understanding the nature and scope of this duty assists the decision maker to resolve numerous professional dilemmas. Consistent with the strategy presented in the framework, the ability to identify instances in which this legal principle applies guides the professional to recognize the "big picture" in practice and diverts the alert decision maker from the often confusing application of conflicting subsidiary considerations, including broad ethical principles and subjective issues.

With regard to the duty to practice reasonably competently, there is much common ground between social work, counseling, psychology, and other allied behavioral health and human service professions. In terms of the essential duty of care owed to the client, professionals in each of these fields face a comparable standard because most of these disciplines offer analogous services, and their members often practice together in interdisciplinary teams in the areas of psychotherapy, school counseling, alcohol and substance abuse treatment, marriage and family therapy, child welfare, forensic assessment, educational testing, probation services, and many others.

The duty to practice reasonably competently is the most fundamental of the legal principles discussed here. In order to understand this concept, however, it is necessary to appreciate the nature and scope of the major behavioral health professions. This task is more imposing than might be expected. In fact, legislatures often have a difficult time defining them, and their elements as recognized in licensing laws vary significantly from state to state. For this reason, these laws do not necessarily provide a good overall definition of competent practice. Nevertheless, they offer an enlightening introduction to the problems associated with defining practice standards.

Legislative Definitions of Social Work

Of the behavioral health disciplines, social work has been the most notoriously difficult to define. As an example, the New Mexico legislature defines the practice of social work expansively as

> a professional service (that) emphasizes the use of specialized knowledge of social resources, social systems and human capabilities to effect change in human behavior, emotional responses and social conditions. (Social Work Practice Act, 1978/1999, §61-31-6(B))

The foregoing definition of social work is broad enough to include almost every professional service known to humankind, and is therefore not terribly helpful in assessing the basic nature of the relationship owed to all clients by social workers. Compare the above definition with the more limited, clinically based one adopted by the California legislature:

> The practice of clinical social work is defined as a service in which a special knowledge of social resources, human capabilities, and the part that unconscious motivation plays in determining behavior, is directed at helping people to achieve more adequate, satisfying, and productive social adjustments. (Clinical Social Workers, 1990/2002, §4996.9)

Unlike the New Mexico definition, which includes elements of psychotherapy, community organizing, administration, and research, the California definition suggests that the most essential definable aspect of social work, from the public perspective, is the practice of psychotherapy, or *clinical* social work. This definition paints social work as a profession similar to psychology, counseling, or psychiatric nursing. Given these wide variations in the public's perception of social work practice, not much can be gleaned from legislative definitions that explains the fundamental nature of the legal relationship between social worker and client.

Legislative Definitions of Psychology and Counseling

Psychology and professional counseling are more limited in their scope of practice and therefore more easily definable by legislatures. In a definition typical of many states, New Mexico describes psychology as

> the observation, description, evaluation, interpretation and modification of human behavior by the application of psychological principles. (Professional Psychologist Act, 1978/1999, §61-9-3(D))

Similarly, New Mexico's legislature defines counseling as

> the application of scientific principles and procedures in therapeutic counseling, guidance and human development. (Counseling and Therapy Practice Act, 1978/1999, §61-9A-3(J))

Counseling includes such diverse areas as

> professional art therapy, professional clinical mental health counseling, professional mental health counseling, independent mental health counseling, marriage and family therapy, alcohol abuse counseling, drug abuse counseling and alcohol and drug abuse counseling. (Counseling and Therapy Practice Act, 1978/1999, §61-9A-3(K))

Despite the more limited range of psychology and counseling, these definitions do not offer much in the way of guidance as to how to carry out these professional activities and what expectations to place on practitioners. In order to better understand these standards, it is useful to examine the courts' responses to this question. Indeed, courts grappling with the problem of defining the nature of the duty owed by professionals to their clients have often looked to *common law* for guidance (*Karen L. v. Dep't of Health and Soc. Svcs.,* 1998). Common law is a body of judicial opinions that cumulatively explain the rights and obligations of all members of society (*Smothers v. Gresham Transfer, Inc.,* 2001). Under the common law system, the law evolves as individual judges examine and apply prior court decisions in the consideration of new and ever-changing factual situations. This process relies on the rule of *precedent*, which requires judges to treat prior court decisions as entitled to respect. By examining common law, it is possible to ascertain first if there is any definable duty imposed on individuals within a given profession, and second, how this duty compares with the responsibilities imposed on all other behavioral health professionals.

In examining the duty required of professionals to their clients, the common law ordinarily looks to statutory standards explaining specifically the expectations placed on the professional (*Dunn v. Catholic Home Bureau for Dependent Children,* 1989). As pointed out above, this presents a difficult problem for judges when the statutory definitions of some professions—most notably social work—can be so vague and variable from state to state (*Horak v. Buris,* 1985; *Martino v. Family Serv. Agency,* 1982). Consequently, courts examining the question of social work responsibility have tended to apply a commonsense standard derived from the expectations imposed on other professionals, and in particular, psychologists. Generally speaking, a social worker, as any other professional, must engage in reasonable conduct (*Roe v. Catholic Charities,* 1992). What precisely is reasonable conduct? Simply put, it is an objective standard that includes engaging in behavior that is considered acceptable to the "reasonable" social worker *(Heinmiller v. Department of Health,* 1995). Similarly, psychologists and counselors are supposed to practice consistently with the expectations placed upon a reasonable member of either profession (*F. G. v. MacDonell,* 1997 (pastoral counselor); *Figueiredo-Torres v. Nickel,* 1991 (psychologist); *Jones v. Lurie,* 2000 (psychologist); *Miller v. Ratner,* 1997 (psychologist); *Sain v. Cedar Rapids Community Sch. Dist.,* 2001 (school counselor)).

Reasonableness can also be understood as a *fiduciary* responsibility imposed on social workers, counselors, psychologists, and physicians, among others. This means that when a trusting client voluntarily seeks the professional's services, and the professional agrees to provide them, the provider undertakes a duty to render the services honestly and faithfully (*Aufrichtig v. Lowell,* 1995; *Eckhardt v. Charter Hosp.,* 1997; *F.G. v. MacDonell,* 1997; *Horak v. Biris,* 1985; *Petrillo v. Syntex Labs., Inc.,* 1986). Specific fiduciary responsibilities may be created by state licensing laws, which, for example, may impose specific practice standards on clinical practitioners. They can also arise when unlicensed persons provide services to clients, which typically occurs when a client seeks specific advice, information, psychotherapy, or other assistance from a person who represents himself to the public as a "counselor" or "therapist."

How does one best ensure that one is behaving in a manner considered to be acceptable by the reasonable professional? The following list summarizes this range of conduct as evinced from a number of court decisions that have defined on a case-by-case basis the reasonable practice standard as it has been imposed on various behavioral health professionals:

- Practicing with reasonable *competence*; this includes practicing with the skill and care expected of a prudent practitioner engaged in the same kind of professional practice, with the same degree of training, in a similar community, and under similar circumstances (*Alejo v. City of Alhambra,* 1999 (social worker); *Figueiredo-Torres v. Nickel,* 1991 (psychologist); *Heinmiller v. Department of Health,* 1995 (social worker); *Naidu v. Laird,* 1988 (psychiatrist); *Roe v. Catholic Charities,* 1992 (social worker); *Sain v. Cedar Rapids Community Sch. Dist.,* 2001 (school counselor)).

Among other things, reasonably competent professional practice has been noted to include the following general aspects:

- Being licensed; this includes practice within the definition of the behavioral health service being offered and according to the licensing law of the state where one practices (*Dunn v. Catholic Home Bureau for Dependent Children,* 1989; *Horak v. Biris,* 1985);
- Having certification in the area of specialization one is practicing in (*State v. Louis,* 1994);
- Engaging in conduct reasonably calculated to help the client (*Roe v. Catholic Charities,* 1992);
- Engaging in appropriate personal conduct that supports the purposes of the professional relationship (*Figueiredo-Torres v. Nickel,* 1991);
- Avoiding conduct that might harm the client in a way that is *foreseeable* to the professional; this requires the professional to take into account the likelihood of injury to the client, and the burden to the professional—financial and otherwise—of guarding against it (*Roe v. Catholic Charities,* 1992);
- Avoiding conduct that may cause foreseeable harm to a member of the public other than the client (such as when the client's threat to commit a violent act against a third party is not acted upon) (*Hertog v. City of Seattle,* 1999 (probation counselor); *Naidu v. Laird,* 1988 (psychiatrist); *Perreira v. State,* 1989 (psychiatrist); *Tarasoff v. Regents of Univ. of Cal.,* 1976 (psychiatrist and psychologist)).

More specific aspects of reasonably competent practice include the following:

- Keeping abreast of professional developments and research in one's area of practice (*White v. North Carolina Bd. of Examiners of Practicing Psychologists,* 1990);
- Practicing according to the public rules and regulations in existence in the state where the professional practices (*Karen L. v. Dep't of Health and Soc. Svcs.,* 1998);
- Practicing within ethical standards (in most situations, this includes practice in conformance with the NASW Code, NBCC Code, or APA Code, as relevant) (*Deatherage v. Examining Bd. of Psychology,* 1997; *Doe v. Finch,* 1997);
- Making appropriate documentation in order to keep track of the client's progress and other continuing issues (*Valcin v. Public Health Trust,* 1984) (hospital);
- Honoring the policies and procedures of one's agency (*Karen L. v. Dep't of Health and Soc. Svcs.,* 1998);

- Obeying the principle of *informed consent* (see chapter 4) (*Modi v. West Virginia Bd. of Med.*, 1995);
- Obeying the principle of confidentiality (see chapter 7) (*Figueiredo-Torres v. Nickel,* 1991);
- Adequately assessing the client and investigating the factual substance of representations made to the professional (*Weaver v. Dep't of Soc. and Health Servs.*, 2001);
- Competent management of client privacy issues (see chapter 7) (*Eckhardt v. Charter Hosp.*, 1997);
- Competent management of the duty to report child and elder abuse, and other legal responsibilities imposed on behavioral health professionals by law (*Tarasoff v. Regents of Univ. of Cal.*, 1976; *Williams v. Coleman,* 1992);
- Cooperating and communicating with other professionals involved in the treatment process—a responsibility that would appear to mandate competence in multidisciplinary planning and coordination of services (*Alejo v. City of Alhambra,* 1999; *Bielaska v. Orley,* 2001; *In re Rebekah R.*, 1994);
- Maintaining appropriate professional boundaries with clients and avoiding inappropriate social or sexual relationships with clients (see chapter 5) (*Heinmiller v. Department of Health,* 1995; *Simmons v. United States,* 1986);
- Designing programs and services using suitable research and investigation (*In re McKnight,* 1990) (developmental disability treatment program);
- Administering programs and supervising employees with due attention paid to agency needs and the client population (*Duran v. Apodaca,* 1980; *Joseph A. v. New Mexico Dep't of Human Servs.*, 1983).

These obligations can be summarized as the *reasonable competence* standard, a doctrine that is summarized in the framework as Principle 1. Observe that the reasonable competence standard does not require perfection, nor does it imply that a behavioral health professional must obtain satisfactory results in all practice situations. Rather, practicing reasonably, as the courts have noted, means practicing with a regard for consequences that are foreseeable to the professional. This concept suggests that reasonable professionals must recognize their limits as individuals. They must also make practice decisions in the context of their standing as members of a professional community within one discipline and also as members of the larger community of allied behavioral health professionals. Conformance with this standard invariably is evaluated according to the practice expectations imposed on behavioral professionals within one community or region. Providing behavioral health and human services inevitably requires a mutual interaction between professional and client whose success depends on the cooperation and effort of both parties. Note also that the courts' interpretation of reasonable competence evolves over time as new judges consider this same standard in the context of changing factual scenarios.

As developments in technology identify new practice techniques and fresh ways (such as the Internet) to disseminate information, expectations imposed on the reasonable behavioral health professional will change as well, especially because the World Wide Web may tend to remove or lessen former regional boundaries. Considering the growing body of research suggesting the importance of incorporating diversity considerations into the practice repertoires of behavioral health professionals, it is inevitable that cultural competence will ultimately be considered a part of the reasonable competence standard.

In other words, one should not spend so much time attempting to memorize the above practice standards as to understand their letter and spirit. This is especially true when one considers the overlap among the behavioral health professions and the tendency of courts to evaluate practice standards on a case-by-case basis according to community standards. Despite this overlap, together with the occasional willingness of health agencies to use behavioral health professionals from various disciplines interchangeably to provide basic mental health services, courts have recognized differences among the professions based on variances in training and responsibilities (*Briscoe v. Prince George's County Health Dep't,* 1991). It is therefore useful to survey some of the unique elements of practice within each of the behavioral health professions—social work, counseling, and psychology—that courts have found to demonstrate the reasonable competence standard outlined above.

Elements of Reasonably Competent Social Work Practice

Courts note that social work is a profession by reason of the foundation of specialized knowledge and skills that are the result of classroom education and field training (*State v. Louis,* 1994). This being said, one is not a "social worker" merely by reason of providing services that social work may comprise, for example, performing psychosocial assessments, data collection, and research (*State v. Louis,* 1994). Consequently, one should describe one's self as a "social worker" only to the extent such a description is consistent with the specialized training one has received (*State v. Louis,* 1994).

What do courts regard as the skills within the specific range of competencies expected of social workers? Among other things, these include the gathering, reporting, and assessment of psychosocial information, the investigation of child abuse and neglect and the protection of children affected by such conduct (*Alejo v. City of Alhambra,* 1999), and individual, marriage, and family counseling (*Horak v. Biris,* 1985). Thus, social work and professional counseling have elements in common. Courts generally are not willing to recognize that social workers are competent to diagnose and treat mental illness or to perform clinical psychological examinations and evaluations for forensic purposes, unless, at the very least, they possess board certified clinical social work status with the additional specialized training that this status implies (*State v. Louis,* 1994).

In their use of an expansive definition of social work, some state legislatures may authorize social workers to practice in areas for which professional standards simply have not been defined. Thus, some states specifically certify social workers to engage in social welfare administration, to practice community organizing, to teach social work courses at the university level, and to conduct social research (see, for example, the New Mexico licensing statute cited earlier), even though courts encountering these practice specialities have noted the difficulty of ascertaining exactly what professional expectations should be imposed upon social workers practicing in these areas (*Horak v. Biris,* 1985). Even though no court may yet have identified practice standards in some of these social work specialties, it is possible for the prudent behavioral health professional to make an intelligent estimate, based on the reasonable competence standard. Indeed, understanding and applying the reasonable competence standard in assessing one's duties as a social worker is the most helpful first step in evaluating professional responsibilities owed to the client, regardless of one's specialty. For example, licensed social workers employed as human service agency administrators in northern New Mexico should estimate their responsibilities to clients and employees by evaluating the skills, training, and care normally expected of prudent program administrators within the same community.

Elements of Reasonably Competent Counseling

The responsibilities of counselors are both similar to and distinguishable from psychologists and social workers. Courts have been willing to impose upon marriage and family therapists, drug and alcohol rehabilitation specialists, school guidance counselors, probation officers, and even unlicensed treatment providers a duty to practice reasonably competently within the scope of their training and according to community standards (*F. G. v. MacDonell,* 1997; *Sain v. Cedar Rapids Community Sch. Dist.,* 2001).

Because counselors offer a wide variety of services, both informational and psychotherapeutic, the key to understanding the extent of any counselor's duty to a client lies in identifying how the parties define the terms of their professional relationship at the commencement of services. If counselor and client mutually agree for the client to receive information or therapy, then the professional has the duty to provide it responsibly. Thus, pastoral and school guidance counselors both form fiduciary relationships with their clients, even though the subject matter of their counseling may be starkly different. (*F. G. v. MacDonell,* 1997; *Sain v. Cedar Rapids Community Sch. Dist.,* 2001).

Counselors assume fiduciary roles in a manner that is similar to psychologists and clinical social workers. In such circumstances, their obligation to practice reasonably competently is comparable to the duty owed by these other mental health professionals. In other situations, however, the role of the counselor is more informational. Such is the case with school guidance counselors, for example. With respect to counselors who disseminate information, the duty to practice reasonably competently extends to the accurate communication of the information that the client has sought. In this sense, the counselor's responsibilities most resemble those of an attorney to a client. Thus, a high school guidance counselor has been held to practice incompetently by giving a college-bound student inaccurate information concerning the course requirements necessary to compete in intercollegiate sports (*Sain v. Cedar Rapids Community Sch. Dist.,* 2001).

With the advent of the Internet, a new market for the offering of clinical services has opened wide, and thus far it seems to have been tapped most extensively by professional counselors. With this in mind, the NBCC has adopted professional standards for Web counseling. Unfortunately, these standards do little to answer the questions that this new technology raises about the ability of Internet based counselors to practice reasonably competently as that standard is defined here. One of the most pressing of these questions is, by what *community* standards should a counselor's practice be judged, when the counselor and client may be separated by thousands of miles? Although as yet unanswered by courts, the likely response to this question is that counselors will be expected, as any other professionals would be, to conform their practice to those standards imposed within both the client's and their own home communities. In other words, the quality of counseling services is likely to be gauged according to regional expectations existing in the communities where both parties are physically situated.

Elements of Reasonably Competent Psychology Practice

Psychologists and other mental health providers bring special responsibilities to their professional relationships with clients. At the very least, reasonably competent practice means that psychologists must diagnose mental illness properly and apply appropriate treatment (*Zagaros v. Erickson,* 1997). Additionally, courts have noted that the psychotherapy relationship is inherently different from all other professional associations. Because of the intensity and emotional closeness of the professional bond between psychologist and client, the capacity for harm to the client is great if the relationship is mishandled. Therefore, the psychologist's personal conduct outside of the professional relationship is relevant in the assessment of professional responsibility, to the extent that it may impact the client's clinical progress. As examples, sexual and inappropriate social relationships with clients are considered malpractice, as is the maintenance of harmful dual relationships with clients, e.g., if a client is hired to work in the psychologist's office (*Overton v. Board of Examiners in Psychology,* 1996).

In addition to the responsibilities noted above, psychologists administer tests, perform psychological evaluations, conduct forensic examinations, and make recommendations in connection with involuntary commitment hearings. Unlike social workers and counselors, licensed psychologists practicing in hospital settings in some areas have attained the right to receive clinical and staff privileges identical to those of psychiatrists (*Reiff v. Northeast Fla. State Hosp.,* 1998). Moreover, psychologists have attained the limited right in New Mexico to prescribe medications (New Mexico Drug, Device and Cosmetic Act, 1978/2002). Sponsors of a bill to introduce similar privileges to California psychologists have suggested (thus far, unsuccessfully) that it would heighten the access of clients in rural and inner city areas to psychopharmacological treatment ("Editorial," 2000). It is plain, however, that extending the pharmacology option to psychologists is also likely to change the definition of reasonably competent practice for these professionals. Given the additional risk of harm to clients that may result from psychotropic medications, the responsibility of prescribing psychologists to protect their clients from foreseeable damage would appear to be heightened.

Consequences for Breach of the Duty to Practice Reasonably Competently

There are several consequences that may arise from a behavioral health professional's failure to practice within the parameters mandated by the reasonable competence standard. These consequences include civil liability, criminal prosecution, and disciplinary action by the licensee's professional board. The nature of each of these remedies will be discussed individually.

Civil Liability

Many of the cases cited earlier began as civil lawsuits seeking monetary damages against a professional accused of violating the duty to practice reasonably competently. As already noted, the duty itself is the result of common law principles developed over the course of time, in large measure the result of extensive litigation. An action alleging that a professional has breached the duty to practice reasonably competently often claims professional malpractice, a *tort*, or civil wrong, for which the victim is compensated through the award of financial relief. Tortious conduct is answerable ordinarily by rewarding the victim with compensatory and, occasionally, punitive damages intended to offset the impact of the harm caused by the misconduct, and, in the case of punitive damages, to punish the wrongdoer and deliver a message to the public regarding the nature of the wrongdoing. The nature and amount of damages awarded the victim ordinarily depend upon whether the malpractice was *negligent* (i.e., accidental), *reckless,* or, on occasion, *intentional.*

Liability, or legal responsibility for malpractice, may be imposed upon the professional and others directly or indirectly associated with the professional's misconduct. Thus, the professional responsible for malpractice may face *direct liability* for the behavior, meaning that the cost of the misconduct is imposed directly upon the responsible professional. Additionally, the professional's employer or agency may face *vicarious liability*, a concept predicated on the principle that an employer stands responsible for the misconduct committed by employees during the course of their employment. Finally, a professional's supervisor may be liable for *negligent supervision* when the supervisor has failed to oversee the professional in a manner consistent with the standards suggested by the duty to practice reasonably competently.

Of the behavioral health professions, courts have been most willing to impose liability on psychologists and professional counselors. This willingness can be attributed mainly to the rather concrete manner in which their professional responsibilities are defined by licensing legislation, and also, perhaps, because these professionals are often privately employed and carry liability insurance. Interestingly, the existence of financial resources available to pay malpractice judgments has itself been cited by courts as a ground for the imposition of liability (*Tarasoff v. Regents of Univ. of Cal.,* 1976).

In the case of social workers, courts have come to different conclusions about whether they should face such liability. Because social workers have until recently worked mainly for the government, courts generally have been reluctant to impose liability upon professionals performing traditional social work functions, such as child protective services. With the entrance of social workers into psychotherapy, courts have begun to examine social worker misconduct in a new light, with due regard for public safety issues caused by the increasing demand for clinical social work services.

Although the tort of social worker malpractice has been recognized by a number of courts (see, e.g., *Horak v. Biris,* 1985), judges have been hesitant to apply the doctrine except in cases in which, first, the duty of the social worker has been clearly or intentionally violated, and second, it has been found consistent with public policy to assess liability. For example, courts have been willing to impose civil liability in a number of cases involving social workers engaged in psychotherapy or counseling, invariably, as the courts have noted, because they have been satisfied with the relatively clear statutory, licensing, and ethical standards governing such social work specialities. Often, courts have analogized this kind of misconduct to psychologist or psychiatrist malpractice (*Horak v. Biris,* 1985). Furthermore, these cases have often involved a willful or deliberate commission of malpractice, such as sexual misconduct with a client, an impropriety so severe, with long-term harm so plainly foreseeable, as to leave the court with no doubt about whether any practice standard has been violated.

In other cases involving social workers in child welfare, courts remain disinclined to assess civil liability. Several reasons have been offered for this. First, courts have noted the difficulty inherent in identifying the boundaries of the professional relationship between the client and social worker offering child welfare services. Second, courts have also offered compelling public policy arguments militating against the imposition of civil damages on child welfare social workers and their protective service agencies. For example, courts examining cases involving social workers participating in child abuse investigations and foster placement have noted that imposing civil liability for reasonable mistakes made during the course of these proceedings would greatly burden already scant social work resources and force social workers to adopt a more defensive posture; this "fear of lawsuit" mentality could be expected to divert child protective service workers from their primary emphasis on the best interests of children (*Karen L. v. Dep't of Health and Soc. Svcs.,* 1998). Courts in such circumstances have tended to resist assigning civil liability in situations in which clear moral blameworthiness has not been demonstrated (*Karen L. v. Dep't of Health and Soc. Svcs.,* 1998).

In addition to lawsuits alleging civil liability for breach of the duty to practice reasonably competently, civil rights litigation is an available tool when a claim arises that a professional has violated the constitutional rights of a client. Under §1983 of the federal Civil Rights Act of 1871, money damages and other forms of relief are available to the victim of such misconduct. Unlike damage claims founded upon the professional's breach of a common law practice standard, the object of civil rights litigation is to seek compensation, and often to secure other forms of corrective relief, from actions taken by *government* agencies, officers, and employees. Thus, state and federal government professionals employed in mental health, child and adult protective services, forensic psychology, veterans affairs, and other areas of public sector practice must be aware not only of the basic duty to practice reasonably competently, but also their responsibilities and rights under the U.S. Constitution.

Behavioral health professionals frequently provide services to clients in the context of a contractual relationship either with an employer or directly with the client. In these instances, the professional not only has the duty to practice reasonably competently, but also has the additional responsibility to honor the terms of the contract. In situations in which this duty has been abrogated, civil litigation alleging breach of contract offers a remedy for the injured client or employer (*Chew v. Meyer,* 1987). Although a comprehensive discussion of contract law is beyond the scope of this book, it will suffice here to note that lawsuits alleging breach of contract must demonstrate that a contract has existed between the professional and the employer or client, that the professional has violated one or more terms of the contract, and that damages have resulted as a consequence (*Roe v. Catholic Charities,* 1992).

Criminal Responsibility

Violations of practice standards that vitally affect the public interest are punishable through the criminal justice system. Unlike tortious conduct, which most often involves negligent or reckless behavior with unintended but foreseeable consequences, criminal conduct almost always involves *intentional* violations of practice standards. Note, however, that some intentional conduct, such as sexual misconduct involving a client, may be simultaneously tortious and criminal. Unlike tortious behavior, most of which is defined in the common law, all criminal conduct must be specifically created by a legislative body and enacted as statutory law in order for it to be enforceable. Criminal prosecution is intended to serve as a deterrent strategy, first by punishing the wrongdoer for the violation of a public standard, and second, by alerting the public to the consequences resulting from the offense (*Grey v. Allstate Ins. Co.,* 2001).

Professional licensing legislation ordinarily contains provisions that encompass criminal sanctions for its violation; thus, breach of statutory provisions such as the duty to maintain confidentiality may have criminal consequences. It is therefore imperative for behavioral health professionals to be familiar with licensing law pertaining to them and the responsibilities imposed by it in the state where they practice.

In addition to criminal sanctions for the violation of licensing requirements, some states have criminalized other forms of professional misconduct that contravene important public standards. With respect to clinical social workers, counselors, and psychologists, the most important example is sexual misconduct. Some states define sexual contact between psychotherapists and their clients, even if it is consensual and performed up to a year after the termination of therapy, as criminal sexual penetration, a felony (see, e.g., Sexual Offenses, 1978/2001, §30-9-10). In explaining society's intolerance for sexual relations between psychotherapists and clients, courts have noted that an important aspect of the therapist-client alliance distinguishes it from virtually all other professional relationships: It is inherently more damaging to the client if it is exploited (*Elliott v. North Carolina Psychology Bd.,* 1997; *Horak v. Biris,* 1985; *Simmons v. United States,* 1986). Specifically, psychotherapy often involves the transference of feelings by the client to the therapist in a way that allows the therapist to assist the client in addressing them. Sexual relationships between the therapist and client distort this process and therefore render extraordinary—perhaps permanent—harm to the client (*Horak v. Biris,* 1985; *Simmons v. United States,* 1986). Considered in this light, states have regarded criminalization of this conduct as an appropriate deterrent strategy.

The duty to report suspected child abuse has traditionally been imposed on medical personnel, teachers, and social workers, among other health and human service professionals. In recent years, this duty has been expanded in some states to impose the same responsibility on all members of the public, with criminal sanctions for its violation. Despite the good intentions of this legislation, it may be the cause in some areas of an increase in anonymous reports of child abuse, a factor that may have been responsible for artificially inflated statistics related to child abuse reporting. Enforcement against members of the public seems questionable in light of the burden it places on untrained individuals to recognize the incidence of child abuse and neglect in all their myriad forms. Regardless of its enforceability against the general public, behavioral health professionals who violate the duty to report remain subject to criminal prosecution as well as civil actions by victims (*Williams v. Coleman,* 1992).

The use of a deterrent strategy has also been attempted in cases involving child welfare social workers. In 1996, two New Mexico social workers were indicted on felony charges that they had negligently permitted physical and sexual abuse to occur by mishandling the foster care placement of a 3-year-old child in the state's custody (Daniels, 1996). The theoretical basis for this prosecution was that the social workers had violated clear and unequivocal practice standards by not adequately monitoring the child's foster care placement. In this instance, the severity of the resulting harm to the client was extreme enough in the eyes of the prosecutors to warrant criminal prosecution. Ultimately, however, the dismissal, refiling, and final dismissal of the criminal charges were played out extensively in regional and national media (Daniels, 1997), with the result that the usefulness of the prosecution in deterring future social work misconduct has been called into question. In light of the extensive burden already imposed upon social work resources in most areas of the country, it is questionable whether the imposition of criminal liability for practice mistakes ultimately serves the purposes intended. Based on New Mexico's experience, a compelling argument can be made that the deterrent strategy advanced by criminal prosecution is best reserved for more deliberate and malicious conduct.

Disciplinary Action

Protection of the public is the most significant reason for requiring licensure of social workers, counselors, psychologists, and other behavioral health professionals (*Heinmiller v. Department of Health,* 1995). Professional licensing boards are granted authority under the laws of each state to regulate each discipline, certify professionals admitted to practice, and impose disciplinary measures for violations of licensing standards. Licensing boards ordinarily have broad legislative authority to establish practice standards consistent with the public interest. Within each professional discipline, these standards generally include requirements that the professional

- Practice consistently with the ethical code established within the discipline
- Be mentally fit to practice
- Practice reasonably competently
- Practice appropriately within the areas authorized by the license class

Both the extent of available disciplinary measures and the manner in which enforcement procedures are carried out vary extensively depending on the state and the profession. It is generally true, however, that licensing boards may refuse to license an applicant, or impose extreme forms of discipline upon a licensee, such as license suspension and revocation, to the extent that it is necessary to protect the public from substandard practice.

Licensing suspension and revocation often occur when a licensing board can demonstrate a threat to the public by way of the professional's demonstrable violation of one or more of the practice standards already mentioned. Clear negligence, criminal behavior, persistent substance abuse rendering the practitioner unfit to practice, and sexual misconduct involving clients or supervisees are all examples of violations important enough to warrant severe discipline.

Disciplinary proceedings instituted by licensing boards must follow administrative procedures governed by state law. The essential elements that must be demonstrated in a disciplinary proceeding are, first, the violation of a practice standard and, second, the threat of harm to the public caused by the violation. Often licensing boards procure the assistance of professionals familiar with practice standards to offer expert testimony interpreting each standard and the significance of its violation. Such testimony is most useful when the expert is able to describe the link between the licensee's violation and the basic duty to practice reasonably competently. Affording this insight ordinarily requires that the expert have familiarity with specific guidelines governing the licensee's specialty area and knowledge of practice standards in effect within the licensee's home community.

Using Reasonable Competence as a Vehicle to Make Professional Decisions: Case Examples

The elements of reasonable competence comprise the first of a series of fundamental legal principles useful in the resolution of a variety of practice dilemmas experienced by behavioral health professionals. To the extent that one can identify a dilemma as implicating the duty to practice reasonably competently, one has a useful tool to identify the choices available and to apply them in an expeditious manner. Several practice dilemmas follow in which the duty is identified and applied according to the decision making framework.

Case Example 1: Individual Therapy in Española, New Mexico

Donald Strom has been a licensed clinical psychologist in Newark, New Jersey, for the past 15 years. A recent transplant to New Mexico, he has opened a private practice in Española, New Mexico, a rural community in the northern part of the state whose population is largely Hispanic. Donald has chosen to practice in Española primarily on the basis of his review of national professional journals, some of which have suggested that community mental health centers have a spotty record nationally in the design and implementation of outpatient services for individuals and families in crisis. Donald fervently believes that his practice will cater to the needs of such persons. His mode of therapy, as honed over the course of his professional career, emphasizes the use of individual counseling and psychodynamic techniques that emphasize self-awareness, personal growth, and enhancement of self-esteem. Donald is aware of his newness to the community, and he believes that what he lacks in regional experience is more than made up for by his filling a critical gap in mental health services. His attitude is inspired in part by the APA Code's Principle F ("Social Responsibility"), which suggests that psychologists have a duty to make known to their community their particular knowledge and skills.

Donald enthusiastically embraces other ethical standards and professional values of clinical psychology, specifically with regard to the need to promote client well-being and self-determination (APA Code Principle D, "Respect for People's Rights and Dignity," and Principle E, "Concern for Others' Welfare"), and he believes that his practice methods are consistent with these standards. He is also aware, however, that the APA Code advises psychologists to "obtain the training, experience, consultation, or supervision necessary to ensure the (cultural) competence of their services" (Ethical Standard 1.08, "Human Differences"). Donald hopes to acquire this cultural competence as he engages in practice, but also believes that, in light of the demand for services, he has much to offer right away as an experienced therapist.

Shortly after the opening of his office in Española, Donald meets Mrs. Manzanares, a 63-year-old retired schoolteacher, who complains of sadness and "nerves," symptoms she attributes to her husband's alcoholism and her "family history" of depression. In addition, she is upset about her teenage grandson, who lives with her and has become increasingly angry and "out of control" in recent weeks. Mrs. Manzanares desperately wants help to deal with her situation. What decisions should Donald make about his intervention?

This case example suggests that Donald has adopted a practice methodology that he has applied successfully for some years. It also indicates, however, that Donald now seeks to introduce this methodology in a new community, and may be prepared to do so without the benefit of sufficient research into community norms and the cultural appropriateness of his techniques. He does this largely on the basis of his years of experience and confidence in his approach. Donald, perhaps, has already sought guidance from a code of ethics, and may have examined the ethical standards previously noted. Donald may feel somewhat conflicted when he attempts to apply the different ethical principles outlined here. As a result, he may offer his psychotherapeutic services to Mrs. Manzanares with the expectation that the exchange between client and therapist will serve as a cultural learning experience for both. What happens if Donald instead seeks assistance primarily from the legal principles outlined in the framework? If he does so, he may first consider the duty to practice reasonably competently.

In this case example, the duty to practice reasonably competently suggests specifically that Donald has the responsibility to practice as a reasonably competent clinical psychologist would in Española, New Mexico. This principle outlines a number of burdens that Donald has before implementing a practice strategy, all of which supersede the broad ethical considerations addressed in the example. First, it suggests that Donald must be familiar with his client's family background, cultural worldview, and relationship both to her family and her community in order to competently assess the client and determine the appropriateness of a practice intervention. Second, Donald has the obligation to be familiar with literature and research outlining practice strategies appropriate for populations living within northern New Mexico. In performing this research, Donald is likely to learn that individual psychotherapy is generally less successful with these populations than family counseling (Bean, Perry, & Bedell, 2001), a practice approach that Donald may be uncomfortable with and unprepared to provide. Nonetheless, the scholarly literature indicates that a psychodynamic approach may simply be wrong for this client.

If Donald applies the duty to practice reasonably competently first in his evaluation of practice choices, he must be prepared to offer reasonably competent services, emphasizing culturally appropriate practice techniques at the commencement of therapy. Even if a pressing need for services exists, and regardless of whether Donald's intentions are ethical and sincere, the duty to practice reasonably competently suggests that a practitioner who has not yet acquired the ability to provide these services simply should not offer them; nor should he provide a client with services she is not reasonably likely to benefit from. With this in mind, Donald must seek alternatives to his initial plan of action consistent both with this principle and the standards emphasized in the ethical code. This may even mean declining to treat Mrs. Manzanares and referring her for services that include family therapy.

Is the practice choice suggested by this discussion overly harsh? Specifically, how does it help Mrs. Manzaneres? The answer to both questions depends on whether the professional believes Mrs. Manzanares is better off being exposed to individual psychotherapy—even if it is not ideal for her needs—than to have no assistance at all. In this scenario, the duty to practice reasonably competently promotes the principle that the professional should "first do no harm." This canon is one of many that find more complete protection in the law than in ethical codes. (Were Donald to review more thoroughly the APA Code, he would in fact uncover a provision addressing this issue, Ethical Standard. 1.14, "Avoiding Harm"; its place alongside competing standards, together with its broad scope, makes it difficult to identify and apply as a first step in this scenario.)

With this case example in mind, the reader is invited to reevaluate vignettes 1, "The Bigoted Client," 2, "The Coffee Shop," and 3, "The Dream Catcher," in terms of the duty to practice reasonably competently.

Case Example 2: Addressing Attrition Among Native American College Students

Mary Vazquez, a certified, master's level counselor, provides guidance and counseling services at a public college in the Four Corners area of New Mexico. This region serves widely diverse communities in Northwestern New Mexico and Southeastern Colorado, including several Indian reservations. Mary is designing a program intervention that will address the problem of high attrition rates among nontraditional students at her college. She is particularly interested in addressing the needs of Native American students, who make up 40 percent of the total student body, a substantial increase over previous years. She is well aware that many of these students are the first in their families to attend college and may require additional support services to assist their adjustment to college life. Aware of her duty to practice as a reasonably competent counselor would in her community, Mary proceeds to study the problems experienced by Native Americans on college campuses. She locates research concerning the Spirit Lake Reservation in North Dakota suggesting, first, that intensive family support should be provided and, second, that basic college courses should be offered to the greatest extent possible on the reservation (Rousey & Longie, 2001). Mary decides to incorporate the results of her research in the design of a culturally appropriate program. She is uncertain, however, whether her college's administration will support any suggestion to offer additional college courses on Indian reservations within the college's catchment area. What steps must she be prepared to take before completing her program design and presenting it to her dean of students?

Both this and the previous case example examine the duty to practice reasonably competently; each focuses on the need to stay abreast of current scholarly literature and research, and to incorporate this information in the design and implementation of programs. In contrast to the situation in the previous case example, in this scenario Mary has researched attrition issues concerning Native students, and has come to certain conclusions that she has incorporated within her proposed program. What then, has Mary omitted? If she understands fully the duty to practice reasonably competently, then she also understands that keeping abreast of national research is one good step in program design. It is, however, only the first step. By incorporating the results of research concerning the Spirit Lake Reservation into her program design, Mary may have overextended the limits of this research in terms of its applicability to her client group. Without undertaking a local need assessment to ascertain the accuracy of these data, she runs the risk both of stereotyping her clients and designing her program incompetently. Indeed, reasonably competent practice means practice that is appropriate based on *community* standards. In the context of program design, it means remaining familiar with scholarly research, but at the same time taking appropriate steps to ascertain the relevance of this research to the community one practices in. In this instance, making an assumption about Native Americans in general, without testing the assumption on the basis of a community need assessment, violates the duty to practice reasonably competently. In this case example, competent practice may be regarded not simply as a legal principle, but also as a useful practice tool that mandates the appropriate consideration of diversity issues in professional decision making.

Case Example 3: The Licensee

Jade Melman, a recent graduate of a master's level program in social work, is anxious to put her newly acquired clinical skills to the test. As part of her graduate program, Jade has completed basic course work in clinical social work practice, psychopharmacology, human behavior in the social environment, and group work. Now licensed in New Mexico as a master social worker, but lacking any advanced clinical training or certification as a clinical social worker, she accepts a position as a psychotherapist at a community mental health center in a small, rural town in New Mexico. The center has been desperate to hire a therapist for some time in order to adequately address the mental health needs of the community. Jade will be practicing under the supervision of the licensed psychologist who oversees outpatient services at the center.

Having reviewed the law in New Mexico governing social work practice, Jade knows generally that clinical social workers certified within that specialty have the authority to diagnose and treat mental illness. She is uncertain, however, about the practice standards that apply to her situation.

The duty to practice reasonably competently suggests several responsibilities that Jade and her supervisor have with respect to the rendering of clinical services. First, Jade arguably does not meet the threshold amount of education, experience, and certification necessary to practice clinical social work competently, at least in the absence of supervision. If she proceeds to see clients without informing them of her training limitations and the extent of her supervision, then clients have the right to assume a level of qualification that should be expected from a trained clinical social worker with the degree of experience that Jade lacks.

In light of the duty to practice reasonably competently, what options do Jade and her supervisor have? For one thing, Jade can assist in the provision of services to her supervisor's clients, a most reasonable arrangement in terms of providing needed services to clients, offering necessary training to an apprentice clinical social worker, and reflecting the manner in which a reasonable therapist practicing in a rural area should be expected both to ensure the competence of the services offered and to provide needed treatment in an underserved area. This arrangement must be explained to clients at the commencement of services, so that they have a realistic appreciation of the professional duties respectively owed to them by Jade and her supervisor and can intelligently consent to receive services.

What exactly should be explained to clients? First, it should be made clear that services will be provided to the client under supervision; second, the nature of Jade's basic credentials; third, the supervisor's credentials; and finally, the nature of the supervision that will be provided to Jade. If this explanation is provided, then clients have a fairer understanding of what services they are receiving and the preparedness of the professionals offering to provide them. In this scenario, offering a clear explanation serves to identify the professional relationships between the client and each provider and the responsibilities expected of all. Jade can enjoy a professional relationship with each client, but from a legal perspective her duty to practice reasonably competently should be assessed according to the expectations imposed on one with her limited training.

What responsibility does Jane's supervisor have? Most importantly, with Jane's limited practice experience explained to clients, the supervisor must be prepared to assume primary authority for the responsible provision of clinical care to each client. Consistent with this responsibility, the supervisor must provide services that match those reasonably expected from one with advanced clinical training. If this is to be accomplished, the supervisor must ensure that Jade's treatment of each client conforms with the reasonable practices of psychotherapists in Jade's community. This responsibility makes the provision of appropriate supervision to Jade a vital duty.

Given the large geographical size of this rural community, the limited number of available services, and the number of other clinicians Jade's supervisor must oversee, it may well be reasonable to extend considerable latitude to Jade in the performance of her job functions, including intake, assessment, and clinical dialogue, provided that Jade's supervisor does not cede responsibility for the essential therapeutic environment until such time as Jade is reasonably competent to manage it.

The professional apprenticeship not only serves the needs of Jade and her supervisor, but also it is a typical way in which clinicians can achieve advanced training while honoring the duty to provide reasonably competent behavioral health care. It is an essential process in the field experience of virtually all clinical providers.

How does application of the duty to practice reasonably competently promote the quality of psychotherapeutic services rendered within a community? Most importantly, it offers a baseline level of protection to the client. This degree of protection may be lacking in some communities where the exigencies created by a lack of mental health resources may be interfering with the enforcement of this standard. As an example, in the Navajo Nation as many as 500 social workers may currently be offering basic mental health services to clients within a community consisting of 26,000 square miles. Of this number, only a handful have advanced clinical social work training and certification. Navajo leaders have become aware of this public health crisis and are forging relationships with professional schools to offer advanced clinical training sufficient to meet this critical need.

When providers understand the boundaries of their own professional competence and are able to communicate this information to clients, a more effective clinical dialogue is opened. This openness leads to more competent assessment, more effective treatment, and plainer expectations by the client. Indeed, defining these expectations appropriately may represent the single most important ingredient in any clinical intervention. The responsibility of a professional to communicate effectively concerning the potential benefits and hazards presented to the client seeking services describes yet another fundamental legal principle whose understanding can assist the decision maker to assess and resolve everyday practice dilemmas. This duty to seek informed consent is related to and interdependent with the duty to practice reasonably competently; it is discussed in more detail next.

4

The Duty to Seek Informed Consent

The duty to practice reasonably competently describes the essential responsibility of behavioral health professionals to render services consistently with the expectations imposed on them within a community. As already noted, a significant part of that duty includes communicating with the client in a manner that facilitates the assessment of the presenting problem, together with the professional's consideration and design of services that address the problem. The *duty to seek informed consent* describes the professional's responsibility to communicate enough information concerning the risks and benefits of the services offered by the professional to allow the client to make a reasoned decision to choose these services. The duty applies to all health and human service professionals, including physicians, attorneys, social workers, counselors, and psychologists.

Similarly to the duty to practice reasonably competently, the duty to seek informed consent actually takes effect even before the client seeks professional help. In this sense, informed consent is a prerequisite to the competent provision of any health service. Indeed, without obtaining it, the professional cannot provide services lawfully. In some circumstances—most notably surgery performed by medical doctors on involuntary patients—it may even be criminal for the professional to provide services to the client in the absence of informed consent (*Bee v. Greaves,* 1984; *Laskowitz v. Ciba Vision Corp.,* 1995). For this reason, responsibilities associated with the provision of informed consent by health professionals are sometimes defined by state legislation. With this in mind, behavioral health professionals should be familiar not only with the common law principles governing informed consent, but also with health and licensing codes in effect where they practice.

The doctrine of informed consent derives from a time-honored common law principle that emphasizes a client's or patient's right to determine the nature and scope of the professional services required, whether these services be in the area of medical treatment, legal assistance, psychological care, counseling, or social work. When a patient or client approaches the professional with a presenting problem, the duty to seek informed consent mandates that the professional assist the client to preserve his or her own right to choose voluntarily the nature and scope of the responsive intervention. Specifically, this means that professionals are obliged not only to describe the services they have to offer, but also to describe alternate means of treating the same problem, together with the risks and benefits presented by each approach. Some professionals may feel awkward doing this when they have confidence in a particular treatment modality or ideological perspective. Even so, it is imperative from the standpoint of protecting the client's basic right to make informed choices about professional services.

The requirement that professionals seek informed consent has been incorporated into numerous professional codes of ethics, including the NASW Code (Ethical Standard 1.03), NBCC Code (Section B8), and APA Code (Ethical Standard 4.02). However, especially in the NBCC provision, more stress is placed upon the requirement that the professional provide "information" to the client than on the need to obtain the client's "consent." The duty to seek informed consent is at first a *legal* principle, the application of which extends to relationships between all professionals and their clients, and whose coverage may be wider than some ethical codes would imply. Therefore, informed consent is one of several basic legal standards whose application in any practice dilemma should be identified first before the ethical guidelines unique to one profession are considered. Adopting this strategy will greatly help the decision maker address numerous practice dilemmas. Furthermore, it will help the practitioner make better practice decisions that advance important societal goals rather than focus on the often conflicting professional aspirations advocated within each behavioral health discipline.

Origins and Elements of the Common Law Duty to Seek Informed Consent

As a legal doctrine, informed consent was recognized initially by courts in the context of relationships between physicians and their patients. At the heart of informed consent is the idea that the patient seeking medical services alone has the right to weigh the risks associated with a particular treatment and then make an individual decision to accept or reject them (*Bee v. Greaves,* 1984; *Rasmussen v. Fleming,* 1987). In formulating the doctrine, courts have been primarily concerned with two different but related freedoms; the first of these is the patient's right to choose services freely. This right can only be secured by demanding full and accurate information from professionals (*Laskowitz v. Ciba Vision Corp.,* 1995; *Mohr v. Commonwealth,* 1995). Second is the right to be free to forgo treatment, a privilege that is often associated with the individual's right to privacy (*Bee v. Greaves,* 1984; *Rasmussen v. Fleming,* 1987). Courts have often described this right in terms of an individual's sense of bodily integrity: the liberty to control and care for one's own physical needs. This right is best preserved when the individual is solely responsible for making choices concerning medical treatment (*Bee v. Greaves,* 1984; *Rasmussen v. Fleming,* 1987).

The first freedom associated with informed consent—the right to choose services—long has been recognized in the case of individuals who seek out the assistance of professionals. The second freedom has been acknowledged in the case of persons against whom involuntary treatment is sought by the government or by treating physicians. This freedom has often been recognized in cases involving the right of nondangerous psychiatric patients and prison inmates to decline psychosurgery and forced administration of psychotropic medication (*Bee v. Greaves,* 1984; *Riggins v. Nevada,* 1992).

Behavioral health professionals concerned with the application of informed consent need to understand each freedom that the doctrine enforces because they will provide services both to clients who seek them out voluntarily and clients for whom services have been mandated, most often by a court (Regehr & Antle, 1997). Note however, that these freedoms are actually related. An individual's choice concerning health services can never be truly "voluntary" unless the individual has information concerning the risks of treatment and the existence of alternative strategies to address the problem (*Laskowitz v. Ciba Vision Corp.,* 1995).

The scope of informed consent has been expanded by courts to include the services rendered by a number of behavioral health professions, including social workers, nurses, psychologists, counselors, and others for whom the requirement of licensure has been imposed by state law (*Laskowitz v. Ciba Vision Corp.,* 1995). As courts have noted, the justification for this broadening of informed consent is that it is an integral part of the duty to practice reasonably competently, a responsibility that applies to all health professionals (*Laskowitz v. Ciba Vision Corp.,* 1995).

The scope of informed consent extends not only to those who traditionally would be considered to have the legal status of "client," but also to other persons, such as human research subjects, whose health and personal privacy may reasonably be expected to be affected by the experimental treatment or research undertaken (*Modi v. West Virginia Bd. of Med.,* 1995; *Stanley v. Swinson,* 1995). Extensive protections requiring the obtaining of informed consent prior to human subjects research are recognized under federal law (Department of Health and Human Services Rules Governing the Protection of Human Subjects, 1991/1994) and under the health and mental health codes of numerous states. When human research subjects also receive or are offered the opportunity to receive services from the researcher, even more difficult informed consent issues arise. These issues are addressed subsequently, and are also the particular subject of case example 8, "The Research Study."

Informed consent has three essential components: First, the client seeking services must be assisted by the professional to have a reasonable understanding of the risks and benefits of the proposed service; second, the client must make a decision concerning treatment that is voluntary; third, the client must have the capacity to choose (*Rasmussen v. Fleming,* 1987). Every behavioral health decision maker must be thoroughly familiar with the components of informed consent, and a detailed discussion of each follows.

Understanding the Risks and Benefits

Each professional has a duty to provide, in a form that can be reasonably understood by the client, the following minimum information:

- The professional's assessment of the client's presenting problem
- The services the professional proposes to address the problem
- The professional's opinion as to the benefits or risks to the client that might result if the client accepts or rejects services
- The nature and availability of alternative services to address the problem

How much information is a "reasonable" amount? The courts have variously answered this question by evaluating

- What a reasonable professional in a particular community should be expected to disclose based on the professional's training and experience; or, in some jurisdictions
- The amount of information that a reasonable person of the client's background could be expected to require in order to choose whether to receive services, i.e., the "objective standard" (*Ashe v. Radiation Oncology Assocs.,* 1999; *Laskowitz v. Ciba Vision Corp.,* 1995).

Consistent with a community-sensitive definition of reasonableness, the cautious decision maker should base the disclosure of information not only on professional training and experience, but also on a consideration of the factors that characterize both the client and the client's community, including age and cultural demographics; these issues are relatively certain to have a role in the client's choice regarding services.

As an example of the burden that informed consent places on a psychotherapist, consider the case of a clinical social worker, counselor, or psychologist specializing in the treatment of mood disorders and substance abuse within a Navajo community in northwestern New Mexico. The therapist must assume that a reasonable client with signs of clinical depression would want to be aware of all modalities available to treat the depression before choosing the one offered by this therapist. Therefore, the professional must be prepared to discuss alternative therapeutic options, including pharmacological, cognitive-behavioral, and culture-specific remedies that the client would likely want information about before making a decision concerning services. This is the case even if the professional is strongly ideologically opposed to any one of these approaches. It would be a mistake if the therapist overemphasized the use of culture-specific remedies or, conversely, underemphasized them. Stereotyping the client threatens informed consent as much as imposing the therapist's own ideological approach does.

In addition to the types of disclosures mentioned above, the professional's lack of experience in, or personal predisposition against, a particular form of service should also be revealed because it may additionally affect the quality of the service delivered. Therefore, the client has the right to consider this point before making a decision about services (case example 5, "The Forest Fire," explores this point in more detail).

In view of the broad duties outlined above, informed consent imposes a burden upon all psychotherapists to have knowledge that extends beyond the bounds of their individual professional disciplines. This may be a troubling thought to some therapists who believe that their training and licensing credentials insulate them from this responsibility. However, from the client's perspective, it is entirely reasonable. A mentally ill client does not feel troubled in a "social work" way, only the sense of affliction. The protection informed consent provides maximizes the chance of recovery by enhancing the client's knowledge about alternative routes to improvement.

One of the additional risks behavioral health professionals should be prepared to discuss with their clients is the existence of any conflict of interest the therapist might have in providing a particular service (*Horak v. Biris,* 1985; *Moore v. Regents of Univ. of Cal.,* 1990; *Petrillo v. Syntex Labs., Inc.,* 1986). Such a conflict is a risk to any client in the sense that it may compromise the quality of the service that the client ought to reasonably expect. Conflicts of interest may include economic interests the professional may have in a particular service, consulting contracts connected with the service, research interests, and external business and social relationships with the client. Some associations, including sexual and inappropriate social and business relationships, may be so innately threatening to the client's best interests that, even with full disclosure, the capacity to give informed consent is jeopardized.

The duty to seek informed consent applies to all behavioral health professionals, sometimes in ways that are not immediately recognizable. For example, in the case of a protective service social worker seeking to place a child for adoption, the duty requires the social worker to advise potential adoptive parents regarding the child's medical and psychological history (*Jackson v. State,* 1998; *Mohr v. Commonwealth,* 1995). In this instance, imposing the responsibility to advise is based on the presumption that the adoptive parents' decision to adopt may in part be based on whether they are able to cope financially and emotionally with children who may have special needs (*Jackson v. State,* 1998; *Mohr v. Commonwealth,* 1995). Reasonable disclosure, in this context, may extend to the conveyance of information pertaining to the birth mother's medical, psychological, and genetic background because adoptive parents are likely to require such information in order to make an informed decision about whether to adopt a child (*Jackson v. State,* 1998; *Mohr v. Commonwealth,* 1995).

In all professional relationships, the duty to seek informed consent mandates a discussion pertaining to confidentiality and its limits because the client's expectation of privacy may be an important motivating factor in the selection of services. At the same time, the client must be made aware of circumstances, such as suicidal ideation or threats of violence, that will require the professional to disclose this information to a third party. Limitations on the rule of confidentiality therefore represent a "risk" to the client that may also influence the choice of services. The professional's duty to disclose the limits of confidentiality is problematic; the very discussion of limits to confidentiality may discourage an already hesitant client from seeking services. Handling of this discussion is therefore best accomplished in a manner that avoids legalistic jargon lifted from the most recent "duty to warn" lawsuit.

At the heart of informed consent is reasonable disclosure. Note that this means disclosure not only to the professional's immediate client (as in the case of the protective service social worker, the child to be adopted), but also to those legally empowered to make decisions on the client's behalf (i.e., the adoptive parents), and other persons who arguably may suffer harm as a result of a failure to disclose (*Jackson v. State,* 1998; *Mohr v. Commonwealth,* 1995).

As noted earlier, advancements in technology—including, specifically, access to knowledge resulting from Internet access—may be changing the definition of reasonably competent practice and lessening the extent to which professional standards vary between communities. The same can be said with regard to the explanation of risks and benefits mandated by informed consent. Thus, if a counselor in Mora, New Mexico, is able to access essentially the same databases of practice knowledge that are available in New York City, then the rural practitioner will likely be held to a higher standard of familiarity with alternative practice approaches and expected to pass this information on to the client. Moreover, as HMOs and other health care providers continue to collect extensive treatment data via computer, they may come under increasing pressure to do a better job of informing potential patients as to the safety of certain health care procedures and the performance records of their providers (Hellwage, 2000). The impact of this pressure may well extend to social workers, counselors, psychologists, and all those behavioral health professionals who provide HMO-sponsored services.

Internet based services raise even more serious questions about the ability of participants to achieve full disclosure of the risks and benefits pertaining to Web counseling. As already noted, Internet based counseling has been embraced by the NBCC for counselors, within certain broadly defined limits. Section B12 imposes only minimal requirements governing informed consent on counselors intending to use the Web. Specifically, it requires them to advise potential Internet clients of the availability of "local sources of care" before any professional relationship is instituted. This provision fails, however, to address the more overriding problem concerning electronic counseling. More specifically, it may interfere with the heart of any professional relationship by diminishing the provider's ability to convey complete information about the services offered and the client's opportunity to present questions concerning these services. Moreover, electronic communication does not provide a comparable substitute for in-person assessment.

Voluntariness

As already noted, behavioral health professionals frequently work with clients who seek their services voluntarily. At other times, they may work with clients who have come to treatment involuntarily, typically as the result of a court order. Each category of client will be addressed separately.

Voluntary Clients. With respect to clients who freely seek the professional's services, the best way to preserve their voluntary pursuit of treatment is to obey the duty to provide reasonably complete disclosure of the risks and benefits associated with the services. Failing to provide this review in essence removes from the client the ability to select the professional's services consciously and ultimately interferes with the client's free-will choices. In this sense, providing reasonable disclosure fosters informed consent. As already noted, such disclosure must include a practical review of alternative approaches to the client's presenting problem, in addition to a full discussion of the services offered by the professional.

The solicitation of clients through advertising and in-person appeals raises important questions concerning the ability of such persons to agree voluntarily to the services promoted. This problem most obviously arises in the context of behavioral health professionals who advertise. It also presents itself in the case of professionals who lecture publicly on clinical or other behavioral health related subjects at academic conferences or through the airwaves. In both instances, the services of the presenter or advertiser may be sought by those who have attended a workshop or watched an advertisement. All too commonly, the indiscreet presenter may be tempted to serve the needs of the often enthusiastic listener and prospective client without explaining the benefits of alternative approaches or drawbacks of the service being promoted.

The significance of this problem may be lost on a generation of behavioral health professionals who regard advertising generally as "legal" and, within limits, "ethical," and therefore promote their services avidly. They are correct in the sense that courts have upheld the right of professionals to solicit clients on the ground that it protects the First Amendment right to free communication and that it promotes the public interest that benefits from the dissemination of accurate information about the availability of services (*Bates v. State Bar,* 1977; *In re R. M. J.,* 1982).

Codes of ethics, including the NASW Code (Ethical Standard 4.07), APA Code (Ethical Standards 3.01–3.06), and NBCC Code (Section F1), generally permit advertising. Moreover, they have adopted the spirit of the court decisions mentioned above by imposing the requirement upon solicitation that it not subject clients, especially the vulnerable, to undue influence. Undue influence is ordinarily presumed to take place when solicitation of clients is done in person, where the solicitor has the opportunity to use personal authority to suggest the need for services. Interestingly, none of the ethical codes cited above absolutely bans in-person solicitation. The APA Code (Ethical Standard 3.06) permits it to the extent that it is "invited," a provision apparently intended to cover public lectures and demonstrations, which in reality may offer the best opportunity for the kind of self-promotion that sometimes challenges the spirit of informed consent.

Ethical codes aside, advertising does raise informed consent problems. Civil malpractice suits based on the violation of informed consent have been brought against health professionals making overtly misleading claims to the public. For example, in *Karlin v. IVF America, Inc.* (1999), a medical clinic's excessively optimistic reports in its advertising and promotional literature concerning its human fertilization program led to the filing of multiple informed consent based claims by disappointed patients. In this case, as in others, the enthusiasm of potential patients to seek the services of the advertiser was plainly driven by the mass market approach of the clinic's promotion. Considered in this light, the most potentially dangerous impact of client solicitation on the client's ability to give informed consent is the interference that it may cause with the client's conscious process of deliberation. When solicitation is carried out through mass media, as it has been done in the recent past with health and mental health services, its greatest impact may well be on the rural, poor, and undereducated people most vulnerable to the effects of this information (Albee, 1999; McMichael & Beaglehole, 2000; Quigley, 2001). Given this fact, client solicitation clearly has the to potential to interfere with the free assessment of treatment alternatives.

The impact of advertising on the voluntary choice of behavioral health services raises interesting questions about the meaning of "voluntariness" in the context of informed consent. The U.S. Supreme Court has suggested that voluntary choice is compromised when a person's "will has been overborne and . . . capacity for self-determination critically impaired" (*Schneckloth v. Bustamonte,* 1973, p. 225). One health care ethicist has proposed a definition that is even more stringent than that of the Supreme Court: Voluntariness exists when there is an "absence of controlling influences" exerted by others and the client retains "the ability to choose either one of at least two options" (Hewlett, 1996, p. 233). To satisfy this definition, the client must be free of manipulation or the selective conveyance of information in order to influence a decision. Under either definition of voluntariness, substantial questions can be raised concerning the impact that direct client solicitation, including advertising, may have upon the ability to provide informed consent.

Undue influence may present significant problems not only when clients are solicited, but also when their participation in research studies is sought by their therapists (Hewlett, 1996). Medical ethicists have noted that, despite the legal restrictions placed upon researchers with respect to the obtaining of informed consent, participants in clinical research are unlikely to be free from subtle influences. Specifically, patients rely upon the position of trust that their physicians retain in order to gain assistance in decision making. Physicians are often perceived as powerful figures whose future care may diminish in quality if the patient declines to take part in the testing of medical procedures or new drugs. Despite the emphasis the behavioral health professions place upon egalitarian service delivery and the client's right to self-determination, there is nonetheless an inherent power differential between these professionals and their clients; this is especially true with respect to the provision of psychotherapy. For clinical social workers, counselors, and psychologists who seek to involve their clients in the research of new treatment modalities, this lesson is an important one; it may persuade such researchers to exercise more care in the solicitation of participants and rely more upon independent, trained personnel, such as client advocates, to explain the risks and benefits of participation (Hewlett, 1996).

Involuntary Clients. Behavioral health professionals often provide services to clients who have not sought them voluntarily. This situation arises regularly in the case of clients who lack some *capacity*, either legal or mental, to make life choices that involve medical and mental health services, among other issues. Clients in this category lack the ability to provide informed consent in a voluntary and knowing way. Included in this group, among others, are persons who have been involuntarily committed for mental health services and individuals for whom life-sustaining treatment is sought against their will. As to the rights of these clients, they are the focus of later discussion.

Other persons present themselves to behavioral health professionals for services because they have been court-mandated to do so, either because of child abuse proceedings or criminal prosecutions. Still other instances arise, such as in the area of probation services, in which a client must submit to drug testing and other conditions of parole or delinquency adjudication. In all of the above circumstances, how can the duty to seek informed consent be compromised without violating the client's fundamental rights?

In reality, the duty to seek the voluntary participation of clients does not evaporate in the case of those who are court-ordered to receive services. In these instances, the satisfaction of informed consent should be understood in terms of the transfer of decision making authority to another legal entity. In the case of individuals under court order, an important state interest usually authorizes a court to assume responsibility for seeking corrective treatment on the recipients' behalf. Often, the state interest involves the protection of a vulnerable person, such as a child caught in an abusive relationship or a victim of criminal conduct. Much like a guardian protecting a ward, the court may approve services that can address the root causes of the aberrant behavior.

Whenever possible, courts ordering services will do so with the client's willing consent. On these occasions, the client's agreement to seek services may provide a means of avoiding or ending litigation that the client is more than happy to endorse. In such circumstances, clients are literally consenting to treatment as a means to avoid a jail sentence or to recover custody of their children; given the situational pressure, however, clients cannot really be thought of as approving services voluntarily. This is especially true considering the routine requirement that treatment progress be reported to a court. Sometimes, court-ordered treatment may be more coercive, with the court mandating a particular treatment plan or course of therapy. In all of these instances, whether the client has given nominal consent or has been ordered to treatment, the professional should regard the *court* as the arbiter of what services are reasonably required; in effect, the court provides informed consent in the client's name.

As an example of substituted informed consent, a respondent in a child abuse proceeding may be ordered by a court to receive individual anger management therapy, parent effectiveness training, or even substance abuse and mental health treatment (Rittner & Dozier, 2000). A criminal defendant convicted of drug possession may be ordered to rehabilitation. Similarly, an individual convicted of aggravated stalking may be ordered to receive both jail time and a program of intensive therapy (see, e.g., Harassment and Stalking Act, 1978/2000, which provides in §30-3A-3.1(C) that a person convicted of aggravated stalking must pay for, participate in, and complete a program of professional counseling). A motorist who has pleaded guilty to driving under the influence of alcohol (DUI) may be ordered to attend victim impact panel sessions and physical handicap educational programming administered by Mothers Against Drunk Driving (MADD) (*State v. Lattimer,* 2001).

In any of the above scenarios, courts are under a clear legal mandate to tailor their orders to address the conduct that has invoked the state interest each court is empowered to protect. If they exceed that mandate by placing excessive requirements or restrictions on a client, courts may violate fundamental constitutional freedoms, including the client's right to privacy. For example, a court that orders an unruly but mentally competent criminal defendant to receive antipsychotic medication during pretrial detention impermissibly invades the detainee's freedom to reject such treatment (*Bee v. Greaves,* 1984; *Riggins v. Nevada,* 1992). Similarly, the increasing tendency of family courts in some areas to impose the requirement of extensive marriage counseling prior to the consideration of divorce may run afoul of the same principle. In both instances, the forced treatment of the client may violate the voluntariness component of informed consent, and thereby unacceptably invade the client's personal privacy. This constitutional doctrine helps to explain why legislatures may avoid enacting mental health treatment components in their criminal legislation, even though compelling research suggests they are so vitally important in the long-term prevention of some types of criminal behavior (Peebles, 1999).

How can the behavioral health professional honor both the letter and spirit of informed consent when working with an involuntary client? First, information must be clearly conveyed to the client at the commencement of services explaining the professional's obligations to the court that has requested the service. This may involve explaining the limits on confidentiality imposed by the treatment situation. Second, the professional must seek the client's voluntary participation in all aspects of treatment to the extent possible. Third, the professional should honor the client's right to receive an explanation of the risks and benefits of the services offered. The fact that the client's treatment may not be voluntary does not eliminate this important component of informed consent.

Capacity

Mental Capacity. Capacity is an important component of informed consent because, without it, a client is unable to comprehend the information required to make an educated decision regarding services. It is related to the voluntariness component in that, lacking capacity, a client for whom services are provided is essentially receiving them involuntarily. Mental capacity can be defined as the ability to participate in a reasoned decision making process regarding the risks and benefits of treatment (*Bee v. Greaves,* 1984). In order to be regarded as having mental capacity, one seeking treatment must have a reasonable understanding of one's own physical and mental condition, the risks and benefits of the services proposed to address the condition, and the consequences of receiving no services at all (*Rasmussen v. Fleming,* 1987). Consistent with constitutional guarantees enjoyed by all adult citizens, persons who have attained adulthood are presumed to have the mental capacity to provide informed consent. This means simply that all treatment decisions that a person with capacity makes must ordinarily be honored, even if they seem to defy common sense or the ideological perspective of the professional provider (*Bee v. Greaves,* 1984). Note that in the case of gravely ill or terminal patients, who otherwise meet the definition of mental capacity, this includes the right to refuse medical treatment (*Rasmussen v. Fleming,* 1987). Clients who are aged, depressed, forgetful, or whose thinking may be mildly compromised, have the same rights. It is an unfortunate reality that these persons are sometimes treated as if they lacked mental capacity.

Under certain circumstances, a family member, guardian, or a representative of the state may seek to demonstrate that an individual lacks the mental capacity to consent to medical, behavioral health, or human services. Frequently this situation arises in the case of the severely mentally ill, the frail elderly, or those with substance abuse-induced psychosis. Less frequently, it arises in the case of persons declining medical services whose conditions are reasonably amenable to conservative treatment. With respect to these individuals, an interested advocate concerned with the patient's welfare, typically a close family member or behavioral health agency, may seek appointment as a legal guardian (see, e.g., Uniform Probate Code, 1978/1998).

The purpose of guardianship is to convey to a concerned individual the legal right to grant informed consent for appropriate medical or psychiatric services on the individual's behalf. Although the legislative standards for the granting of guardianship vary from state to state, a patient's inability to provide informed consent is a critical component. Consistent with the spirit of informed consent, even when a patient fails to meet the legal standards governing mental capacity, it is appropriate that a guardian reasonably consult with the patient in order to ascertain where possible the patient's wishes concerning treatment and living arrangements. In some situations, guardianship may be expressly limited by the granting court in such a way as to narrow the guardian's authority to specific medical conditions or areas of decision making, or to impose clear responsibility upon the limited guardian to consult with the patient on important matters pertaining to care and living arrangements. In some states, legislation may provide for the appointment of a treatment guardian whose responsibility extends solely to mental health care issues.

Guardianship is conferred at the conclusion of a court proceeding in which a person's lack of mental capacity is demonstrated. It is often granted in conjunction with conservatorship, in which an individual or organization—the conservator—is granted the legal authority to manage the person's financial assets. State laws governing guardianship and conservatorship typically require that a person's mental capacity be demonstrated on the basis of, among other things, a review of the person's psychosocial functioning. Such a review is often undertaken by behavioral health professionals acting in the capacity of *visitors* appointed by the court. In conjunction with expert medical witnesses, visitors assist the court in the consideration of the person's capacity for informed consent regarding both health care decisions and financial estate management.

Alternatives to guardianship exist that avoid the extreme measure of removing from an individual all right to decision making. A more satisfactory approach involves prior planning, including the identification of surrogate decision makers capable of making important life choices on a person's behalf in the event of incapacity. Surrogate decision makers may face alternatives that include various health care options, including end of life decisions and the termination of artificially maintained medical treatment. All states have provisions allowing these *advance directives* to be designated by a mentally competent person. Under the Uniform Health-Care Decisions Act (1993), presently in effect in New Mexico, Alabama, Delaware, Hawaii, Maine, Mississippi (and its adoption being considered in others), the process for appointing surrogate decision makers has been liberalized, allowing the choice to be made by a *power of attorney*. The Act even contains a provision (§5) entitling health care decisions to be made by a close family member or friend if the patient has not completed a power of attorney in advance (see, e.g., New Mexico's version of the Uniform Health-Care Decisions Act, 1978/1997).

Persons who lack mental capacity often are sufficiently ill to warrant more invasive treatment. In such instances, the mental health codes of all states provide a mechanism through commitment proceedings in which to mandate treatment for these patients. In such instances, the heightened procedural standards of most states require not simply that patients lack the capacity to consent to treatment, but also that they be demonstrated harmful to themselves or others. This elevated standard is the culmination of a series of court decisions (see, e.g., *Commonwealth v. Bruno,* 2000; *Kansas v. Hendricks,* 1997) recognizing that the state's interest in confining a person for mental health services does not arise unless a specific threat to the health and safety—either the person's or the public's—is demonstrated. State legislatures also have expanded the use of civil commitment proceedings as a means of providing alternative mechanisms for the institutionalization of criminal sexual predators (*Commonwealth v. Bruno,* 2000; *Kansas v. Hendricks,* 1997).

Various constitutional protections, including the Fourteenth Amendment's due process clause, govern the extent to which a person can be involuntarily confined for mental health treatment (*Commonwealth v. Bruno,*

2000; *Kansas v. Hendricks,* 1997). One doctrine, the *least restrictive means* principle, holds that a person's right to personal privacy supersedes a state's power to confine involuntarily unless it can be demonstrated that this measure is the most minimally invasive way to provide appropriate psychotherapy. Even then, constitutional doctrine mandates that commitment be avoided unless the state can demonstrate that the patient is likely to benefit from treatment (*In re Mental Illness of Thomas,* 1996). Consistent with these constitutional protections, federal and state mental health laws and administrative regulations provide a series of protections to institutionalized patients, including, for example, the right to freedom from excessive medication, the right to an appropriate diet, the right to adequate medical attention, the right to a humane physical and psychological environment, and the right not to participate in experimentation without informed consent (see, e.g., Personal Rights of Residential Clients, 1978/1989; Restatement of Bill of Rights for Mental Health Patients, 1991/2000).

Legal Capacity. The requirement of legal capacity can be understood as a means of protecting vulnerable members of society from seeking services that they lack the ability to choose in an informed way. Imposing the condition of legal capacity on informed consent supports a presumption that minors ordinarily lack the reasoning sophistication to consider the risks and benefits of alternative behavioral health services. Therefore, in many circumstances, only an adult or legal guardian of a child under the age of 18 years can provide informed consent on behalf of that child. Legal capacity additionally supports the *doctrine of family privacy*, which guarantees the solitude of the parent-child relationship and the principal authority of parents to raise their children and consider their best interests without interference either by the state or by outside professionals (*Gruenke v. Seip,* 2000; *M. L. B. v. S. L. J.,* 1996).

Only in a few circumstances does public policy presently allow informed consent by minors, most notably when important public health concerns mandate it, and children are deemed sufficiently mature to choose particular services. These situations are defined starkly differently under various states' laws but often include provisions comparable to New Mexico's:

- The receipt of noninvasive mental health services, including psychotherapy and verbal counseling, by any child (Children's Mental Health and Developmental Disabilities Act, 1978/1995, §32A-6-14(A));
- The receipt of more invasive psychotherapy, including psychotropic medication, by older children (over the age of 14) (Children's Mental

Health and Developmental Disabilities Act, 1978/1995, §32A-6-14(E));
- Voluntary admission of older children (over the age of 14) for residential treatment for mental disorders (joint parental informed consent must also be obtained) (Children's Mental Health and Developmental Disabilities Act, 1978/1995, §32A-6-12(B));
- The termination of life sustaining treatment by a terminally ill minor (joint parental informed consent must also be obtained) (Uniform Health-Care Decisions Act, 1978/1997, §24-7A-6.1);
- Requests for HIV/AIDS testing (Human Immunodeficiency Virus Test Act, 1978/2000, §24-2B-3);
- The receipt of all services by children who have become legally emancipated (Emancipation of Minors Act, 1978/1995, §32A-21-5).

In addition to these common provisions, some states recognize several more controversial situations in which minors can grant informed consent for services. Most notable of these are the receipt of abortions and the obtaining of contraceptive information. Presently 26 states entitle minors to consent to receive contraceptive services and abortions, either with or without parental notification (Alan Guttmacher Institute, 2002). The right to receive prenatal care and delivery services is guaranteed to minors in some states, as is the right to seek medical treatment in an emergency when parental consent is impossible to obtain. In two states, Alabama and South Carolina, minors over the age of 14 and 16, respectively, currently can grant informed consent to most types of medical care (Consent for Health Services, 1975, §22-8-4; Legal Capacity of Minors, 1985, §20-7-280) (in South Carolina, legal capacity to consent is restricted to nonsurgical health care). Given this diversity in regional interpretation of the legal capacity rule, the reader is encouraged to consult state law to identify specific situations in which minors may obtain services independently.

Note that an individual who lacks legal capacity but fits one of the state-defined exceptions outlined above may still lack mental capacity to voluntarily consent to services. In such circumstances, treatment guardianship together with parental cooperation may be necessary in order to ensure safe and appropriate treatment.

As a general rule, the exceptions to legal capacity enforce a growing nationwide public policy supporting early intervention in the treatment of emotional and mental conditions, substance abuse, and teenage pregnancy. An area of pressing national concern involves the right of a minor to consent to an abortion. States that predicate a juvenile's right to obtain an abortion upon a parent's informed consent or judicial waiver are, in the opinion of at least some courts, interfering with the right of a woman to control her own body and destiny (*Planned Parenthood v. Farmer,* 2000). Thus, even when state legislatures decline to recognize statutory exceptions to the requirement of legal capacity, courts may be willing to create them in limited circumstances; this is particularly true when it comes to the promotion of public health.

Exceptions to legal capacity may occasionally present challenging issues for behavioral health professionals who work with children and teenagers. In these instances, the rights of children and parents alike must be thoroughly surveyed with respect to the legal principles governing them. Several of these, including the duty to practice reasonably competently, the duty to seek informed consent, and the duty to preserve confidentiality, are often implicated simultaneously whenever behavioral health or human services are provided to children. A review of the case examples presented later demonstrates this point. Additionally, behavioral health professionals who understand informed consent and the public policy behind exceptions to legal capacity are in a unique position to lobby for legislative changes in areas that promote the well-being of young clients who presently lack the legal standing to seek health and mental health services.

Similarly to the rule of mental capacity, legal capacity is intended to support the voluntary choice of services by clients. Specifically, the doctrine supports the concept that, in most instances, the provision of services to a child unable to appreciate the consequences of a choice really amounts to the involuntary imposition of services on that child. The legal capacity doctrine promotes the idea that, except in the limited circumstances outlined above, a parent's surrogate decisions are invariably more likely to preserve a child's best interests.

Legal capacity additionally helps to explain how court-ordered services can be provided to clients consistent with the letter and spirit of informed consent. As the discussion on voluntariness disclosed, courts can attain the right to make decisions on a person's behalf when important public policy demands that the community be protected from the consequences of the person's behavior. This concept may be understood equally well in the context of capacity. A person who commits a crime or engages in conduct that may be threatening to the welfare of others is understood in a limited legal sense to lose the right to consent to treatment options that may protect the interests of those endangered by the person's conduct.

Just as they must understand effective strategies to present services to involuntary clients, behavioral health professionals should adopt decision making strategies with mentally and legally incapacitated clients that honor the philosophy underlying informed consent. As with involuntary clients, incapacitated clients have at least some ability to reason, feel, and participate in the services they are receiving. Behavioral health professionals must seek to engage them in aspects of decision making in a manner that both recognizes the policy behind vicarious consent and is also respectful of human dignity. How is this objective best accomplished with incapacitated clients? In the case of older children and functional adults, it is appropriate to seek consent from the client in addition to the parent or guardian. Although the social worker must respect the authority of the guardian to make ultimate treatment decisions, it is consistent with competent clinical practice to seek the voluntary participation of the protected client. Thus, psychotherapists, child welfare workers, and other behavioral health professionals should, where appropriate, seek consent from underage clients and medically fragile adults, toward the end of engaging the client in the therapeutic process.

Informed Consent and the Fear of Liability

There appears to be widespread fear within the medical and behavioral health professions concerning potential liability for violation of the duty to seek informed consent. Most of this fear seems to have arisen from the reputed increase in civil lawsuits regarding informed consent and other malpractice issues. This fear has resulted in a corresponding expansion of the emphasis that professionals place on the preparation and completion of "informed consent forms" by clients prior to the institution of services. Indeed, some professionals seem to equate the duty to seek informed consent as described here with documentation. They do not have identical meanings. Although the informed consent form may be intended to assist professionals to limit liability for claims that they have violated informed consent, it does not always accurately demonstrate that informed consent truly has been obtained. When a boilerplate form is placed in front of a client before any substantive discussion between professional and client, then by definition it cannot substantiate informed consent. In such instances, the form serves more as a documentation of the client's request for treatment.

The best strategy for avoiding informed consent based malpractice claims is to follow the guidelines discussed. Once attained, informed consent should be documented with the client's approval in a format both parties are willing to review, reconsider, and modify as services are designed and redesigned by both client and professional (*Kovacs v. Freeman,* 1997).

Consequences for Breach of the Duty to Seek Informed Consent

As noted, professionals have a duty to seek informed consent both from their clients and from those, such as research subjects, who may be affected by their conduct. Similarly to the duty to practice reasonably competently, the duty to seek informed consent may be enforced not only by clients but also by persons who suffer foreseeable harm as a result of the professional's failure to honor it. In fact, violation of the duty to seek informed consent is itself a breach of the duty to practice reasonably competently. This point is not purely academic. In many states, violating the duty to seek informed consent is recognized by courts as an independent ground to impose civil liability upon a behavioral health professional if a client or research participant suffers damages as a result of the violation.

Many civil lawsuits have been brought on behalf of mentally ill individuals from whom informed consent was not sought in medical or psychiatric research, or during the provision of new or experimental psychiatric services (*T. D. v. New York State Office of Mental Health,* 1995). Other cases have involved the failure of human service agencies to provide complete and appropriate information to adoptive parents concerning the birth family's medical and psychological history (*Gibbs v. Ernst,* 1994; *Jackson v. State,* 1998). Damages claimed in these cases have covered such diverse areas as physical injury, psychological trauma, and, in the case of adopting parents, the cost of raising a child with extensive medical bills (*Gibbs v. Ernst,* 1994; *Jackson v. State,* 1998).

Remedies sought in medical or psychiatric research cases have included not only the award of money damages, but also on occasion court orders enjoining the offending clinician, researcher, or behavioral health agency from engaging in the conduct complained of (*Kus v. Sherman Hosp.,* 1995; *T. D. v. New York State Office of Mental Health,* 1995). Periodically, courts have faced large-scale informed consent violations committed by state-sponsored institutions against particularly vulnerable adults and children (*T. D. v. New York State Office of Mental Health,* 1995). Such cases often have involved the involuntary medication of psychiatric patients or prisoners in penal institutions. Invariably, state officials defending these cases have sought unsuccessfully to explain such violations in terms of the need to "control" patients, the public policy favoring important medical research, or the logistical burden of seeking guardianship or other substituted consent from the individual patient's representative.

All of the practices noted above have been recognized to violate victims' fundamental right to privacy. On occasion, they have mandated wholesale changes in state regulations governing institutional mental health services and research. Indeed, informed consent is considered such an elemental human right that one court has recognized the standing of a medical researcher at a major university to contest his firing after "blowing the whistle" on the questionable practices of experimenters studying the relationship between passive smoking and contact with radioactive materials (*Stebbings v. University of Chicago,* 2000).

Excessive zeal in conducting forensic research lies at the bottom of the apparent mistakes made in the criminal investigation of suspected child sexual abuse in the now notorious *McMartin Pre-School* case in California. In 1983, a social worker spurred on by a single allegation of sexual abuse against teachers at the preschool proceeded to interview hundreds of children in an effort to uncover additional instances of abuse (*Buckey v. County of Los Angeles,* 1992). The social work investigator, apparently convinced that the abuse had taken place, asked persistent, leading questions, even after children had denied that any abuse had occurred. The investigator's heartfelt belief that child abuse is deeply rooted in American society was allowed literally to drive her forensic research to the extent that it took precedence over the direct, factual information offered by the children. Considered in the context of informed consent, children were subjected to questioning that was arguably coercive, and it rendered their participation essentially involuntary. Moreover, it led ultimately to the dismissal of a number of indictments in the criminal case against the *McMartin* defendants and also to extensive revisions in the management of child abuse investigations.

Violation of informed consent represents the breach of a practice standard essential in all behavioral health professions. Consequently, violating the standard can have licensing consequences (see, e.g., *Modi v. West Virginia Bd. of Med.,* 1995), or even criminal ramifications (*State v. Watkins,* 2000).

Psychotherapists in Colorado have been convicted of reckless child abuse and sentenced to jail time in connection with the death of a 10-year-old girl subjected to "rebirthing therapy" (Mercer, 2001; Nicholson, 2001; Rouse, 2001; *State v. Watkins,* 2000). The treatment, which involves simulation of the birth process by bundling the child in blankets as a purported therapy for childhood attachment disorder, is intended to allow the child to "rebond" with her mother through the simulated experience of birthing (Mercer, 2001). Instead, in the Colorado case it resulted in the child's smothering. The therapists reportedly failed to respond to the child's screams for help, apparently convinced that this expression of anxiety was a critical component of the therapy. Insofar as the therapy became involuntary, the therapists' reputed approach represents not simply criminally negligent practice, but also the utter repudiation of the doctrine of informed consent.

Using Informed Consent as a Vehicle to Make Professional Decisions: Case Examples

Informed consent is one of the most useful legal principles for behavioral health professionals to understand and apply in everyday decision making. Because it sets so many of the basic ground rules for the professional-client relationship, identifying informed consent dilemmas can greatly assist the decision maker in getting to the heart of an otherwise perplexing practice problem. In this respect, informed consent addresses the essential tasks of the professional relationship, including client assessment, the establishment of rapport, discussion of the client's expectations regarding the services to be provided, the engagement of the client in the design of services, and other important areas that often determine the success of an intervention.

Many of the issues associated with informed consent also promote important professional ethical principles, such as the promotion of client self-determination and well-being. As the decision making framework suggests, however, understanding informed consent as an enforceable legal responsibility underscores the behavioral health professional's duty to identify and apply it (along with the other primary legal principles identified in this book) first when important practice decisions are to be considered.

The subsequent case examples not only demonstrate the usefulness of informed consent in evaluating complex practice situations, but they also highlight its application in cross-cultural practice. This should not be surprising, because diversity has such a significant impact on the quality of the professional relationship between providers and their clients. Illustrative examples highlighting the diverse populations of New Mexico follow next.

Case Example 4: The Welfare Office

Katrina Montez, a 68-year-old widowed housewife living in Artesia, New Mexico, has applied for income support, including Temporary Aid to Needy Families (TANF), food stamps, and other public assistance programs. Artesia is a town of about 10,500 in southeastern New Mexico and has a majority Anglo population with a significant Hispanic minority. At the time of her application for benefits, Katrina is given informational materials relevant to her case that explain generally her rights and obligations under each program. Some of the materials are in comic book form and are available in English and Spanish. A posted sign on one of the walls of the welfare office outlines the rights of the applicant, such as, e.g., the right to appeal denials of benefits. Detailed administrative rules and regulations describing income and other program conditions are not provided, but they are available through the Internet and by request. The applications Katrina has to complete require, among other things, her verification of income and her attestation as to the amount of property she owns. Katrina's primary language is Spanish, and her ability to read is limited.

This case example represents a nontraditional application of the informed consent doctrine in the sense that it involves the delivery of human services, rather than health or mental health care. Nevertheless, informed consent governs the professional relationship here every bit as much as it does the relationship between a clinical provider and a client. The decision maker who recognizes the application of informed consent in this case example will obtain useful assistance in identifying responsibilities that apply to behavioral health professionals in all of the administrative responsibilities of practice, including client intake, assessment, and claims processing.

In this scenario, the requirements of informed consent are challenged by language barriers that may seriously impede Katrina's understanding of her rights and obligations under government programs. Can dissemination of general information about Katrina's rights and obligations be presented to Katrina in a form that reasonably ensures her comprehension of what she is receiving and what her responsibilities are for receiving it? The answer will depend in large measure not only upon the paperwork Katrina is required to sign, but also on the quality of the dialogue between Katrina and her case worker before, during, and after her application for benefits. If a fully bilingual professional is not provided to Katrina at the time of her intake, then her informed consent cannot reasonably be obtained nor can the rushed, bureaucratic atmosphere of a typical welfare office justify the avoidance of this responsibility. If it is provided, then informed consent must continue throughout Katrina's involvement with the government programs, and cannot cease with the application process. It must even include competent advice to Katrina concerning possible alternatives to some of the public assistance programs that Katrina seeks. Considering the community in which Katrina lives, a welfare worker should be reasonably familiar with the role of extended family ties in providing economic support to individual sustenance (Harris, 1998) because such information is likely to have an impact on the client's expectations and ability to conform to the requirements of the welfare programs. Katrina cannot be expected to access this information without ongoing professional assistance. Therefore, the agency's promotion of Internet use as a means of obtaining the required information may be high-tech but not entirely appropriate.

Courts have demonstrated that a failure to honor informed consent by government employees can be legally enforced. Indeed, government agencies and their employees have suffered civil sanctions for professional misconduct in connection with representations made to clients during the welfare application process (*Reynolds v. Giuliani,* 1999). In 1999, New York City welfare workers evidently pressed by the responsibilities imposed by administrative reform legislation acknowledged turning away applicants for assistance and failing to provide prompt access to food stamps and Medicaid; in response, a federal judge ordered the city to retrain workers, revise benefit applications, and increase the visibility of posted signs outlining applicant rights (*Reynolds v. Giuliani*, 1999).

Case Example 5: The Forest Fire

Noel Patrick practices individual and family psychotherapy in Los Alamos, New Mexico. A licensed independent social worker, Noel has 10 years' experience in the treatment of anxiety disorders. In his practice, Noel emphasizes cognitive and behavioral techniques that increase the capacity of the client to identify and address specific life stressors that precipitate anxiety attacks. Noel's new client, Peter Baca, is one of many San Ildefonso Pueblo members employed at the nearby Los Alamos National Laboratory. An engineering technician, Peter has sought Noel's assistance in dealing with his "nervousness." Evacuated from Los Alamos along with thousands of others during the Cerro Grande forest fire of 2000, Peter has since had vivid dreams in which he finds himself trapped at the end of a long evacuation line of cars unable to leave the town site to return to the Pueblo. His stress has started to interfere with his employment, and he finds that he is unable to concentrate. Peter also reports that he is drinking heavily and fears it may be getting out of control.

Noel assesses Peter's symptoms using the *Diagnostic and Statistical Manual of Mental Disorders* (*DSM-IV*) (American Psychiatric Association, 1994). Initially inclined to regard Peter's symptoms as evidence of posttraumatic stress disorder (PTSD), Noel is also a committed and culturally sensitive therapist. He therefore seeks more information about the personal significance of Peter's symptoms. During comprehensive interviews with Peter and additional research into the assessment of stress in American Indian clients, Noel has also evaluated the degree of Peter's cultural affiliation with the Pueblo. After exploring a number of treatment options with Peter, Noel notices Peter's favorable reaction to a traditional approach involving consultation with a tribal healer (Villa, 2001). This approach is not familiar or even comfortable to Noel, and he does not personally share the opinion that it accurately characterizes Peter's ailment. Nevertheless, he regards it as in Peter's best interests and therefore accompanies Peter on a consultation visit with a tribal medicine man.

In this case example, Noel's assessment raises questions about the therapist's unintentional stereotyping of a client in a manner that may influence the client's informed choice of a treatment approach. In his zeal to be culturally responsive, Noel may have overreacted to his client's favorable response to a suggested course of therapy and understated his own preference for a treatment strategy he is more familiar with. Furthermore, in the course of pursuing cultural relevance, Noel risks engaging Peter in an approach with which Noel has neither personal nor professional experience. Apart from the more obvious questions raised about Noel's duty to practice reasonably competently, specific informed consent questions are raised here. In contrast to case example 2, "Addressing Attrition Among Native American College Students," this scenario additionally involves a kind of misrepresentation by the professional to the client. If Noel engages in this therapy without genuinely adhering to the belief system that lies at its heart, professional dishonesty compromises the relationship between client and professional. What happens, for example, if the treatment is ineffective and Peter seeks an explanation for its failure?

Noel's situation may be comparable to that of a psychiatrist in West Virginia who applied "depossession therapy" in the treatment of a patient who allegedly believed he had been possessed by spirits (*Modi v. West Virginia Bd. of Med.,* 1995). Not actually believing in the client's possession, the doctor nevertheless hypnotized the client while chanting incantations in an effort to rid the patient of his own destructive beliefs. The West Virginia Medical Board regarded this conduct as inconsistent with the duty to seek informed consent. Specifically, the Board noted that a therapist has a responsibility to help the patient make choices from among *all* available practice alternatives. Thus, remaining silent as to one's professional orientation out of the concern that it might interfere with a client's own belief system is paternalistic, deceptive, and countertherapeutic (*Modi v. West Virginia Bd. of Med.,* 1995). In the case of cross-cultural practice situations, it may inspire the otherwise well-meaning professional to expect unreasonably that clients of one ethnic heritage will act uniformly, and that they will forego treatment unless it is provided consistent with traditional cultural beliefs.

What should Noel have been prepared to do in this case example? First, he might have disclosed fully the existence of multiple treatment approaches, including the *DSM-IV*-inspired approach consistent with Noel's professional orientation. Second, Noel should have shared fully his own predisposition toward the conservative, Western approach. This choice might seem distasteful to a clinical social worker concerned with imposing an external belief system upon the client. Nevertheless, it would appear to be a required element of informed consent. In other words, the client should expect to receive the therapist's own opinion, and the therapist should be prepared to offer it in a nonpatronizing manner. Third, if, upon full disclosure of alternative approaches, Peter had selected a traditional Native American approach, Noel might then have suggested collaboration with a Native healer, who could assume responsibility for culturally based, alternative services (Villa, 2001). In this manner, Noel would have avoided imposing a particular service on the client at the same time as he remained faithful to his own professional ideology.

Case Example 6: The Guidance Counselor

Isaac Depuis is a middle school guidance counselor in Albuquerque, New Mexico. He has a master's degree in guidance and counseling and is licensed in New Mexico. Roscoe Manygoats, a 12-year-old seventh-grader of Navajo heritage, is referred to Isaac after persistent "acting out behavior" is reported in class by the homeroom teacher. The behavior consists of cutting classes, schoolyard fights, and clownish conduct in class. During a series of three 45-minute counseling sessions, Isaac learns that Roscoe has little contact with his father, who is divorced from his mother. Additionally, Roscoe's mother has remarried, and Roscoe does not get along with his stepfather. Isaac suspects mild depression and schedules Roscoe for twice weekly counseling sessions.

The rules of informed consent suggest that in many states (including New Mexico) children such as Roscoe have the legal capacity to seek or refuse verbal counseling and psychotherapy; children over the age of 14 can even consent to receive medication. In this case example, the clinical relationship between Roscoe and Isaac must be based on the same precepts that govern any association between client and therapist. Here, however, the administrative authority that Isaac would appear to have over Roscoe may lead him to diagnose and prescribe treatment in essentially the same manner that a teacher prescribes homework. As with any adult client, Roscoe has the right to a full and competent assessment of his problem, including its potential cultural aspects, together with the freedom either to accept or forgo services. This fact imposes a particular burden upon Isaac to ensure the voluntariness of the services proposed, and it is also especially difficult for Isaac politically in a school where the guidance counselor's role is regarded as more disciplinary than clinical.

When a child consciously seeks services for a self-identified mental health problem, the therapist is required to provide full disclosure of the alternative treatment approaches. The same rule applies to a child for whom "treatment" is instituted at the behest of the professional. Assuming, then, that Isaac can obtain Roscoe's informed consent to counseling, Roscoe is still entitled to an explanation of his problem and a discussion of all appropriate treatment options. This may open the door to still additional informed consent problems because Roscoe lacks the legal capacity to consent to at least one treatment option—a referral to a physician for medication that may be appropriate for him if he is in fact clinically depressed. Roscoe may be more than willing to consent to confidential, individual counseling with Isaac, but unwilling to explore options that may require the active involvement of his mother. Informed consent additionally suggests that Roscoe must be advised of his right to confidentiality, limitations upon that right, and Isaac's duty to report certain kinds of conduct, such as suspected child abuse, that may be revealed in the course of counseling.

Precisely what are Roscoe's mother's informed consent rights in this situation? If Roscoe has behavioral problems that affect his performance in school, plainly Roscoe's mother has the right to disclosure of this information, consistent with her caretaking duties as Roscoe's guardian. It does not mean, however, that she has the right to know the substance of the clinical discussions between Isaac and Roscoe, at least to the extent that such disclosure is not necessary for the continuation of Roscoe's treatment. This material is private, as appropriate clinical practice standards demand. Suppose that, in the course of Roscoe's counseling, Isaac determines that Roscoe's condition may warrant medication, or that his problem calls for more invasive treatment, such as family therapy or medication? At this stage, Isaac is obliged to advise Roscoe's mother, and to seek both Roscoe's and the mother's consent in the referral for services.

In this case example, the application of informed consent standards, including the rules relating to legal capacity, work to protect Roscoe's right not to have services imposed upon him. The idea that Roscoe enjoys this right of personal privacy may surprise anyone who has attended middle school. Nevertheless, it exists, within boundaries, at least with respect to the student's freedom from more invasive interventions, such as prescribed therapy. As the court in *Gruenke v. Seip* (2000, p. 307) observed, students have the right not to be forced to disclose personal matters, and "school-sponsored counseling and psychological testing that pry into private family activities can overstep the boundaries of school authority."

It may seem that the doctrine of informed consent imposes an extraordinary burden on the unsuspecting school guidance counselor in this case example. In reality, it spells out a strategy for effective behavioral health practice that enhances the best interests of the client. The public school has long served as an institution in which both socialization has been accomplished—occasionally imposed—upon students. Forced acculturation unfortunately has been true with respect to minority, and particularly Native American children, on whom clinical diagnoses sometimes have been stamped more frequently than on other children. Given this fact, strict interpretation of the rules of informed consent serves to guarantee the right of the student to a sense of personal integrity that is conducive to mental health and academic success. Therefore, the ability of a behavioral health professional to identify the informed consent issues within all areas of practice is essential. As with each of the basic legal principles discussed in this book, minor regional variations exist, and the competent professional must become familiar with these local differences.

Case Example 7: The Faith Based Service

A church-administered counseling program in rural northern New Mexico offers mental health and support services to young women who have become pregnant. The program mission emphasizes the reinforcement of spiritual values, education, financial responsibility, and the enhancement of self-esteem in girls experiencing the consequences of teenage pregnancy (Corcoran, 2001). Consistent with the strong family ties that are an important part of this predominantly Hispanic community's cultural heritage, counseling often includes the extended families of young women who have sought services from the program. The average age of young pregnant women seeking services is 15 and one half, and for this reason the program's emphasis on family solidarity is particularly important. The program advocates for the family's continuing involvement in support for the mother. Birth control and abortion violate the religious ethic advanced by the church, and program counselors are advised by the clinical director to stress the moral and spiritual concerns favoring childbirth.

Melissa Zak recently has started her new job as a counselor within the program. A clinical social worker with several years of experience offering comparable services to clients in a secular project in Boston, she is aware of the church program's ethic, but also believes in the importance of helping her young clients to help themselves. Melissa believes that the only way to advance this ideology is to maximize the amount of information that clients receive. In view of the program's philosophical positions, she is prepared to adopt a "low profile" during her initial months in her position, and then plans to seek a healthy dialogue with the clinical director about suggested changes in the program's framework.

The program's restrictions also interfere with Melissa's duty to seek informed consent from prospective clients. By discouraging Melissa from discussing contraception and abortion as alternative treatment approaches available by law, clients are not able to make a fully informed decision to accept the counseling services offered by the church. Melissa herself may already recognize this point, and perhaps has understood before assuming her new job that the program's restrictions might present an obstacle that she would have to surmount in order to provide reasonably competent services to clients. In the meantime, however, she seems resigned to addressing the problem by enforcing her employer's policies. This approach may be a conservative choice intended to extend her professional life at the agency, or it may reflect the respect she is willing to pay to the program and to the clinical director. If the program has effective elements that Melissa endorses, that bring families together, and are regionally and culturally appropriate, it may simply be hard to criticize it. Regardless of Melissa's motives, however, her strategy does not address the informed consent problem that presently exists.

Young women in New Mexico and other states have the legal capacity to provide informed consent for mental health services, even if they still are minors. Melissa is obliged to seek this consent by describing all treatment strategies reasonably available to her clients. She cannot evade this responsibility by honoring the church's restrictive policy. Unless she resolves this point with the clinical director, her professional relationships with potential clients are undermined before they begin. She may wish to discuss this issue with the clinical director in a manner that honors the spirit of the program's founders, but also respects the minimum standards imposed by the duty to seek informed consent. Melissa may recommend, for example, that the church amend its informed consent policy to explain all options available to the client, along with an explanation of the program's religious orientation. She may recommend additionally that an appropriate referral system be implemented to place clients in communication with alternate service providers. It is perfectly appropriate to discuss one's faith based perspective, provided different available approaches are also discussed with the client.

Case Example 8: The Research Study

Patricio Ortega, an adjunct research professor at a university school of psychology, is undertaking a scientific study to survey the presence of mental health problems among the elderly within a multicultural community in northern New Mexico. As part of the study, Patricio will conduct interviews with community members and distribute several assessment instruments commonly used by behavioral health professionals to identify depression and anxiety disorders. Treatment will be offered as necessary to study participants at the university's mental health clinic. Consistent with federal policy (Department of Health and Human Services Rules Governing the Protection of Human Subjects, 1991/1994), Patricio has prepared an informed consent form in English and Spanish that outlines the benefits and risks that are expected from the research. He has obtained informed consent forms from a population of 75 Hispanic participants, 20 Anglos, and 5 Native Americans.

Undertaking human subjects research is a minefield for behavioral health professionals not entirely familiar with informed consent. As already noted, federal policy has been developed to extend informed consent protections to human research participants, and it requires the establishment by research institutions, such as universities and medical facilities, of *institutional review boards* (IRBs) to monitor the satisfaction of informed consent. It is important for the researcher to know and apply the rules of informed consent discussed here in addition to relying on the IRB process to sort out informed consent issues. The reason is that understanding the basic elements of informed consent often provides better initial guidance for the administration of research projects than do the confusing and sometimes contradictory professional standards adopted by state and private institutions for the review of research proposals. Often, this review is undertaken by an insular group lacking the time to give research proposals significantly more than the minimal examination for compliance with federal and state regulations governing IRBs. Indeed, even psychological testing proposed at major research institutions is occasionally prone to insufficient review (Lehrman & Sharay, 1997).

One of the most prolific dangers connected with institutional research concerns the failure to fully advise already ill participants of the risks posed by the research (Lehrman & Sharay, 1997). For example, in some research the testing of mentally ill subjects may exacerbate symptoms; in other instances the questioning of those who have been mentally ill in the past may promote a relapse of the earlier symptoms (Lehrman & Sharay, 1997). Moreover, an inadequate research design, including the use of instruments whose cross-cultural application has not been demonstrated, may lead to the over- or underreporting of mental health symptoms by subjects who simply do not understand the questions being posed. If clinical services are then offered to test study participants, some may ultimately agree to an unnecessary intervention. In other words, the satisfaction of informed consent depends upon a culturally competent research design.

What do these issues reveal about how Patricio should undertake his research study? In this case example, Patricio must have his research proposal evaluated by the university's IRB to determine the expected benefits of the research, the anticipated risks, and the quality of the informed consent that is to be sought. However, even if the IRB approves Patricio's research design he still must take reasonable steps to verify the regional and cultural appropriateness of his research design. Additionally, he should implement such procedures as are necessary to ensure that the risks and benefits of participation are truly understood. This may present a significant problem when subjects are frail or vulnerable, where language or literacy barriers exist, or when cross-cultural communication may influence the expectations of the parties.

In this scenario, in order to ensure that study participants truly understand the risks and benefits presented by the research, Patricio and his staff must be willing to dialogue with study participants both before, during, and after the research. This step promotes issue clarification and support of the participants. Reliance solely upon an informed consent form to provide this information may well violate both the letter and spirit of informed consent, especially when the form may be nearly unintelligible to the reader (Lehrman & Sharay, 1997). Even if participants cannot understand the form, *orgullo* and *verguenza* (pride and shame, respectively) may well lead the reader to claim understanding. For these reasons, Patricio should consider the use of trained, multilingual clinical assistants who are available to provide ongoing reinforcement to study participants and who can facilitate the communication of informed consent between Patricio and the subjects.

Patricio must also be prepared to ensure the voluntariness of his participants' involvement. Where Patricio has advised prospective study participants that he is prepared to offer clinical aftercare services to them, both their voluntary consent to the research and the integrity of their responses to test questions are questionable; stated simply, the possibility of aftercare may unduly influence participants to take part in the study.

An additional informed consent problem is caused if study participants ultimately accept Patricio's offer to provide clinical services to them; specifically, the link between the research and the services raises a question as to whether the services have really been sought voluntarily. Furthermore, Patricio's own involvement in the research may limit his ability to obtain informed consent for his clinical work with participants. The reason is that his willingness to provide treatment is at least partly grounded in his professional interest in the research study, including the scholarly writings and potential financial remuneration that may result. The effect is to create a conflict of interest that may influence the treatment stance he takes with his future clients; at the very least, it threatens the independence and integrity of the clinical services and therefore compromises his clients' best interests (*Moore v. Regents of Univ. of Cal.,* 1990). The conflict is a risk prospective clients need to be aware of.

For the foregoing reasons, Patricio best obeys the principle of informed consent if he refrains from offering any clinical services to participants until after the research study has been completed. Once he does make the offer of services, he must clearly explain the conflict of interest arising from his involvement in the research study. As a safe approach that honors the letter and spirit of informed consent, Patricio may wish to dissociate himself from the aftercare program entirely, leaving the provision of clinical services to a therapist not directly involved in the research.

5

The Duty to Identify the Primary Client

Some of the basic legal responsibilities that underlie the professional relationship between behavioral health providers and their clients have already been the focus of much discussion here. Specifically, reasonable competence in the delivery of services and the pursuit of informed consent in professional relationships are two fundamental duties that promote the best interests of clients. Recognizing the importance of satisfying these duties may therefore help the professional to make practice decisions more effectively and expeditiously.

Where a behavioral health provider offers services to a single client, the duties imposed by a professional relationship may be identified in a fairly straightforward manner. Often, however, professionals work not with individual clients, but with client groups that include marital couples, families, civic associations, and on occasion, entire communities. Sometimes services are provided primarily to one family member, such as a child, whereas other family members, such as parents, have important peripheral interests in the quality of the services provided. Public sector professionals are often called upon to provide services simultaneously to a government agency and to individuals who come into contact with that agency. In all of the above instances, it may sometimes become difficult for the conscientious professional to identify the client(s) to whom professional duties are primarily owed.

Identifying the primary client may also be critical when multiple parties are involved in the referral of a client for services, or in the payment for those services. For example, when a client is court-ordered to receive treatment, or referred to a behavioral health provider by another professional (such as an attorney or primary care physician), or when a client seeks reimbursement for services through an insurance company or other third-party payor, the provider's judgment may be influenced by professional or business obligations to these third parties. In such circumstances, understanding how to identify the primary client may be of critical importance in evaluating how the professional's responsibilities must be exercised. Identifying the primary client may also be a helpful way to resolve practice dilemmas in which multiple parties are involved and seemingly conflicting interests are at hand.

The *duty to identify the primary client* requires that the decision maker take the following steps:

- Identify the person(s)—the primary client(s)—with whom the provider has agreed to establish a professional relationship. The primary client(s) may be an individual, family, or vulnerable population to whom the professional has agreed to provide relevant services, or whose interests the professional is legally bound to protect.
- Identify the professional duties owed to the client, e.g., the duty to practice reasonably competently, the duty to seek informed consent, and the duty to maintain confidentiality.
- Perform the duties owed to the client(s).

As with each of the basic legal principles, following the steps mandated by the duty to identify the primary client will support clients' best interests and also maximize the likelihood that important societal goals enforced by the duty are advanced. As the decision making framework suggests, the duty to identify the primary client should be considered, along with the other basic legal principles, as a first step in the decision making process. As the subsequent case examples demonstrate, a decision maker who can sort through a practice dilemma to identify the professional duty owed to a primary client has an important aid in the resolution of the problem.

The duty to identify the primary client often is inadequately explained, or, even worse, confused, by professional ethical codes. For example, the NASW Code, the NBCC Code, and the APA Code all express important but broad aspirational ideals governing practice, including the advancement of human welfare and social justice, but they pay little attention to identifying specifically *to whom* these obligations are primarily owed. None of these professional codes actually defines the term *client*, which is essentially a legal concept. Most confusingly, the NASW Code's Preamble describes *client* not in its strict, legal sense, but rather loosely as a term "used inclusively to refer to individuals, families, groups, organizations, and communities." This interpretation omits any discussion as to the manner in which the professional relationship is created and seems to suggest instead that the provider owes duties to all elements of society simultaneously, whether services are sought voluntarily or not. This important failing sometimes leads code users to categorize certain practice situations involving multiple parties as ethical "conflicts of interest," where the law actually may suggest otherwise. In light of this fact, the decision maker who recognizes and applies the duty to identify the primary client *before* undertaking a review of any of the ethical codes will avoid this unnecessary confusion.

Establishing Professional Relationships With Clients

Professional relationships between behavioral health providers and their clients are inaugurated in a variety of ways. Some begin when a person voluntarily seeks out the services of a professional to assist with the person's own problem, such as a mental health issue. Others start when the professional's services are engaged vicariously on behalf of a family member, e.g., when parents seek a provider's assistance on behalf of a minor child. On other occasions, the social worker's, counselor's, or psychologist's services are sought by another professional, such as when an attorney refers a client for a mental health consultation. Sometimes clients are ordered to seek services by courts, e.g., when criminal defendants or respondents in child abuse proceedings are directed to receive counseling. A professional relationship between a government agency and a client is created when legislation directs the agency to protect the best interests of certain vulnerable members of a community, such as the victims of abuse and neglect. When the agency hires behavioral health providers, such as child and adult protective social workers, or forensic psychologists, their professional relationships with the endangered clients commence the moment that they accept public employment.

Regardless of the diverse ways in which behavioral health providers begin their affiliation with clients, the end result is the establishment of a professional relationship. A professional relationship with a client is established when the provider voluntarily agrees to provide services to an identified individual or group (or voluntarily agrees to represent the interests of a legally protected class of vulnerable persons), and the client (or, if the client lacks capacity, the client's surrogate) voluntarily agrees to accept them (*In re Investigation of Underwager,* 1997 (psychologist-client relationship); *People v. Simms,* 2000 (attorney-client relationship); *Zinermon v. Burch,* 1990 (civilly committed mental patients and hospital)). The individual, group, or class that is the chief beneficiary of the professional service is the primary client. The professional relationship is sometimes memorialized by a contractual agreement, expressed either verbally or in writing, in which the parties mutually agree on the services to be provided, including the cost, if applicable, of the services. This relationship imposes a number of burdens on the professional, including, most notably, basic legal responsibilities.

Note that the legal definitions of professional relationship and client serve an important purpose consistent with communitarian principles. First, they emphasize the point that the fundamental responsibilities owed by all behavioral health professionals to their clients are essentially the same. This fact is often confused by technical variations in the ethical standards and aspirational ideals expressed by individual professions. It is important for behavioral health and human service providers to understand that the professional relationship imposes standards of care that transcend the values of particular professions and unite all providers in their commitment to the protection of client welfare. This commitment is essentially the same whether the professional service offered is medical care, legal services, psychological assistance, counseling, or social work. Therefore, contrary to the myriad of aspirational values that ethical codes identify, the law recognizes that behavioral health professionals have their limits. Awareness of this fact can inspire a modicum of personal humility in the provider, as well as a measure of comfort in the realization that the law does not expect omnipotence from behavioral health professionals.

Informed Consent and the Professional Relationship

Creation of a valid professional relationship with a client depends on the receipt of informed consent from the client or a surrogate representing the client's best interests. Honoring the duty to seek informed consent protects the client's privacy and self-determination, and it is consistent with competent practice. Behavioral health and human services are often sought on behalf of underaged, infirm, or incapacitated persons by a parent, guardian, or other representative. In these circumstances, the legal capacity to provide informed consent is retained by a party best able to protect the vulnerable client's interest. Although informed consent is not provided by the incapacitated client, he or she is the primary client in the resulting professional relationship to whom the provider's central legal responsibilities are owed. For example, in the case of a mother who brings her young child to a family physician for a medical consultation relating to the child's hyperactivity, informed consent is provided by the mother; the primary client, however is the child. The physician owes specific legal duties to that child, including the duty to practice reasonably competently. If important risks and disclosures pertaining to the treatment of hyperactivity are not discussed with the mother, then she cannot provide informed consent. In this instance, the professional's failure to seek informed consent violates practice duties owed to the primary client, i.e., the child.

Professionals often owe independent duties to a person who provides informed consent on behalf of a vulnerable client. For example, a parent or guardian may contract with a therapist to offer clinical services to a child. Failure to provide these services may represent a breach of contract with the parent warranting legal relief.

Guardians, surrogates, and other individuals who have the responsibility to make informed decisions on a vulnerable person's behalf themselves have a legal duty to that client to act with reasonable care in making such decisions. This fiduciary duty means that the law imposes a commitment to prudence and trustworthiness that obliges the fiduciary to make reasonably competent decisions that protect the health and property of the vulnerable person. For example, if a guardian were to consent to a course of "rebirthing therapy" treatments for a minor ward, the fiduciary duty might well be violated.

Identifying the Primary Client in Practice With Families and Groups

Behavioral health professionals who practice with families and groups often provide services to a number of clients simultaneously in counseling, psychotherapy, community organizing, and other areas. The fact that family or group forums are used to provide services does not detract from the fact that each and every member of a client group enjoys the status of a primary client. Each individual is therefore entitled to the rights and protections afforded to primary clients. This entitlement may prove troublesome for the professional who regards the family, group, or community singularly as "the client." Indeed, it could prompt otherwise cautious professionals to broaden the scope of their services in such a way that appropriate attention is not paid to the right of each individual to such legal protections as informed consent and confidentiality. In group settings involving vulnerable individuals particularly subject to group influence, the ability of such individuals to communicate effectively with the facilitator may be compromised. The careful professional therefore needs to prepare for group practice in a way that respects the basic rights of all members. Precautions may include holding individual informed consent dialogues with all group members individually before their admission to the group. Consistent with the requirements of informed consent, these dialogues should address the risks and benefits unique to group treatment modalities.

Group practice presents unique challenges for the behavioral health professional concerned with honoring the legal rights of each individual member. Upholding confidentiality, for example, may be burdensome where group facilitators have no control over the activities of members outside of the group session, and where they themselves may interact with individual group members away from the group setting.

Identifying the primary client presents special considerations for those behavioral health professionals involved in practice with large groups, such as social workers active in community organizing, political advocacy, and regional economic development. In fact, the concept of identifying a primary client may seem unnatural to a professional used to practicing in informal settings with spontaneously created coalitions of community members or civic associations. Nevertheless, the duty to identify one's primary client is as necessary a task with large groups as it is with individual clients, and for all the same reasons. The duty means literally that every member of a community for whom services are voluntarily provided is a primary client of the professional who undertakes such services. Moreover, it implies a responsibility on the part of the organizer to seek informed consent from these potential clients. This concept should give pause to any organizer who believes that professional responsibilities do not apply in this area of practice.

The difficulty of defining reasonably competent practice in macro-level human services, such as community and political organizing, has bedeviled judges, some of whom have been unable to ascertain exactly what practice standards should be expected of such professionals (see, e.g., *Horak v. Biris,* 1985). This fact notwithstanding, if one considers case examples 2, "Addressing Attrition Among Native American College Students," and 12, "The Anti-WIPP Organizer," it will be noted that each addresses program development and organizing issues in minority communities, and each demonstrates the vital safeguarding role that identifying the primary client plays in the promotion of individual well-being and community diversity. Indeed, if the community developers in each case example fail to undertake a community assessment that tests the applicability of their research to the local population, then they truly are disregarding their duty to identify the primary client(s). Appreciating this point in community development, political organizing, and agency administration puts these areas of behavioral health and human service specialization in the same legal context as more traditional practice methods. Specifically, it demands adherence to minimal legal responsibilities as surely as in the case of conventional practice with individual clients and modest family groups.

Identifying the Client in Public Agency Practice

Identifying the client in public agency practice is a task required of every professional who accepts employment with the government. In contrast to the relationship between private sector professionals and their clients, the association between government servants and their clients is expressly defined by law and advances special societal goals. The aspiration government agencies most often voice in the design and implementation of health and human services is best described by the legal/philosophical doctrine known as *parens patriae,* which means literally the "'parent of his or her country' and refers to the role of the state as sovereign and guardian of persons under legal disability" (*Kelm v. Kelm,* 2001, p. 301 n.1) (quoting *Black's Law Dictionary* 1137, 7th ed., 1999). According to *parens patriae*, the government has a moral obligation to protect the interests of those vulnerable citizens unable to protect themselves (*In re Kendall J. and Darris P.,* 2000; *Kelm v. Kelm,* 2001; *Steele v. Hamilton County Community Mental Health Bd.,* 2000).

Over the last 100 or more years, state legislatures have cited *parens patriae* in the creation of extensive child welfare, adult protective service, mental health, and other government bureaus charged with the administrative responsibility of protecting the public interest in each of these respective areas. These departments are sometimes described as *executive agencies* because typically they are placed under the ultimate administrative authority of the chief executive of a jurisdiction, such as a governor, at the state level, or the president, at the federal level. The terms *public agency* and *government agency* are used interchangeably here to describe these service bureaus.

As an example of the legal responsibilities of government agencies, state legislation creating human services departments has given such bureaus broad authority to administer public welfare, food stamp, and medical assistance programs for needy persons (*State* ex rel. *Taylor v. Johnson,* 1998). Similarly, many state legislatures have addressed the needs of mentally ill citizens by establishing community mental health boards empowered with the authority to house incapacitated persons and provide treatment both voluntarily and involuntarily (*Steele v. Hamilton County Community Mental Health Bd.,* 2000). Additional legislation in most states has created public agencies charged with the responsibility of administering child welfare, mental health, and other programs offering protection to vulnerable citizens.

All government agencies have a particular administrative burden defined by law, and they carry out this responsibility through the promulgation of rules and regulations governing their internal agency practices. Rules and regulations have the force of law and must be consistent with the public policy, also known as *authorizing legislation*, that creates each agency and empowers it with governmental authority. According to their authorizing legislation, and in a manner consistent with their rules and regulations, government agencies are entrusted to hire qualified public personnel whose ultimate responsibility is the enforcement of each agency's governmental purpose. In the case of agencies that protect specific public interests in the areas of child welfare, mental health, and juvenile probation services, behavioral health professionals are largely responsible both for providing direct agency services and for administrative functions.

In a very real sense, a behavioral health professional who accepts a position within a public agency assumes the agency's legal obligation to a specific vulnerable population. Put differently, the professional accepts the agency's service population as a primary client, and assumes the same legal obligations as are owed to any client with whom a professional relationship is established. Thus, behavioral health professionals who work with the kinds of public agencies listed below assume as their clients the populations indicated:

Table 1: Primary Clients of Public Agencies

Agency or Bureau	Primary Responsibilities	Client Population
Child Welfare	Investigation of Child Abuse, Neglect	At-risk and Vulnerable Children
Health	Maintenance of Public Health	The Public
Mental Health	Maintenance of Public Mental Health Protection of Mentally Fragile	The Public Mentally Fragile
Adult Protective Services	Investigation of Abuse of Physically and Mentally Fragile Adults	Physically, Mentally Fragile Adults
Corrections	Protection of Public Welfare Through Deterrence and Rehabilitation of Inmates	The Public
Income Support	Protection of Public Welfare	Vulnerable, Income-deprived Members of the Public
Education	Promotion of Public Schools	School Children

The advantage of understanding the public agency professional's role as a duty owed to a specific class of primary client is that it helps to identify the legal obligations owed to that group. As an example pertaining to government-employed social workers, consider the specific legal obligations that child protective service professionals agree to undertake when they provide services to the public. Most importantly, they agree to represent the interests of the population of vulnerable children in the region served by their agency. Included among the responsibilities owed to this client population are the duty to practice reasonably competently and the duty to maintain confidentiality. In this context, reasonably competent practice means that a child welfare social worker must adequately investigate reports of suspected child abuse or neglect, and must in the child's best interest keep the identity of the presumed victim confidential. Similarly, a psychologist employed by a community mental health center must capably examine severely depressed or psychotic patients for signs that they may be a threat to themselves or others. Finally, as case example 4, "The Welfare Office," demonstrates, a social worker employed by an income support bureau must obtain informed consent from a client applying for government benefits. The same is asked of a public school guidance counselor offering services to school aged children.

In many instances, members of the vulnerable client groups served by public agencies lack legal or mental capacity to provide informed consent for health and human services. This is the case, for example, with children and mentally fragile persons. In these instances, the role of the public agency is in the nature of a guardianship, with the agency obliged to protect the interests of its wards and to consent to services that best meet their needs. Some agencies literally become the legal guardians of their vulnerable populations, as is the case with child welfare agencies that obtain custody of abused children whose legal rights as natural parents have been terminated by a court. In such instances, agencies have on occasion failed notoriously. In New Mexico, during the early 1980s, civil rights litigation challenged the management of the foster care system by New Mexico's Human Services Department (*Joseph A. v. New Mexico Dep't of Human Servs.,* 1983). Specifically, this public agency was charged literally with abandoning its wards—abused and neglected children placed in foster care—by failing to keep track of their whereabouts and further neglecting to provide suitable, permanent home placements. In this respect, the *Joseph A.* case is representative of litigation initiated in a number of states seeking the reformation of inadequate foster care programs. The *Joseph A.* case was an important factor motivating the creation of a new, cabinet-level government agency—the Children, Youth, and Families Department (CYFD). As with similar statewide bureaus operating elsewhere, CYFD bears primary responsibility for administering child protective services in New Mexico.

Some behavioral health academicians and ethicists raise the question of whether professional values are consistent with public sector practice. In particular, they raise the argument that a government agency professional cannot observe important aspirational ideals promoted by the behavioral health disciplines, such as the promotion of client self-determination, the enhancement of client well-being, and the pursuit of social justice, while representing a public policing authority. This argument makes three erroneous assumptions that ignore important legal principles governing behavioral health practice:

First, it dismisses the doctrine of *parens patriae*, a societal value whose enactment into child and adult protective service legislation must be embraced by all professionals, as well as by participating members of a community. Compliance with this law, as the decision making framework suggests, is to be expected as much from behavioral health professionals as from all other citizens within a community. Moreover, it must guide the manner in which each professional interprets its own professional ethical codes.

Second, it ignores the desirability of encouraging behavioral health professionals to devote their practices to particularly vulnerable client groups, such as at-risk children who may vitally need their services. With respect to professionals who enter the public sector, commitment to a specific client group is not only mandated by law, but it is also critically necessary for reasonably competent practice. More than that, a commitment to a class of clients tends to make professional ethical ideals more realistically attainable. It has already been noted that a weakness of ethical codes generally is that they express a laundry list of aspirations that sometimes encourage the belief that professionals must be all things to all people simultaneously. The NASW Code, with its excessively broad concept of *client*, tends especially to promote this diffusive sense of responsibility among social workers. While the encouragement of social accountability is a noble ideal, it tends also to account for the early professional burnout suffered by many providers. Indeed, it may be the primary ingredient in the role confusion expressed by many behavioral health professionals unable to reconcile the seemingly conflicting ethical burdens that guide daily practice (Bakker, Schaufeli, Sixma, & Bosveld, 2001; Schaufeli & Enzmann, 1998). In contrast to this philosophy, the law identifies and limits the nature of the professional relationship between every provider and client. This fact alone provides a reason for considering all practice decisions in the legal context suggested by the decision making framework.

Identifying and Performing Duties Owed to the Primary Client

The duty to identify the primary client includes the responsibility to assess all professional obligations owed to that client. Each of these, including the duty to practice reasonably competently, the duty to seek informed consent, the duty to treat clients and co-workers with due process and equal protection, and the duty to maintain confidentiality at times extends not only to the primary client but also to other members of the public who reasonably may be affected by the professional's conduct. Thus, behavioral health professionals providing services to a primary client who threatens violence have a responsibility to protect the identified victim (*Tarasoff v. Regents of Univ. of Cal.,* 1976). Similarly, public agency professionals have the obligation to enforce constitutional protections that extend to federal and state employees. Finally, behavioral health and social researchers have the duty to seek informed consent from and maintain the confidentiality of participants, even though, strictly speaking, such participants may not normally meet the definition of primary client suggested here.

Despite the occasionally broad application all of these basic duties have to the general public, they apply most strictly within the unique relationship enjoyed by the behavioral health professional and primary client. They promote the quality of the professional alliance by requiring the provider to honor its importance above all other social and business entanglements. A key element of this responsibility is the professional's obligation to avoid conflicts of interest, or "dual relationships." It is an inherent part of the commitment owed to the primary client, and enhances the provider's ability to honor all other legal obligations.

Avoiding Conflicts of Interest

On occasion, a provider's ability to perform the duties imposed by the professional relationship may be compromised by significant factors external to the relationship. For this reason, avoiding conflicts of interest is an important legal responsibility that applies whenever a behavioral health provider anticipates forming a professional relationship with a primary client. Conflicts of interest include

- Social or business associations with the primary client
- Social or business associations involving a third party to the professional relationship
- Professional responsibilities imposed by law or by agency obligations
- Proprietary or research interests in services that are being offered to the primary client
- Business associations with insurance companies, health maintenance organizations (HMOs), and other third-party sources of payment for the primary client's services

Each of these categories of conflict may occur either before or after the professional has entered into a formal relationship with a primary client, and the client either may be aware or lack knowledge of the conflict's existence.

When a primary client is unaware of the existence of a conflict, the professional's failure to discuss its impact interferes with the client's ability to give informed consent because it denies the client information that might reasonably be relied upon to make a voluntary decision about whether to accept services. For this reason, failure to reveal a known conflict of interest to an unaware client violates a fundamental legal principle—the duty to seek informed consent—applicable to behavioral health professionals.

Some conflicts are so inherently disruptive to the client's decision making capacity, e.g., sexual and inappropriate social and business relationships, that, even if the client is a willing participant in the external alliance, its manipulative power undermines the client's ability to consent to professional services voluntarily. Under these circumstances, simply revealing this point to the client is not enough to salvage the professional relationship. Maintaining a relationship under such circumstances also violates the duty to practice reasonably competently. Therefore, the best overall strategy for avoiding conflicts of interest is to obey the following rule: Consider the impact of any conflict of interest on the professional relationship by reviewing the conflict's effect on the duties to practice reasonably competently and to seek informed consent.

Understanding the range of impact that conflicts of interest can have on the creation and maintenance of professional relationships is critical for the decision maker. For this reason, each conflict category is addressed individually in light of the rule suggested above.

Social and Business Associations Involving the Primary Client. Social and business associations with clients can interfere with the ability of the behavioral health professional to make independent judgments necessary for reasonably competent practice. When a conflict of interest based on a social or business association threatens to interfere with a professional relationship, the provider involved must make a reasonable evaluation of the extent to which the association may pose a risk of harm to the primary client. Consistent with reasonably competent practice, discerning professionals facing such conflicts must consider and apply standards that prevail within the communities where they work, together with treatment alternatives reasonably available to prospective clients. In addition, clients' own psychosocial and cultural backgrounds must be assessed in an effort to estimate the risk of harm.

When a behavioral health professional considers entering into a clinical association with a social acquaintance, the impact of the personal connection is a necessary element of the discussion of risks and benefits essential for informed consent. Note that, with the exception of certain types of exploitative social and business associations that are inherently threatening to the client, the law places no absolute restrictions on the provision of professional services either to social acquaintances or relatives. As noted earlier (see vignette 2, "The Coffee Shop"), professional ethical codes all echo this legal principle. For example, the NASW Code (Ethical Standard 1.06) suggests that "dual relationships" with clients are to be avoided to the extent they threaten a "risk of exploitation or potential harm to the client." Similarly, the NBCC Code (Sections A8, A9, and B9) places a burden upon counselors to avoid the "misuse of their influence" and associations that threaten impartiality and independent judgment. Finally, the APA Code (Ethical Standard 1.17) mandates that psychologists avoid business and social associations that impair objectivity, interfere with effective service delivery, or are exploitative. Of these code provisions, only the APA's indicates that the extent of harm or exploitation may depend profoundly on community norms, and therefore implicitly grants some leeway to psychologists practicing in rural areas. With this singular exception, the ethical codes cited simply do not address the impact of cultural and regional context on professional and personal conflicts.

Summarizing the issues discussed above, the following rule offers the most effective strategy for assessing conflict of interest dilemmas involving social or business associations: Consider a decision to enter into a professional relationship where a social or business association with a client already exists by thoroughly reviewing the decision's effect on the duties to practice reasonably competently and to seek informed consent.

As a way of examining the operation of this rule, consider the case of a 55-year-old, lifelong resident of Truth or Consequences, New Mexico. The man knows virtually everyone in town, including the certified alcoholism counselor at a local rehab program. Faced with his own severe drinking problem, the man seeks treatment from the program and its counselor. Strictly speaking, the counselor has a conflict of interest with the man because of their social acquaintanceship. However, based on regional community standards, this social association might not reasonably be expected to have an impact on the counselor's ability to provide independent, appropriate services. Moreover, there are no feasible alternatives to providing these services locally. Indeed, denial of services on the basis of a presumed conflict might well prove fatal to this prospective client. At the same time, the duty to seek informed consent requires the counselor to explore the potential impact of the social affiliation on the budding professional relationship.

Entering into social relationships with clients *after* the professional association has commenced should invoke the same legal review outlined above. In other words, consider a decision to socialize with a primary client after a professional relationship already exists by thoroughly reviewing the decision's impact on the duties to practice reasonably competently and to seek informed consent. For example, in vignette 2, " The Coffee Shop," the decision maker performed a conflict of interest analysis and ethical review suggesting that brief social contact with the client was appropriate. In completing the analysis the counselor most likely received some assistance from applying the legal rule described above. The present discussion suggests that the thorough professional would at the least want to examine the duty to practice reasonably competently in order to evaluate the potential impact the coffee shop encounter could have on the clinical relationship. One might find good therapeutic reasons to believe that accepting the cup of coffee supports the client's clinical progress, and none that indicates it is threatened by the coffee. As vignette 2 suggests, the impact of socialization on the professional relationship should be evaluated with respect to regional and cultural standards. Familiarity with the way people behave in Truth or Consequences is likely to lead the prudent professional to conclude that the duty to practice reasonably competently is, after all, not compromised by a cup of coffee.

In addition to demonstrating the usefulness of a conflict of interest analysis, vignette 2 also shows that many ethical standards simply restate preexisting legal principles. With this in mind, the cautious practitioner can gain much from a thorough survey of the law governing a practice problem.

Some social alliances are so inherently destructive to the professional relationship that they are defined as malpractice, as is the case with sexual associations between psychotherapists and their clients. In some states, this kind of behavior is criminalized. Sexual relationships between other health and human service professionals, e.g., social workers, physicians, nurses, and attorneys, are somewhat more complicated to analyze because the purposes of these professional relationships are not as immediately and irreparably harmed as the psychotherapeutic bond is. Nevertheless, if one performs a thorough conflict of interest analysis, any sexual relationship with a client would appear to compromise the professional's ability to deliver services objectively (i.e., reasonably competently and with informed consent), and be so inherently coercive as to substantially interfere with the client's ability to consent voluntarily to the professional relationship. This is the position adopted by the NASW, APA, and NBCC Codes. Social workers, for example, are admonished in the NASW Code's Ethical Standard 1.09(a) "under no circumstances to engage in sexual activities or sexual contact with current clients, whether . . . consensual or not." Similarly, the APA Code (Ethical Standard 4.05) warns psychologists not to engage in "sexual intimacies" with current clients. Finally, counselors are advised flatly in NBCC Code Section A(10) that "sexual intimacy," together with physical and romantic intimacy, is unethical. These clear standards may be the most binding and enforceable in all three ethical codes, a fact reflected in data suggesting that sexual misconduct accounts for the most instances of disciplinary actions by licensing boards against behavioral health professionals nationally (Berkman, Turner, Cooper, Polnerow, & Schwartz, 2000).

Providing services to clients with whom a past sexual liaison has existed also has the strong potential for undermining the professional relationship. The conflict of interest analysis suggested here should lead the decision maker to conclude that this kind of situation blurs professional boundaries, threatens exploitation of the client, and compromises the ability of the provider to offer reasonably competent behavioral health services, regardless of the specific nature of those services. For this reason, ethical codes take a strong stand against the provision of clinical psychotherapy services to partners of a past sexual relationship (see, e.g., the NASW Code's Ethical Standard 1.09(d) and the APA Code's Ethical Standard 4.06) but do not rule out the provision of other human services to such individuals. No such prohibition is imposed against counselors in the NBCC Code, nor does it seem to apply to social workers not engaged in psychotherapy. Considering the fact that counselors and social workers frequently engage in such diverse fields as school based counseling, program development, community organizing, and other human services not involving direct psychotherapeutic interaction, this interesting omission leaves the behavioral health professional without specific ethical guidance covering these practice situations. Here again, the decision maker is urged in such contexts to complete the conflict of interest analysis suggested here.

Engaging in sexual liaisons with former clients also raises significant conflict of interest questions. In this circumstance, the professional relationship technically has terminated before the commencement of the sexual association. Even here, however, there exists a risk to the former client that the lingering impact of the prior professional relationship may be used coercively as a means of manipulating the person into the sexual affiliation. This danger is especially acute where psychotherapy has been provided. In such cases, the intense professional relationship that existed during the formal treatment phase has a permanent effect on the continuing mental health of the client. Therefore, the progress the client has made may be jeopardized if the relationship with the past therapist becomes inappropriately personal. Viewed in this light, a psychotherapist should regard any professional relationship and the duties imposed by it as existing beyond the formal termination date of services.

The present conflict of interest discussion might reasonably lead a decision maker who has provided clinical services to a client to conclude that involvement in a sexual relationship with the former client violates the duty to practice reasonably competently because it could be expected to have an impact on the client's continuing health. This is the position of many state legislatures, which have criminalized sexual relationships between psychotherapists and former clients where the professional services have only been terminated for a short time (as an example, one year in New Mexico) (Sexual Offenses, 1978/2001, §30-9-10(A)(5)). Even when such conduct is not criminal, it still may be so inherently harmful to the former client as to constitute malpractice. This danger may or may not be present in the case of sexual relationships between other human service professionals, such as social workers and counselors providing nonclinical services, and their former clients.

Ethical codes in the behavioral health disciplines (see, e.g., the NASW Code's Ethical Standard 1.09(b), the NBCC Code's Section A10, and the APA Code's Ethical Standard 4.07(a)) suggest that sexual relationships with former clients are to be avoided and place the burden on professionals seeking to engage in such relationships to demonstrate the absence of exploitation. In the case of counselors and psychologists, this burden includes the passage of at least two years since the termination of services.

Is it possible for the professional to overcome the presumption that sexual relationships with former clients is inherently harmful? Consider the case of a social worker or counselor serving as a hospital patient advocate. The patient advocate's services during the client's one-day hospital visit consist of presenting the client's grievance concerning the hospital's food to the administrative staff. Ten years pass, and the advocate has been reintroduced to the former client at a social event; she and the client now independently wish to pursue an intimate personal relationship. Whether the relationship should be avoided depends in large measure on the advocate's assessment of the potential harm to the former client. Applying the test suggested above, the advocate might reasonably conclude that the former professional relationship terminated at the time of the client's hospital discharge, and that the professional relationship that previously existed has no continuing impact on the client's present well-being.

Acceptance of a gift creates a conflict of interest for the behavioral health professional if the gift is substantial enough to influence the professional's subjectivity or it threatens to distort the client's expectations regarding services. Thus, if psychologist Dr. Malfi accepts Tony Soprano's cash gift for her "good work this week," Dr. Malfi can reasonably expect that the acceptance of the gift will encourage Tony to expect more clinical successes in future weeks.

As with other conflict of interest dilemmas, it is helpful for decision makers to assess their responsibilities regarding gifts in terms of the duties relating to informed consent and reasonably competent practice. As an example, reconsider the counselor's acceptance of the dream catcher in vignette 3. Taking the gift probably creates no unreasonable client expectations that harm the professional relationship. Moreover, it is consistent with regional and cultural expectations that help to identify standards of reasonably competent practice and informed consent in the community of Farmington, New Mexico.

Occasionally, state legislation defines the extent to which behavioral health professionals—especially government employees—can accept gifts. Typically this legislation is defined in terms of a dollar amount. Considering this fact together with the two situations noted above, the decision maker's best strategy for making a choice concerning a client's gift is to consider it only upon a thorough review of the duties to practice reasonably competently and to seek informed consent, as well as any applicable law governing the receipt of gifts by public employees.

Gift acceptance should also be considered in the context of ethical standards governing conflicts of interest. The general theme of these standards echoes the legal rule cited above: Avoid risking the harm or exploitation of a client, and abstain from exploiting the client or taking unfair advantage.

Mastering this concept, together with the definitions of reasonably competent practice and informed consent, offers to the decision maker the best overall preparation for conflict situations, especially because it most effectively encourages the consideration of cultural and regional context.

Business associations between behavioral health providers and their clients present a comparable threat to the integrity of the professional relationship. A variety of business relationships—from formal to informal—can link professionals and their clients, and the more rural a community is, the more inevitable is a conflict of interest. A professional may drink coffee at a coffee shop whose owner is a primary client. A professional may simultaneously buy a car from, and provide services to, the lone car salesperson in a small town. A professional may exchange services with a physician, or may offer treatment to a public school teacher who teaches the professional's child. The range of interests cited here demonstrates that there can be no reasonable legal or ethical rule barring outright the existence of a business association between professional and client. However, one should consider the effect of a business association on the professional relationship by a thorough review of the duties to practice reasonably competently and to seek informed consent.

This strategy requires the professional to consider the business association by reference to its impact on the competent provision of services to the client, the professional's ability to make impartial clinical choices on the client's behalf, and the client's continuing expectations regarding services. Consistent with standards governing competent practice and informed consent, these legal principles must be applied with reference to community and cultural expectations. Thus, in all of the business conflict situations cited above, a professional might reasonably offer services to the client and maintain the business association where

- It is consistent with community and cultural expectations
- The professional is treated similarly to any other business customer
- The business association does not otherwise exploit the client such that the benefits of the business association might reasonably alter the client's expectations concerning the professional service
- The professional seeks informed consent, i.e., the professional discusses the risks presented by the business association as a condition to providing professional services

Consider the example of a licensed counselor who receives an offer of a personal loan from a bank vice president, also a client, based on the vice president's "vouching for the good reputation and credit worthiness" of the counselor. The counselor's application for and acceptance of the loan exploits the professional relationship with the vice president in a way that is burdensome. Specifically, there is a danger that the bank president may expect quid quo pro from the counselor in the delivery of future clinical services, a belief that clouds understanding of the risks and benefits offered by the counseling. In this situation, the imposition that the business exchange places upon the professional relationship is so extreme that no amount of open discussion between professional and client can overcome it. In informed consent terms, the risk created by the loan guarantee offered by the banker is not likely to be overcome simply because both parties are aware of it.

Compare this situation with the other business and social conflicts described earlier. The difference here is not only in degree, but also in the role that the exchange of money has in defining the professional relationship. Because the professional relationship itself often involves a business exchange, including payment for services, additional financial entanglements between the provider and client may alter or confuse, at least in the mind of the client, the clear contractual agreement that should form the basis of the parties' essential bond.

Social and Business Associations Involving a Third Party. Social and business associations that involve the provider, a client, and a third party may also interfere with the professional relationship. These types of situation arise when the client's or provider's mutual social or business association with another individual threatens to have some impact on the professional relationship. This may occur when the professional and client both share a close friendship with another person, or when the professional has a business relationship with a member of the client's family, or even when the professional has a close social or sexual relationship with a member of the client's family. As with other conflicts, this kind most clearly threatens the bond between professional and client when it interferes with the client's voluntary consideration of the risks and benefits attending services, and with the professional's ability to exercise independent judgment.

If, for example, a psychologist provides psychotherapy to the teacher of the psychologist's child, a thorough discussion of the conflict's existence may be sufficient to allow the client to consider freely the potential impact of the external association upon the services; the client may quickly reject its importance, and openly consent to treatment. Suppose, on the contrary, that the psychologist's association with the teacher has been a tempestuous and confrontational one, and in the recent past the two have quarreled publicly during school board meetings over the quality of teaching (including this person's skills) at the community elementary school. Perhaps the teacher sees therapy not only as the best way to address long-standing emotional problems, but also as a method of mending fences with the psychologist on a social level. In this rather unlikely predicament, the cautious professional might find, even after a full discussion of risks required by the duty to seek informed consent, that the parties' past history is bound to intrude into the clinical dialogue. In this circumstance, a subsidiary issue—the teacher/student/parent triangle—may play an excessive role in the teacher's decision to seek services. Considered in another light, the professional's duty to practice reasonably competently is compromised by this turbulent social history.

Other social associations involving the provider and a third party may threaten the professional relationship in a more immediate way. A common example of such a circumstance is sexual contact between the provider and a close friend or relative of the primary client. This situation may impose such a great burden on the client's expectations concerning services that, even with the provider's full disclosure of the risks, the potential for psychic harm to the client is too foreseeable to permit the establishment of a professional relationship.

A legal approach to risk evaluation is also implied by professional ethical codes, which essentially require the professional to assess the potential for harm to the client when triangular social associations are involved. For example, the NASW Code (Ethical Standard 1.06) suggests that such relationships should be avoided "when there is a risk of exploitation or potential harm to the client." The APA Code (Ethical Standard 1.17) takes essentially the same position, as does the NBCC Code (Section B9). As with conflict situations presented here, the decision maker managing dilemmas that involve third-party relationships should consider them by thorough application of the duties to seek informed consent and to practice reasonably competently.

Conflicts Created by Legal Responsibilities and Agency Obligations. Services provided to a primary client may be limited by the law or by professional responsibilities that the behavioral health provider owes by reason of agency policy or other employment obligations. For example, professionals have a legal obligation to report suspected child abuse and to protect the client and other members of the public from the client's threats of violence. The professional's duties in these instances may clearly affect the nature of services rendered to the client, and they may supersede other responsibilities ordinarily owed to a client, such as the maintenance of confidentiality. Thus, in these instances, the conflicting obligations owed by the professional plainly create a conflict of interest. As with any other conflict, the professional must manage it in a manner that satisfies the duty to practice reasonably competently and the duty to seek informed consent. The latter responsibility suggests that the provider should disclose legal responsibilities as one of the "risks" created by the professional relationship.

Any behavioral health provider, and particularly one offering direct clinical services, must struggle with the impact that the disclosure of legal responsibilities may have on the professional relationship. To a shy or sensitive client entering psychotherapy for the first time, the recitation of legal responsibilities by the clinician can have a chilling effect on the client's willingness to disclose information. This is especially true where the provider treats informed consent as a formality, rather than a continuing dialogue between professional and client. The discussion concerning the professional's legal responsibilities calls for the exercise of good clinical skills and presents one more argument in favor of an open, relaxed, informal, and ongoing clinical conversation concerning informed consent issues. In fact, the competent therapist should discuss the meaning of informed consent itself, so that the client plainly understands the purpose underlying the revelation of risks and benefits.

As noted above, behavioral health professionals practicing with public agencies frequently have a legal responsibility to protect the interests of a class of vulnerable clients. Often, however, these professionals also provide services to other members of the public who do not fall within the protected class. For example, the legal responsibility imposed on child welfare social workers is to protect the interest of vulnerable children who may be threatened by abuse or neglect. These children, in effect, are the primary clients of the agency social worker. In the course of performing a vital public service, the agency social worker may be called upon to provide rehabilitative assistance to the family of a vulnerable child. Indeed, such assistance is frequently mandated by children's courts facing the problem of family violence. In such cases, a child's custody may hinge on the parents' successful completion of parenting classes, individual therapy, anger management training, or a family preservation service (FPS) program. FPS programs are short-term, intensive interventions that are intended to prevent the removal of children from the homes of families who have experienced abuse or neglect (Littell & Tajima, 2000). FPS programs typically last no more than four months but provide up to 15 contact hours per week in home based counseling, parenting skills education, and similar clinical services (Littell & Tajima, 2000). Spurred on by federal legislation, including the Adoption Assistance and Child Welfare Act of 1980, and by federal dollars from the Omnibus Budget Reconciliation Act of 1993 (OBRA) and the Adoption and Safe Families Act of 1997 (ASFA), most states have adopted FPS programs (Littell & Tajima, 2000).

When clinical services, including counseling, psychotherapy, and FPS programs are provided by the child welfare agency itself, the recipients of the services become the agency's secondary clients. Secondary clients may be defined as clients to whom services are provided peripherally as part of the agency's satisfaction of its legal responsibilities to a primary client.

In any child welfare case involving a youngster who is threatened by suspected abuse or neglect, the child and parents have interests that are, at least for the moment, in conflict. Parents usually wish to get well and improve their parenting skills. However, these goals in the long run may or may not be realizable. More immediately, they desire to have their custody rights ensured. Their children, on the other hand, have a state-supported interest in being protected and parented according to minimal standards. This conflict presents a significant burden for the social worker, who may be forced to alter, limit, or otherwise moderate the services provided to the secondary client on the basis of a primary responsibility to the vulnerable child. For example, the parents' progress in a parenting class facilitated by the social worker will help to determine whether they maintain custody of the child. A social worker convinced of the need to remove the child permanently from the parents' custody may allow this fact to direct the services rendered during the family intervention. Moreover, statements made by the parents during counseling may relate directly to their continuing fitness to be the child's custodians. Consequently, the parents' expectation of confidentiality does not exist to the extent that the social worker's revelation of information is necessary for the protection of the child.

Child welfare agencies that acknowledge the conflict of interest created by the situation described above may make efforts to contract with independent clinical providers to offer family services to secondary clients. In poor and rural communities, however, neither the funds nor the providers may exist in sufficient numbers to make these independent services routinely available. Even when independent clinicians are available, they may frequently work in close concert with child welfare agency employees and so have clinical stances regarding their clients that are somewhat predetermined by their professional positions. Even if independent clinical services are offered, family preservation programs are invariably administered by clinical social workers employed by the child welfare agency itself. How, then, can the public agency social worker or administrator resolve this significant conflict of interest? As with any conflict of interest, the most appropriate initial strategy is the legal analysis suggested here. Specifically, the duties to practice reasonably competently and to seek informed consent must govern the resolution of this dilemma.

In any scenario involving FPS or similar programs, the parents may have been court-ordered to receive services. Therefore, they may lack legal capacity to consent to the services and are at least in this sense involuntary. Nevertheless, the social worker's duty to seek informed consent suggests that the parents are still entitled to a full disclosure of risks and benefits presented by treatment, and that a candid discussion of these risks and benefits may help to make the parents more willing participants in the clinical work. At the same time, the social worker has a duty to the primary client—the vulnerable child threatened by troubled parents—to remove the threat of danger and ensure a secure home environment. This responsibility imposes limitations on the social worker's professional relationship with the parents, and these restrictions must be disclosed to the parents as risks imposed by therapy. For example, the social worker must explain that the child welfare agency's primary legal responsibility is to the child and that family therapy serves essentially as a means toward protecting the child's best interests. An additional issue raised by the duty to seek informed consent is the professional's responsibility to assess fully all relevant clinical issues affecting the parents' relationship with the child and to disclose treatment options available for such issues. Thus, alcoholism, substance abuse, and significant mental illness may have an important role in the underlying parenting problem (Rittner & Dozier, 2000), and parents have the right to receive information about responsive interventions.

An intensive service such as family preservation often represents a last ditch effort to reunite the family, and it may prove ultimately to be unsuccessful. Informed consent suggests that this reality must be adequately related to the parents. The social worker's legal responsibility to the child includes violating confidentiality with the parents in the event that they reveal matters in therapy that have a bearing on the child's safety, or, indeed, if the therapy itself is not sufficiently effective to warrant reunification of the family. On the plus side, benefits offered by intensive therapy may include a healthier family and restored custody, and these factors are an equally important topic of an informed consent discussion. Regardless of the outcome of therapy, the clinician may count on being called upon in court to offer an opinion about the parents' progress; this situation ultimately places the therapist in the position of supporting a particular custodial outcome that runs counter to the legal stance of at least one of the parties. Planning for this eventuality may at least unconsciously make the clinician an advocate for a particular result even before therapy begins.

The foregoing discussion of informed consent issues unfortunately does not satisfactorily resolve the conflict of interest facing the social worker. Even if the risks and benefits are disclosed candidly and the parents become willing participants in treatment, the social worker is still faced with two disturbingly conflicting responsibilities: On the one hand, the social worker wishes to undertake therapy to reunify the family. On the other hand, the therapy itself may place the child at an even greater risk in the event family reunification is accomplished. Still again, the social worker's recognition of the legal responsibility to protect the child may be so focused as to limit or remove the objective orientation to therapy necessary for effective clinical practice. Even if the social worker can focus on clinical responsibilities, inadequate specialized training may result in superficial services that fail to address contributing problems such as mental illness and substance abuse. Therefore, regardless of how the informed consent problem is resolved, difficult questions remain about the competence of clinical services offered by child protective social workers and their agencies to secondary clients.

This conflict of interest is not one of the social worker's making. It is a catch-22 injected into state children's codes by a federal mandate—the Adoption Assistance and Child Welfare Act of 1980—that places manifestly contradictory responsibilities upon child welfare workers. Specifically, by this federal decree, state child abuse legislation must require public agencies both to protect the interests of children and to attempt family reunification where possible. In an effort to address both the rights of families and the protection of children, such legislation impedes the accomplishment of both objectives; it effectively creates a dilemma that cannot be resolved consistently with the agency's obligation to provide reasonably competent services to both the primary and secondary clients.

As already noted, where clinical services are available and child welfare agencies are directed by courts to provide them, these agencies may contract with independent providers to offer treatment to secondary clients. Alternatively, courts may decree in their child welfare dispositions that such treatment be sought by parents independently from an unnamed provider. For the reasons already noted, some parents—primarily rural, poor, and minority—are more likely to receive these services from the child welfare authority itself.

Changes in federal law under the Adoption and Safe Families Act of 1997 have forced states to streamline *permanency planning*, the process by which child welfare agencies organize the long-term care of children whose families fail to rehabilitate themselves sufficiently to be reunited. In these circumstances, agencies must hasten preparations for adoption by close family members or foster families, or, in the alternative, long-term family foster care or guardianship by persons who do not choose to adopt (Wattenberg, Kelley, & Kim, 2001). ASFA has directed states to hasten children's court proceedings relating to the termination of parental rights in child abuse, neglect, and abandonment cases. In such cases, the required procedures may result not only in the accelerated transfer of child custody to the state, but also in the expedited termination of parental rights and adoption of children placed within the foster care system. The system mandated by ASFA may ultimately be in the best interests of children who have experienced severe abuse and neglect, but it also raises important questions about the capability of state welfare authorities to reunify families in a shortened time frame. When mental health, alcoholism, or substance abuse problems have a significant impact on family relationships (Rittner & Dozier, 2000) but cannot reasonably be addressed within a matter of months, the competence of the clinical services that are provided to parents must be questioned.

Ultimately, threats to the competency of services offered to children and their parents affect the rights of both groups. These threats may rise to the level of constitutional violations when fundamental liberties, such as the right to due process and family privacy, may be implicated. It remains for future judges to sort out the constitutional problems that may be raised by child welfare legislation and corresponding agency conduct. In the meantime, however, a conflict of interest analysis suggests several immediate responses to the problem:

First, ordinary clinical services for secondary clients must be provided by independent contractors not under the administrative management of the child welfare authority. The urgency of this point is based not only upon the need to provide the most competent clinical services available, but also to ensure the confidentiality that is vital to the therapeutic relationship. Ultimately, legislatures should consider the redesign of family preservation services, which should be organized independently and publicly funded under the aegis of an appropriate governmental authority, such as a public health agency, more suited to the care and maintenance of vulnerable families. Available services must be expanded to address contributing causes of child abuse and neglect, such as mental illness and substance abuse. While clinical family services remain under the administrative management of child welfare agencies, more open acknowledgment of persistent conflicts of interest should take place. In the same manner that hospitals provide patient advocates to address specific grievances regarding care, child welfare agencies should be prepared to offer secondary clients the services of trained liaisons available to facilitate communication between service providers and recipients.

The responsibility to address conflicts of interest must additionally be borne by children's courts. These courts often make dispositions and approve treatment plans that call for specific family interventions. The burden for designing and implementing these programs often becomes the obligation of child welfare agencies that are understaffed and ill equipped to provide them. Social workers and children's court attorneys should actively lobby courts to tailor child welfare orders consistent with the informed consent and competent practice standards discussed here. Additionally, courts would do well to consider the implementation of support programs to monitor the progress of parents receiving clinical interventions from child welfare authorities. Similarly to court-appointed special advocates (CASAs) assigned in many state children's courts to observe and report on the progress of children in child welfare proceedings, court-assigned parent mentors could significantly assist fragile parents, many of whom are as emotionally brittle as their children (Calkins & Murray, 1999). An added benefit of this approach would be to provide courts with an independent, objective assessment of parental response to clinical services.

Child welfare agencies that acknowledge the important conflict of interest created by the delivery of family preservation services make an effort to separate the delivery of clinical and investigative services. Thus, "family preservation units" are created to provide expressly clinical services, and agency social workers are typically shunted into either investigative or clinical roles. Overall administrative management remains, however, under the leadership of a single child welfare agency, and this creates a problem in the delivery of reasonably competent services to secondary clients. In apparent recognition of this problem, no less an authority than the National Commission on Child Welfare and Family Preservation has made an as yet unheeded proposal for the radical reorganization of child welfare service delivery (Schorr, 2000).

The distinction between primary and secondary clients discussed here underscores an important point about many behavioral health and human services offered by public agencies. For instance, a certified counselor employed by a prison system to provide clinical and other services to inmates essentially has two sets of clients—the public at large (i.e., those interested in the prisoner's rehabilitation), to whom the counselor, by assuming employment, owes a primary obligation, and prisoners, who, in truth, are secondary clients. Similarly, a forensic psychologist employed by a state mental health facility may be court-appointed to diagnose the mental competency of a violent offender in an effort to assist the court in its determination of the offender's criminal culpability or mental capacity to stand trial. In effect, the psychologist's primary client is the state on whose behalf the psychologist has been appointed to render an opinion about the offender's dangerousness, amenability to rehabilitation, appreciation of the difference between right and wrong, and other issues (*Hafner v. Beck,* 1995). At the same time, the diagnostic process is a service being administered to this secondary client, whose future care and rehabilitation may depend on the accuracy of the diagnosis.

These conflicts of interest are most serious to the extent they make the reasonably competent delivery of clinical services to the secondary client impossible. As with families involved in child abuse proceedings, the constitutional rights of other secondary clients, such as prisoners and forensic patients (i.e., persons adjudicated incompetent to stand trial or not guilty by reason of insanity), may be compromised by severely inadequate treatment (see, e.g., *Duran v. Apodaca,* 1980). Within privatized prisons and forensic treatment centers, the monitoring of service delivery may be even more limited, with an extra bureaucratic layer making the oversight of inmate services even cloudier.

With the foregoing discussion in mind, the need is apparent for a set of clear legal rules that summarize the standards discussed in this section governing the provision of services to secondary clients. The following principles offer a general strategy for addressing situations involving primary and secondary clients: First, the behavioral health professional should identify the primary client and the legal responsibility owed to that client. Second, the professional should identify the secondary client. The professional should offer services to the secondary client only if they facilitate the professional's duty to the primary client and are *peripheral* in nature. This is the situation when case assessment, investigation, and diagnostic services are required in order to protect the best interests of the vulnerable group the professional is required to protect. As illustrations, a social worker's assessment of a family experiencing child abuse, a psychologist conducting a forensic examination of a violent offender, and a county coroner's completion of an autopsy are all peripheral services offered in the interest of satisfying important state interests. Third, all other services to secondary clients should be offered only when they can be provided reasonably competently and with informed consent. Ordinarily, this will be the case only when the secondary services are provided by a professional administratively separate from the agency responsible for primary clients, such as an independent contractor hired for this express purpose, and only when confidentiality can be honored. Thus, a professional serving a primary client must generally avoid simultaneously providing services such as psychotherapy, family preservation services, counseling, and other substantive services, to secondary clients.

The Professional's Proprietary Interest in Services. Similarly to the professional's interest in a research project or the use of advertising in soliciting clients, other proprietary or business factors with which the professional is associated may have a role in influencing the client's entry into a professional relationship. In some instances, the provider may have a personal or financial interest in a treatment modality that is offered to the client. This type of interest creates a conflict between caregiver and client that may threaten the integrity of the professional relationship. For example, the fact that a physician has staff privileges at a hospital may inspire a recommendation to admit an ill patient to that hospital. In a series of related federal cases that have alerted the public to the potential abuse of this proprietary interest, a major for-profit hospital system partly settled government allegations that it offered salary bonuses and other direct financial incentives—labeled "kickbacks" by the U.S. Justice Department—to staff physicians based on their referral of Medicaid and Medicare patients (*In re Columbia/HCA Healthcare Corp. Litig.,* 2001). Unsettled questions include the government's remaining allegations that the hospital system used a "physician syndication" strategy offering doctors investment opportunities in member hospitals as a means of fostering physician loyalty (Taylor, 2001).

Another major HMO settled a lawsuit instituted by the Texas attorney general challenging the use of financial incentives to physicians in the reduction of health care costs (*State v. Aetna U.S. Healthcare, Inc.,* 2000). Pursuant to the settlement agreement entered into in the *Aetna* case, the HMO was prohibited from using inverse compensation schemes that reward physicians who minimize their patients' consumption of medical services, including doctor visits and referrals for laboratory testing. The effect of financial incentives on the delivery of health care services continues to pose a major threat to the delivery of competent health care and the exercise of independent clinical judgment by providers in the twenty-first century.

As another instance of a conflict stemming from a professional's proprietary interest in services, consider the example of a psychologist who has written extensively on the use of eye movement desensitization and reprocessing (EMDR) a controversial treatment whose proponents claim facilitates the brain's processing of information and painful emotions in sufferers of posttraumatic stress disorder (PTSD) (Davidson & Parker, 2001). Influenced by intense scholarly interest in this field, the professional wishes to attempt this therapy with a new patient complaining of persistent memories of a car accident. Alternatively, a mental health facility specializing in the treatment of depression may advertise its program to the public motivated jointly by a desire to increase public awareness of mental health issues and by its interest in getting new patients.

As with all of the other conflicts of interest detailed here, the situations described above endanger both the voluntariness of the client's choice of services and the professional's ability to exercise free and competent judgment on behalf of each client. Similarly to the resolution of all other conflicts, a provider holding a proprietary or business interest in services offered should assess the impact by considering and applying the duty to practice reasonably competently and the duty to seek informed consent. At the very least, the existence of the business or proprietary interest must be disclosed to the client. Failure to do so denies the client information that could reasonably play a role in the client's decision to enter into the professional relationship.

In many circumstances, the proprietary interest is both a reasonable and necessary part of the professional relationship. As already noted, many professional relationships themselves involve a business exchange and are fee generating. As with most behavioral health services, the provider has both a right and a need to be paid for rendering the services. Where, however, the business interest eclipses the professional's ability to provide competent services, the purposes of the professional relationship are fundamentally violated. Consider, for example, the case of a physician paid a salary bonus by a hospital based on the number of patients admitted. Here, the financial motivations both of the hospital and the physician appear to supersede independent medical judgment in a manner that is overtly threatening to the patient. The salary incentive in this case represents such a strong potential inducement to the physician that it sabotages the objectivity required to render an accurate assessment of each patient's health. In an era in which managed care, profitability, and cost containment have become operative principles within the health care industry, these financial factors may continue to tempt hospitals and physicians to engage in the kind of practice highlighted in this example. Indeed, the elevation of cost containment to a place of preeminence threatens to undermine the competent provision of health care to patients.

In the case of the psychologist and PTSD patient noted earlier, the psychologist may reasonably be able to assess and treat the patient even in the face of strong personal professional interest in EMDR therapy. Indeed, it is eminently reasonable to expect a behavioral health professional to pursue scholarly endeavors within a practice specialty and to share the benefits of this scholarship with potential clients. In fact, the duty to seek informed consent requires the disclosure of professional opinions relating to clients' problems, together with a discussion of alternative treatment methods that may be of comparable assistance. To the extent, however, that the psychologist allows an interest in EMDR to cause an incomplete assessment of the client's mental health issues or otherwise allows a devotion to this treatment modality to avert a discussion of other options, such as cognitive behavioral and medicinal strategies, the provider renders an incomplete and incompetent service.

Relationships With Third-Party Payors. The duty to identify the primary client requires behavioral health providers to preserve the integrity of the professional relationship and to protect it from personal, social, and business interests that may compromise it. The steps outlined here present a strategy for defending the professional's relationship with the primary client in a variety of hazardous situations. A key element of this approach requires the professional first to ascertain who the primary client is in settings in which that individual's identity may not always be obvious.

One of the reasons that identifying the primary client may present a challenge is that the busy professional often works in conjunction with third-party payors, including insurance companies, health maintenance organizations (HMOs), government agencies (such as Medicaid and Medicare) and other payment sources—often close members of the client's own family—that underwrite the client's care and support the provider's practice. Often these persons and entities have an important role in financing or otherwise facilitating the client's entry into the professional relationship, and for that reason, their role in making services available may be critical.

Third-party payment relationships may be initiated by the client or the professional. They are instituted by the client when the client makes a request for reimbursement from a payor—typically an insurance company—for professional services. Often the provider agrees to manage the paperwork involved in filing for insurance benefits on the client's behalf because this service benefits both parties to the professional relationship. On other occasions, the third-party connection is initiated by a provider who agrees to offer services to clients as a member of an HMO. The professional benefits from associating with the HMO, which provides a financial incentive by ensuring a steady source of clients but is subject to the policies and guidelines governing the HMO agreement.

In any third-party relationship, the professional's association with the third-party payor is not a professional relationship as defined here, nor does the provider owe the payor the duties associated with that relationship. Instead, it is a contractual one in which the professional agrees to perform services on the client's behalf and to receive payment, at least in part, from the payor. The client's relationship with the third-party payor likewise is a contractual one, and its responsibilities are defined in the insurance agreement entered into by the parties. The duties prescribed for the professional relationship are owed solely to the client. In contrast to the other conflicts of interest described here, those involving third-party payors concern businesses and governmental agencies that have a direct and immediate concern with the client's care based on their financial relationship with the professional and client. As already noted, cautious providers must take steps to ensure that these obligations do not interfere with the professional relationship established with each client.

Because they play such an extensive role as gatekeepers in the delivery of health care services to the public, the interests of third-party payors are sometimes elevated inappropriately when the professional responsibilities of behavioral health care providers are assessed. The conflict of interest thus created may seriously hamper the honoring of essential legal responsibilities owed to clients or may put an inordinate amount of pressure on the provider to tailor the professional relationship in a way that satisfies the third-party payor's requirements and expectations. As with all of the conflict of interest scenarios described here, the decision maker facing conflicts involving third-party payors should assess each conflict by considering the legal duties to practice reasonably competently and seek informed consent.

A classic example of the manipulation of a professional relationship for the payor's benefit is the provision of hospital perinatal care. Pursuant to an HMO's requirements, hospitalization benefits may only be required for a limited number of days, irrespective of the professional preference of the attending physician, who may regard more extended hospitalization as in the best medical interests of the mother. In this instance, early release of the patient plainly violates the duty to provide reasonably competent medical service. To the extent the provider deviates one bit from prudent medical judgment in order to satisfy the HMO's reimbursement limit, an essential legal duty to the patient is violated.

A similar result occurs in the case of a psychologist who may be persuaded to diagnose a mental health condition in a manner that ensures the client's maximum coverage under available insurance. Some government health programs, such as Medicaid and Medicare, rely upon a cost containment system that employs the use of *diagnostic related groups* (DRGs) (Rosenberg & Browne, 2001). Under this approach, the payor limits insurance coverage to a maximum amount established for a particular medical or psychological condition. DRGs serve as a means of limiting the overall amount spent by the payor for health care by requiring providers to anticipate the cost of care through the *prospective payment system* (PPS). Unfortunately, DRGs also serve as a strong motivation for behavioral health care providers to adjust the services rendered based on their knowledge of the maximum covered amount.

Consider the case of a depressed client who seeks the services of a licensed psychotherapist for treatment. Upon a review of the client's insurance coverage, the therapist discovers that the client is limited to 20 sessions per year of individual counseling. Based on this formulation, the therapist engages in a course of time-limited rational emotive behavioral psychotherapy (Yankura & Dryden, 1997). This approach might be chosen in part because of the scholarly research suggesting its effectiveness, but also because the therapist recognizes that the client will be unable to afford traditional long-term care. If this decision is assessed according to the legal conflict analysis presented here, the practice of tailoring services to insurance coverage limits violates the professional's duties to provide reasonably competent care and to seek informed consent from the client. Both duties are implicated because the provider who defines or adjusts services to fit the requirements of an insurance policy is failing to apply the independent clinical judgment that is an important part of the professional relationship. Moreover, the provider who depends upon an insurance policy to define the extent of the services offered may be tempted to deny full disclosure of this information from the unsuspecting client. Even if the professional candidly discloses that a treatment option has been chosen on the basis of the limits of the client's insurance coverage, and the client freely consents to such treatment, the services may simply be inappropriate for a person who requires a more extensive intervention.

Limitations imposed by insurance coverage may inspire professionals not only to adjust their services but also sometimes to downright misrepresent them. The incidence of Medicaid and insurance fraud among behavioral health professionals is on the rise, or at least is being increasingly reported, and the government is taking a more active stand in combating it (Sparrow, 1998; Stefl, 1999). Fraudulent reporting of insurance claims is due at least in part to the pressure imposed on therapists to characterize services consistent with coverage limits. In the *Modi* case cited earlier, involving the use of "deposession therapy" to rid a patient of his belief that he was possessed by demons, a psychiatrist allegedly reported the treatment to the patient's insurance company as "psychotherapy" for billing purposes. In a lengthy disciplinary complaint citing billing misrepresentations and informed consent violations, an appellate court remanded the case to the licensing authority to allow it to specify more definitively the licensing standards by which the complaint had been brought. The case unfortunately suggests the occasional futility of attempting to define the expectations concerning professional conduct in terms of broad, aspirational principles. It also demonstrates that this problem is not unique to social work, counseling, or psychology.

A credible argument can be made that the use of DRGs by government programs and insurance plans violates the duty to provide informed consent because it substantially interferes with the voluntary and unimpeded consideration of treatment alternatives available for client care. Indeed, the prospective payment system itself implies that the consideration of cost is to be an inherent part of service delivery, a concept that is fundamentally at odds with the free choice mandated by informed consent.

Too often the pressures imposed by managed care have had tragic consequences for professionals and clients inspired to make important medical decisions on the basis of insurance limits. The severest consequences of these pressures may well fall on the backs of poor people most dependent on the prospective payment system in effect in government-sponsored health insurance programs. The most bizarre example of this may have occurred at a private hospital emergency room in San Francisco, where a homeless trauma victim with a four-inch knife still protruding from his stomach was apparently discharged without further treatment (Russell, 1996). Under Medi-Cal, California's health insurance program for the poor, the hospital was required only to evaluate and stabilize the man. According to this presumed authority, physicians elected to release the man after determining that his vital signs were stable, his internal organs had not been perforated, and the wound, although bleeding, was not bleeding profusely. The hospital's internal investigation revealed no wrongdoing and no action inconsistent with the terms of the man's insurance coverage (Russell, 1996).

Relationships with third-party payors impose certain constraints upon clients and professionals relating to the receipt of payment. The fact that the provider owes a central legal obligation to the primary client does not nullify obligations to third-party payors; it simply separates them from the scope of the professional relationship. Both clients and providers owe contractual responsibilities to payors. Among other things, these include the prompt reporting of claims and the accurate description of services rendered. Compliance with this obligation on occasion requires some lapse in confidentiality between the client and the professional, and the competent provider obtains this solely with the consent of the willing client. The fact that confidentiality may be waived to some extent does not allow the payor unbridled access to the client's records; indeed, without an express waiver, these remain confidential. Other legal aspects of the relationship between clients, professionals, and third-party payors are generally defined by the insurance codes, health legislation, and contract law of individual states.

Behavioral health professionals who write grant applications often design interventions with rigorous attention to the requirements of the granting authority, which may be either a government or private source. Granting authorities represent a unique kind of third-party payor that agrees contractually with grant writers to underwrite individual services, professional salaries, and program costs. Professionals who rely on grant money have the same aspirations regarding their relationship with the granting source as those providers who rely on insurance reimbursement: They are motivated to satisfy the terms of the grant application. In contrast to other kinds of third-party relationships, the associations between grantees and their patrons are subject to far less public scrutiny and regulation. Although a grant may be audited to ensure financial compliance, the consequences to the grantee for fiscal mismanagement may be limited to nonrenewal of the grant or, at worst, recollection of grant money. For this reason, the behavioral health care of clients being served by a grant may be at greater risk. Consider the example of a community mental health program administrator who, in anticipation of an audit, hurriedly directs program staff members to review client records compiled over the past two years for completeness, and also asks that "cosmetic changes" be made to "clean up" notes and add demographic information. Favorable numbers may please the grantor, but they remain inconsistent with the agency's duty to the primary client to maintain accurate and complete records of services provided.

The custody of client records may confuse the relationship between professionals, clients, and third-party payors. In an effort to obtain easier access to these records some HMOs have instituted the practice of claiming an ownership interest in the records maintained by providers who affiliate with the HMO (*Maio v. Aetna, Inc.,* 2000). The intent of this practice appears to be to subvert the duty of confidentiality imposed by the law on professional records and files maintained by a provider on clients. Legally, these records have been recognized historically as the property solely of the professional and/or the client. Under most states' health and professional codes, clients have the privilege of reasonable access to records and a right to have their confidentiality maintained. The strain that a third-party payor's asserted ownership interest may have on the professional relationship has been the subject of at least one lawsuit challenging the practice (*Maio v. Aetna, Inc.,* 2000). Future legal actions may continue to raise questions about the destructive impact it may have on the professional relationship between providers and their clients.

Confusion over the ownership of records also sometimes occurs when a client seeks to transfer files from a professional with whom services have been discontinued. As already noted, the law generally recognizes that clients have a property interest in professional records and notes prepared on their behalf (*In re Application of Casillo,* 1992). At minimum, the law requires that professionals cooperate in the transfer of records when the client switches providers. With respect to some professionals, such as attorneys, the law of some states actually recognizes the client as the absolute owner of his or her files, subject only to a retaining lien, or security interest, held by the professional for any outstanding fees (*Sexton Law Firm v. Milligan,* 1997). Considered in this light, the professional relationships developed by attorneys and their clients give specific proprietary rights to the client in the work product—including documents, case records and attorney notes—prepared by the attorney. Given the efforts of third-party providers to expand the scope of their involvement in the professional relationship, it would not be surprising for progressive courts in the near future to reconsider and redefine the respective record ownership rights of all behavioral health and human service providers and their clients.

Clients' ownership interest in professional records remains one of the unfortunate and unnecessary secrets complicating the relationship between clients, providers, and third-party payors. As with many aspects of behavioral health and human services, this secret may be kept by all those interested in containing costs, including the expense of photocopying on behalf of clients who lack adequate resources. Regrettably, some providers deny or limit adequate access to clients wishing to review their records, sometimes under the limited protection of professional codes that understate the extent of each client's ownership interest. The NASW Code (Ethical Standard 1.08), for example, admonishes social workers only to "provide clients with reasonable access to their records" and to "limit clients' access . . . only in exceptional circumstances when there is compelling evidence that . . . harm (would result)." The NBCC Code, Section B5, most closely approximates the law governing ownership of client records when it declares that the "physical records" are "property of the counselors or their employers," but that the information contained in them "belongs to the client." The APA Code (Ethical Standard 5.10) effectively evades the question by advising psychologists that ownership "is governed by legal principles," and that the psychologist's responsibility is to make records "available" to clients according to "reasonable and lawful steps" in accord with each client's "best interests."

In reality, the ownership interest that courts recognize clients to hold probably makes their right of access to records more extensive than these codes imply (*Wear v. Walker,* 1990). Any behavioral health professional relying on the above-quoted words to protect a vulnerable client from access to candid case notes might be surprised to face a lawsuit seeking recovery of the original documents. A client's legal ownership interest in these records simply reflects an important component of the professional relationship: the professional's duty to make competent records of the services provided. The right is also based in part upon the business exchange that underlies many a professional relationship: The client pays for services and, therefore, has a proprietary interest in the documentation made by the professional. As with other important legal protections, this one effectively supports the best interests of all primary clients.

Understanding the client's ownership interest in records reinforces the point that, in most circumstances, the client is the primary director of the professional relationship, in accordance with principles underlying informed consent. The client's proprietary right also supports professional accountability. Denying access to records interferes with the client's right to be fully informed about the services rendered by the professional. In fact, it may frustrate the client's right to substitute the services of one professional with another. If a public health facility denies access to records, it may even violate constitutional standards governing due process and personal privacy (*Huether v. District Court,* 2000).

Most courts have been reluctant to recognize the client's property interest in records as anything greater than a right to reasonable access, with the singular exception of legal service recipients (*Cynthia B. v. New Rochelle Hosp.,* 1983). Nevertheless, the behavioral health professional's recognition of the client's prerogative as a property interest, as opposed to a right of inspection subject to the provider's discretion, may inspire more open access. It is important to note that, in circumstances in which the client lacks legal capacity, mental capacity, is emotionally vulnerable, or is the secondary client of a public agency, the right of access to records—especially hospital records—may be starkly limited. State law must be consulted in individual cases to determine the extent of these limitations.

Consequences for Breach of the Duty to Identify the Primary Client

Where a professional's failure to identify the primary client leads to incompetent practice or the neglect of informed consent, the offending practitioner may face the civil, criminal, and disciplinary remedies outlined earlier. The risk that one may violate one or more legal principles governing practice is greatest where a third party unduly influences the professional relationship with the primary client.

Identifying the primary client presents a special burden for public sector behavioral health professionals who function in forensic psychology, child welfare, public mental health services, school based counseling, and other programs administered by public agencies. In agreeing to assume a public trust on behalf of a vulnerable class of citizens, public agency providers essentially represent the government in each professional decision that they make. Therefore, mistakes made by these professionals are not only personal, but also governmental. Such errors represent a threat not only to the individual clients involved, but also to the public interest in general.

On occasion, budgetary and administrative exigencies dominating the public sector's delivery of behavioral health and human services are so severe as to result in the inadequate design or implementation of child welfare systems, public assistance programs, mental health institutions, educational organizations, and other domains that are the concern of government agencies. As noted previously, conflicts of interest involving budgetary and administrative issues can cause a professional to practice incompetently or violate the duty to seek informed consent. Where this occurs at the government agency level, an entire class of service recipients—whose number can range from the hundreds to the millions—may be harmed simultaneously. On occasion, such harm may become the subject of a class action lawsuit in which a single client, or small group of clients, sues on behalf of a larger class of service recipients in order to seek judicial relief from the practices of a public agency. The relief granted in a class action suit can include the award of money damages, the issuance of an injunction against agency practices, or an order mandating program changes by the public agency.

Mistakes by public officials can violate important constitutional provisions that protect citizens from excessive government intrusion into personal privacy. This right to individual privacy—a fundamental constitutional cornerstone—has a significant role in framing the professional relationship that each client develops with government behavioral health and human service agencies. Thus, when public agency personnel practice incompetently, or fail to seek the informed consent of clientele, these violations may rise to a level of constitutional significance.

Using Identification of the Primary Client as a Vehicle to Make Professional Decisions: Case Examples

As with other essential legal responsibilities, recognizing and applying the duty to identify the primary client can assist behavioral health professionals to evaluate seemingly complex practice scenarios. In contrast to the broad, aspirational, and often conflicting ideals set forth in professional codes of ethics, the principles underlying the duty to identify the primary client set the basic parameters defining boundaries between professionals, their clients, and third parties. In this respect, the duty to identify the primary client builds upon responsibilities underlying the duty to practice reasonably competently and the duty to seek informed consent. For these reasons, all of the preceding duties should be considered as a first step when the professional encounters practice dilemmas that involve third parties to the professional relationship. Because regional and cultural issues often play a significant role in presumed conflicts of interest between the professional and the client, some of the case examples that follow highlight the usefulness of identifying the primary client in cross-cultural practice. Illustrative examples are drawn from practice with the diverse populations of New Mexico.

Case Example 9: The Single Psychotherapist

Amy Rivera, a single mother and licensed psychotherapist in Santa Fe, New Mexico, works four days per week at a community mental health center. On her day off, she provides services to a cooperative child care program that requires each participant to supervise the young children of program members one day per week. On the day that Amy is responsible for child care, she receives a call from a local school principal requesting that she make arrangements to come to the school. A bus accident has caused a number of injuries, and Amy's clinical services are urgently required to provide crisis counseling to the accident victims and their families. Amy could arrange for substitute child care, but it would require her to contact each of the other parents and the substitute service would be at her own expense.

This dilemma is a variation on a classic exemplar often presented in behavioral health ethics texts. It is sometimes described as a conflict of interest that pits the requirements of the provider's private life against potentially superseding professional obligations. If characterized in this way, the dilemma is misleading and unfairly depicts the professional's choices. Analyzing the dilemma becomes especially confusing if the decision maker seeks initial guidance from an ethical code, a set of ideological perspectives, or personal values. In contrast, if the duty to identify the primary client is applied in this dilemma, Amy will recognize at first that she has established no professional relationship with a client and owes no specific legal duty to an identified person. If she has any legal obligation at all, it is in her role as a parent and substitute caretaker, and it is owed to her own child and the additional children in her temporary custody.

Before one jumps to the conclusion this is a crass and hypertechnical assessment of a public tragedy, consider the benefits of a legal analysis on all those involved. First, if Amy falsely assumes in this scenario that an official duty obliges her to provide a service, she takes on a risk she may simply be unprepared to accept and unreasonably elevates a presumed responsibility above her personal commitments. If Amy makes this mistake, or instead seeks guidance initially from an ethical code or her own philosophical convictions, she may easily be overwhelmed by a multitude of considerations. In reality, no legal conflict of interest exists in this dilemma. Amy's obligations here are strictly personal, and as a compassionate professional—but cautious mother and caretaker—she can reasonably decline to offer services.

How callous is this decision? Honoring one's personal commitments before making a decision to undertake a professional relationship may be the surest way to provide competent services once one voluntarily enters into a professional relationship. In Amy's situation, a rushed decision may do more damage to her own family than it does good for the prospective clients. The risk to these clients includes an incompetent clinical intervention by a therapist preoccupied with partly resolved personal responsibilities. The concern and panic caused by the bus accident may or may not require the assistance of crisis counselors, and a surge to offer them runs the risk of imposing services on people who have not voluntarily sought them.

Clearly, Amy owes the children in her charge her primary attention. Her personal credo may inspire her to offer services voluntarily at a time when she can competently present them and has satisfied her immediate obligations to her family and friends. In this way, both Amy and her prospective clients will be more likely to have entered the professional relationship thoughtfully and voluntarily.

Amy's dilemma highlights a misapprehension about behavioral health services that may represent the most serious cause of professional burnout. Specifically, it underscores the point that a professional's obligations are neither unceasing nor boundaryless in their extent. Ethical codes sometimes add to the professional's role confusion by reciting broad goals that are well intended but at times unattainable, most notably by failing to define adequately the meaning of *client*. Until a professional relationship is formed and a legal bond between a provider and primary client is established, most ethical aspirations simply cannot be enforced.

Reconsider the above case example based on a few factual changes. Specifically, suppose that Amy has already established a professional relationship with a client that she has been treating some weeks for an anxiety disorder. Amy learns from the client by telephone that her client's child was involved in the bus accident. In this situation, Amy's alternatives should be assessed in terms of her duty to practice reasonably competently. Under these circumstances, she may be unable to schedule an office visit but be available to provide further consultation by phone. If she does this, Amy should be prepared to offer reasonably competent services consistent with her professional relationship to the client. On the contrary, should she see her role purely as an informal "head to cry on," her stance may be both exploitative and countertherapeutic.

Yet another variation on the above scenario is faced frequently by child welfare social workers in connection with services they provide to families involved in abuse and neglect proceedings. Even though their main legal duty extends to their primary clients—the vulnerable children of a community whose interests these professionals have voluntarily agreed to protect—parents involved in children's court cases sometimes look to social workers for reassurance and counseling, even as the child abuse proceedings press forward. On occasion, social workers are contacted beyond their normal office hours to address parental crises and to provide consultation and other services associated with their positions. In many circumstances, the social worker may feel obliged to provide this assistance in the fulfillment of a sense of ethical and personal obligation. Before this choice is made, however, it is appropriate for the professional to evaluate carefully the extent of the legal obligation owed to the primary client, together with the limitation that this places on interactions with secondary clients.

Social workers are sometimes called upon to engage in dialogues with secondary clients—perhaps parents and adult family members involved peripherally in abuse proceedings. This type of interaction may be offered in a way that blurs the professional boundaries existing between the parties and misrepresents the professional stance that the social worker must adopt concerning a vulnerable child. Recall that important questions have been raised here about the conflict of interest created by this kind of situation, and the competence of a public agency professional to provide clinical services to secondary clients. Moreover, it is questionable whether this type of support is consistent with the child's best interests. Aside from these points, if the social worker is not "on call" and not bound by terms of employment either to offer such services or to be available after hours, it is not advisable to provide them. The risks created by such efforts far outweigh the potential benefits that may arise from them. Moreover, the availability of a social worker for service that transcends the professional responsibility to the primary client may take an enormous toll on the professional's own mental health. As already noted, this legal conflict of interest contributes to a confusion in professional roles that often plays a significant part in the generally high employee turnover rates within public child welfare agencies nationally (Graef & Hill, 2000).

Case Example 10: The Full-Service Office

Allan Korn is a licensed psychologist self-employed in Farmington, New Mexico. Specializing in the treatment of depression, he is a qualified provider under a group health insurance plan, from which he draws a significant number of referrals. Allan has a receptionist who assists him with greeting and intake of clients. When a new client comes in for services, the receptionist, Alice Contreras, routinely distributes a client information form that requests personal data, insurance coverage information, a brief medical history, and also requires the client to provide a brief description of the present problem. Vera Tom, a Navajo woman who has recently been laid off from her job as a maintenance worker, schedules an appointment to see Allan for therapy. Vera fills in the information form and includes her group health insurance number. Vera has had some high school, but has never sought professional help before and has difficulty answering some of the questions. Vera asks for assistance from Alice, who takes the form from Vera and asks her the questions indicated on the form. Listening to Vera's answers, Alice fills in the answers. Additionally, Alice makes a copy of

Vera's insurance identification card as Vera explains that the insurance is "still good for six months."

Vera next proceeds to have her initial appointment with Allan. On the way out, she notices a sign in the office that reads "We will be happy to assist you in the filing of insurance claims, but please remember that the client has the responsibility to pay for all service rendered." Vera asks Alice about insurance claims, and Alice obtains Vera's signature on an insurance claim form. Vera does not review the form carefully. After eight weeks of therapy with Allan, Vera receives a computer generated letter from Allan's office requesting payment in full for the unpaid balance of the office bill. Vera visits Allan's office and asks Alice to find out about the insurance. Upon calling the insurance claims office, the secretary advises Alice that the wrong form has been filed and that no reimbursement has been sent to Allan's office. Alice repeats this information to Rita, then hands Rita another form and suggests that she "walk it in" herself to the insurance claims office in order to save time. As Alice explains this new, more urgent approach, "we really need some payment on the bill."

This scenario depicts an unfortunate "run around" involving third-party payment that is all too common in behavioral health service delivery. At its simplest it represents a business conflict of interest between Allan, Vera, and the insurance company. Specifically, Allan maintains an ongoing business relationship with the company to the extent that he keeps claim forms on hand, routinely assists in the preparation and submission of these forms, and benefits from the insurer's frequent reimbursement of client services. The business association also, however, requires Allan to complete paperwork and file claims, which requires a personal and financial commitment. Allan, like some professionals, seems willing to honor this burden only to a point. He delegates responsibility for claim filing to his receptionist, uses office signs to advise clients of their independent responsibility for bills, and, unfortunately, when the conflict becomes somewhat cumbersome for him, essentially absolves himself—through his receptionist—from further responsibility for the claims process.

Allan must reassess his responsibilities to Vera using the legal conflict of interest analysis presented here. Specifically, he should identify candidly his legal duties to this primary client and attempt reasonably to fulfill them. In this scenario, Vera has reasonably anticipated that she would receive assistance in the claims process and has entered into the professional relationship expecting this assistance. Given Vera's experience and background, her reliance on this help is to be expected all the more. In assessing his duty to practice reasonably competently, Allan should recognize that this includes assisting clients with the filing of necessary paperwork. He undertakes this responsibility both by communicating it at the commencement of services and, along with Alice, engaging in conduct that becomes part of the professional understanding between his clients and him.

Courts today have recognized that professionals who agree to assist with clients' paperwork filing have a legal responsibility to do so reasonably competently (*Chew v. Meyer,* 1987). They have noted additionally that, with the complexity in service delivery created by reliance on third-party payors, claims assistance and client advocacy in the pursuit of reimbursement often become expected components of the professional relationship and important parts of the services rendered by health care providers (*Chew v. Meyer,* 1987).

Where there are cultural differences between client and professional, or the client may be particularly vulnerable because of a lack of familiarity with third-party claims applications, claims assistance may become even more vital. Once this advocacy is offered, neither the provider nor a clerical assistant can withdraw it on the empty assertion that it is the client's ultimate responsibility. In the present case example, however, this legal conclusion represents only the first part of the picture. Allan should recognize additionally that it is inappropriate to seek payment immediately from Vera when she has not been responsible for the careless filing of her claim. In this respect, Allan is responsible not only for reasonable competence in his clinical practice, but also for ensuring his staff's prudent completion of their administrative responsibilities. When clerical mistakes cause foreseeable harm to the client, Allan is responsible. This *vicarious liability* for the conduct of his employees requires Allan to take measures to correct the problem, not the least of which is to modify his payment arrangement with Vera to allow time for the filing of the insurance claim.

The assumption of clerical responsibilities is not always a happy one for the busy professional. However, where the provider benefits as much as the client from the third-party relationship, these responsibilities must be assumed if the professional is to practice competently. In rural areas, where the client may expect a more informal and communicative helping relationship with the provider, the reasonable professional must tailor practice to reflect clients' needs and expectations.

Case Example 11: The Voc Rehab Counselor

Lucy Chambliss works as a vocational rehabilitation counselor at a residential training center in Albuquerque, New Mexico. One of her clients, Larry Delgado, is a 13-year-old with mild developmental disability and conduct disorder. Larry was placed by his parents at the residential program about six months ago and has received individual counseling from Lucy during that time. Lucy also serves as a house parent at the cottage in which Larry is housed.

During the six months that Lucy has worked with Larry, she has observed substantial improvement both in Larry's behavior and in his attention to his schoolwork. The Delgados visit Larry bimonthly, at which time they confer with Lucy concerning their son's progress. As a result of her work with Larry, Lucy has begun to feel that further institutional care is not appropriate and that Larry belongs at home with his family.

During their most recent meeting with Lucy, the Delgados have expressed their pleasure at the apparent improvement in Larry's conduct. When Lucy suggests that further institutionalization might not be helpful for Larry, the Delgados disagree, noting that Larry has made great strides in the preceding six months. Moreover, they note, Larry has been the primary source of friction in their marriage, and the respite Larry's residency at the center has given them has made home life more bearable for them and their other young children.

Lucy's options in this scenario are most easily addressed if she first considers her duty to identify the primary client. Despite the role of Larry's parents in placing Larry in institutional care, Lucy's primary client is Larry. Consequently, she owes Larry a duty to practice reasonably competently. Although the interests of Larry's parents are peripherally important in the sense that they have authority to provide informed consent for any treatment on Larry's behalf, it is *Larry's* well-being that must be of paramount concern to Lucy. If, in her professional judgment, Larry's best interests are not served by continuing placement at the training center, then she must so advise the Delgados. They may have important personal reasons for Larry's continued placement out of the home, but if, in Lucy's independent clinical judgment, placement does not correspond with Larry's health and continued progess, she cannot proceed to provide reasonably competent services.

Lucy may well regard her position in this scenario as an uncomfortable one. She may have developed a friendly working relationship with the Delgados and may feel obliged to honor their choices regarding Larry's care. These impressions may be strengthened by cross-cultural considerations that suggest to Lucy, a compassionate counselor who believes in client self-determination, that she must demonstrate respect for the Delgados' right to make independent choices on behalf of their family. In honoring her duty to the primary client, however, Lucy must take literally her central concern with Larry's progress.

In identifying her primary client, Lucy should consider the impact of informed consent. The Delgados have the legal capacity to make decisions on Larry's behalf, and Lucy must discuss with them all reasonable risks and benefits of the care options available to Larry. As the guidelines for informed consent indicate, Lucy has the responsibility to discuss fully her own professional opinions with the client (or those responsible for making decisions on the client's behalf), especially when these views contradict the client's or decision makers' interpretation of the problem. In the present case example, the duty to seek informed consent requires Lucy not to allow her respect for the Delgados' worldview to silence her communication of a professional opinion. How effectively and sensitively Lucy expresses this judgment to the Delgado parents may well determine what decisions they make about Larry's care.

Lucy must recognize from the outset of her conversations with the Delgados that her duty to practice reasonably competently mandates that she identify, assess, and, if necessary, report, instances of suspected child abuse and neglect. In the unfortunate event that the Delgados are unable or unwilling to assume responsibility for Larry's care, it is incumbent upon Lucy and her supervisors to report the threat posed to Larry's well-being. Cautious communication of this point may help the Delgados to reassess their position regarding Larry's institutionalization.

Staff counselors and other behavioral health providers in the lower echelon of employees at mental health institutions may feel overwhelmed at the responsibility placed on them to identify and represent the best interests of the primary client. They may be familiar with the administrative routine at their agencies, may contemplate the burdens that third-party funding places on client services, and may actively participate in their institutions' zealous solicitation of new clients. These issues may place pressure on employees and administrators to maintain amicable relationships with the families of clients. The inducements created by funding considerations may be a powerful incentive in the decisions made on their clients' behalf, and cautious agency employees may not be anxious to make waves. Nevertheless, every behavioral health professional involved in long-term care for institutionalized clients must be prepared to answer the following question: Can the provider lawfully maintain a professional relationship with a client for whom no further services are available, or who is not likely to benefit from further treatment? The answer, under a strict interpretation of the duty to practice reasonably competently, is plainly no.

The question Lucy has been called upon to ask in the present case example has been posed in a variety of behavioral health contexts. For instance, its consideration in the delivery of mental health services is at least partly responsible for the deinstitutionalization of many chronically mentally ill patients who had previously been consigned to "warehousing" in state facilities (see, e.g., *Jackson v. Fort Stanton Hosp. & Training Sch.,* 1990; *Wyatt v. Fetner,* 1996).

Case Example 12: The Anti-WIPP Organizer

A national environmental organization, *Cleanspace*, has decided to take a decisive stand against a proposed waste isolation pilot plant (WIPP) in southern New Mexico. The plant will receive radioactive waste from various points around the nation and will store them in an underground facility that will be constructed together with a series of access roads leading to it. Civic leaders in Carlsbad are hopeful that the plant will bring more employment to a depressed economy, as plentiful oil and mining jobs have declined in recent years. Scientists are also interested in the new plant because it may offer an ideal location for an experimental physics lab. Construction of the lab would bring even more jobs to the community.

Cleanspace has retained the services of a community organizer to coordinate an effort against the construction of the plant. The organizer has a master of social work degree and has received additional training at the organization's training center in Washington, D.C. Cleanspace advocates against the storage of nuclear waste in populated areas and the transport of hazardous materials on public highways (Thrower & Martinez, 2000). In its training program, Cleanspace teaches social action techniques (Pilisuk, McAllister, & Rothman, 1996), which involve the use of a confrontational approach to mobilize activity against unwanted development projects and to promote public awareness of the health impact of various environmental hazards. Furthermore, Cleanspace's training program emphasizes the use of aggressive lobbying activities at the federal, state, and regional levels. Cleanspace tends to staff its community organization projects with graduates of its training program, who receive their salaries from the organization.

Jarrod Heatherton, a recent graduate of Cleanspace's training program, has just arrived in New Mexico to open the organization's field office in Carlsbad. Jarrod plans to hold an open house to celebrate the opening of the office and to allow an opportunity for meeting the public. Sympathetic legislators have been invited to attend. In addition, Jarrod plans to commence his organizational activities with a public demonstration against the WIPP project. He has sought a municipal permit for a public demonstration against the opening of the WIPP site.

This case example demonstrates the usefulness of applying the duty to identify the primary client in the field of community organizing. As in all other behavioral health and human services, community organizing should be understood to involve the establishment of a professional relationship with one or more primary clients.

The use of terminology associated with the duty to identify the primary client may seem awkward when it is applied outside the realm of health and mental health care. Even so, the duty is no less applicable here than it is in the delivery of clinical services. Consider the responsibilities that the duty imposes on Jarrod in this scenario, and the impact that they have on his planning of services. First, Jarrod must establish a professional relationship with one or more identified clients through the seeking of informed consent. According to this scenario, however, no primary clients have as yet sought Jarrod's assistance nor have they granted informed consent to the intervention that Jarrod has planned. Indeed, at the moment, the intervention Jarrod has designed is being *imposed* rather than arrived at through any reasonable assessment of community need. Moreover, Jarrod appears ready to actively recruit participants in a way that violates not only informed consent principles but also ethical standards governing the solicitation of potential clients.

In this case example, there are many potential clients whose interests Jarrod ultimately may come to represent, including members of the community who are affected by the proposed WIPP project and may need a community based intervention to advance their position. However, the duties to practice reasonably competently and to seek informed consent require that Jarrod ascertain the needs of his potential clients in a way that does not presuppose the outcome. In order to do this, Jarrod may appropriately use any one of a number of reasonable methods to assess his community; regardless of which community assessment Jarrod chooses, its purpose must be to identify what his clients want and need.

If Jarrod plans his assessment thoroughly, he may find that there is wide diversity of opinion within the community about the WIPP project. If he surveys opinions among Hispanic and Native American citizens, he may discover some support for the project and the jobs it will bring to an economically disenfranchised segment of the community. He may also find concern about the health impact of the project, but also an unwillingness to support a confrontational effort that further isolates this underclass from the economic mainstream of the community.

If Jarrod freely discusses the risks and benefits of Cleanspace's approach, he and his potential clients may reasonably conclude that a social action approach will not serve their long-term interests. Informed consent guidelines suggest that it is appropriate for Jarrod to discuss Cleanspace's preference for the social action approach but only if he also reveals the risks presented by this strategy. Such risks might include, among other things, jeopardizing the ability of minority workers to obtain future employment in a community dominated financially by a new industry. After a discussion of these risks, all may conclude that an economic intervention that supports job creation and fiscal revitalization of the city may more adequately address the immediate needs of the numerous poor and unemployed among the city's minority populations. Additionally, working to develop a broad, economically based coalition may help to interest community members who presently support the WIPP project in the environmental issues advocated by Cleanspace.

Even if Jarrod and his potential clients openly discuss the risks and benefits created by a social action strategy, and in the event all elect to pursue Jarrod's strategy (thus satisfying the requirements of the duty to seek informed consent), Jarrod's approach still may be inappropriate for a community in which environmental and economic issues should more properly be addressed in a unified manner, and with extensive long-term planning. Put differently, Jarrod's limited social action approach may offer a strategy that fails to address competently the needs of his community.

In this scenario, Jarrod's organizational approach thus far has been driven by the organization—Cleanspace—that has trained him and underwritten his effort. If he permits Cleanspace's philosophy to direct the services he ultimately offers community members, he is effectively allowing a third party to predetermine the extent of his professional relationship with his prospective clients. This problem is conceptually similar to the one faced by psychotherapists who feel constrained to diagnose a mental health problem in the manner that ensures the greatest reimbursement from a third-party payor. Thus, the impact of a conflict of interest may be as far-reaching on the community organizer as it is on the psychotherapist. In both instances it may interfere with the professional's ability to practice reasonably competently. In Jarrod's case, this includes the freedom to design a community intervention that appropriately addresses the need of his clients and is based on their voluntary and knowing consent.

The duty to identify the primary client suggests that an otherwise well-meaning professional can threaten the interests of potential clients by allowing the funding requirements or ideological positions of a financial backer to drive a professional intervention. As in all areas of behavioral health and human services, a failure to observe this duty may fall most heavily on the backs of poor clients for whom assistance is underwritten by a third-party payor, a government agency, or a charitable organization. One of the important legal premises underlying the duty to identify the primary client is that the rights conferred by the professional relationship apply irrespective of whether payment has changed hands between provider and recipient. Specifically, the privileges of a client receiving free services are no less apparent than those enjoyed by paying clients. Therefore, the fact that services may be charitable does not excuse the provider from the responsibility of designing and implementing them competently and with informed consent.

Case Example 13: The Faith Based Service Revisited

Please reconsider the scenario described in case example 7, "The Faith Based Service." Recall that the counselor in this scenario, Melissa Zak, is struggling with the religious principles that guide service delivery in a church based counseling program.

As the duty to identify the primary client suggests, a conflict of interest is created between a behavioral health provider and client when their professional relationship is influenced by a third party. This point has important relevance for Melissa in her effort to provide appropriate assistance to her clients. As in case example 12, "The Anti-WIPP Organizer," the services that are offered by the church have in large measure been defined by the strong philosophical principles advocated within its program. The restrictions imposed on Melissa not only limit the nature of the counseling she may provide, but they also apparently conflict with Melissa's own ideological position regarding counseling. If this is the case, then Melissa's conflict of interest may be irreconcilable, because her independent clinical judgment is excessively hampered by the limitations forced upon her. She cannot presently offer competent services to clients unless her philosophical orientation to counseling is reasonably consistent with her program's. Simply put, if this consistency does not exist, Melissa cannot work for the agency. If she evades this point in the interest of planning a more strategic time for addressing it in the future, she virtually ensures that any service she provides to her clients will be deficient. The need to get a job can be a powerful incentive to understate one's professional philosophy to potential employers. It may even inspire a reasonably well-intended job searcher to accept a position in the hope of ultimately reconciling an ideological conflict with the employee. This strategy, however, is plainly inconsistent with competent professional practice, and it subverts the duty to seek informed consent from prospective clients.

Case Example 14: The School Social Worker

Gaspard Fontaine is employed as a school social worker in the Pecos, New Mexico public school system. Gaspard's school social work position is legally mandated by the Individuals With Disabilities Education Act (IDEA) (1975/2001), which promotes the interests of educationally disabled children attending school. Among other things, the law guarantees the right of such children to a "free appropriate public education" (FAPE), uniquely tailored to meet the educational needs of each child.

Through an assessment and planning process, IDEA requires that an individually planned educational program (IEP) be jointly designed by an "IEP Team" to address the special learning needs of each child, and provide appropriate support services, such as remedial education and individual counseling. IDEA strongly encourages schools to *mainstream*, that is, to allow the disabled child to be educated together with nondisabled peers (*Alabama Coalition for Equity, Inc. v. Hunt,* 1993; *Oberti v. Board of Educ.,* 1993). IDEA also requires that parents of children entitled to an IEP must be included in the plan's design. Finally, IDEA mandates that the school provide children and their parents with adequate support services—including social workers, counselors, and psychologists—to assist them in planning and implementing the IEP. Occasionally, parents disagree with the IEP established by the school for a child. IDEA grants these parents the right to an administrative appeal before a hearing officer and ultimately the right to challenge a negative result through court proceedings.

One of Gaspard's important roles is to participate with the IEP team in the formulation of appropriate educational plans. Gaspard also provides counseling and other supportive services to children and their families, and in this capacity is administratively responsible to his school principal and local school board. According to his job responsibilities, Gaspard also helps parents to advocate for themselves throughout the entire IEP design process. Occasionally, he is called upon to testify about his recommendations in administrative proceedings concerning the IEP.

Gaspard presently is working with the Ramirez family: Ernesto and Sylvia and their daughter, Amalia, a fifth-grader at the school. Amalia is developmentally disabled and has also been diagnosed with attention deficit disorder. Her primary spoken language at home is Spanish. Ernesto and Sylvia speak little English and can read and write only in Spanish. During the development of Amalia's IEP, Gaspard communicates with both parents in Spanish, of which he has a working knowledge. Gaspard has advised the Ramirez family that the school system's budget is limited, and that only one bilingual teacher is available possessing the special education skills necessary to accommodate Amalia's needs.

Gaspard regards himself as a mediator, and seeks to reconcile Amalia's best interests with what the school board's budget will reasonably allow. Given Amalia's special needs, Gaspard suggests that Amalia be enrolled in a special education class together with other similarly disabled children, where she can receive more individualized attention. At Gaspard's initial meeting with Amalia's parents, they have consented to the proposed plan. After discussing it further at home, however, they have more fully realized that the plan means isolating Amalia from her friends at school. Treating Amalia as "different" violates the family's values, and they believe it to be inconsistent with her best interests. They wish to discuss this matter further with Gaspard.

This case example depicts a common conflict of interest that affects school social workers, counselors, and psychologists. In this scenario, Gaspard has established a professional relationship with a primary client—Amalia Ramirez. At the same time, however, his administrative relationship with his school board and its principal threatens to impact the quality of the services he offers Amalia, as well as his ability to offer independent, objective guidance to the family. This may already be reflected in Gaspard's communication to the parents concerning the school board's limited funds.

School social workers in Gaspard's position may face additional pressures from teachers with whom they interact daily to help them in their quest to keep class sizes reasonable and to avoid taking on additional responsibilities with special needs students that might detract from the attention owed to other students. Indeed, Gaspard attends staff meetings with faculty and support personnel, at which time these concerns often are voiced openly.

The tasks required as part of the duty to identify the primary client call for Gaspard to honor his commitments to practice reasonably competently and seek informed consent; with respect to the latter responsibility, it is owed to the Ramirez parents. The present case example suggests, however, that these commitments may already have been compromised. Amalia is entitled to mainstreaming, and, as IDEA mandates, it is consistent with her best educational interests, which Gaspard is duty-bound to represent. In fact, it may be *required* under federal and state laws and administrative regulations governing the formulation of IEPs. However, Gaspard appears willing to allow school budgetary issues to influence formulation of Amalia's IEP. If Gaspard is later called upon to testify before the school board—and in any subsequent court challenge to the IEP—he may continue to find himself subtly influenced to endorse recommendations that are consistent with the school district's financial constraints. He may be asked by the Ramirez family to justify his position in terms of Amalia's best interests, a task that may be difficult to accomplish.

Gaspard's conflict of interest in this scenario may also threaten his ability to seek informed consent from the Ramirez parents. First, Gaspard owes to the Ramirezes the delicate responsibility of explaining the conflict. The same subtle administrative influences already described may limit Gaspard's free discussion of all available educational alternatives, together with the risks presented by isolating Amalia in a special education environment. These influences notwithstanding, Gaspard must be prepared to discuss the effect that this course of action may have on Amalia's language development, and the possible delay it could cause in Amalia's cultivation of English language skills. Gaspard's limited Spanish language ability may make it difficult to explain the more intricate aspects of the risks and benefits presented by the proposed IEP. This type of language problem may greatly amplify the existing hazard created by Gaspard's relationship with his school board and principal. The Ramirez family's hesitance to accept Gaspard's initial recommendations already suggests that his initial communication with them has been flawed.

Even if Gaspard ultimately can obtain informed consent from Mr. and Mrs. Ramirez, his conflict of interest raises substantial questions about his ability to perform effective client advocacy in his role as a school employee. This role requires the independent development of an educational plan that promotes Amalia's best interests, and it puts him in a position potentially antagonistic to the administrative personnel that supervise him and pay at least part of his salary. Interestingly, a substantial portion of Gaspard's salary is underwritten by an IDEA grant, a fact that further complicates his relationships with the school board. Similarly, his associations with fellow staff members may present comparable influences. These social and economic pressures offer a powerful incentive for Gaspard to temper the assertiveness necessary to represent Amalia adequately. If the most appropriate IEP for Amalia requires her placement in a regular schoolroom, together with individualized attention both from the home room teacher and a special education instructor, Gaspard's present suggestion falls far short of it.

To some extent, *every* professional employed by someone else has an inherent conflict of interest with the client. When one performs services that are salaried, or whose provisions are determined by an agency budget, these variables may affect the competence of the services rendered to clients. At one time or another, all diligent agency professionals will raise significant questions with their own employers concerning the constraints that agency budgets or policies place upon client services. In most of these situations, however, professionals find themselves requesting their agencies' financial and policy assistance in honoring legal responsibilities to individual clients who have fallen through administrative cracks. In such circumstances, the professional's continuing role within the agency is not usually in direct conflict with the agency's interests. Put another way, this kind of conflict does not ordinarily hamper the professional's ability to offer reasonable services consistent with most agency policies and procedures.

What makes Gaspard's conflict extreme is that his role has been designed and largely funded by a federal law—IDEA—that designates Gaspard as an advocate for the best interests of educationally disabled children. This professional role frequently involves the formulation of individualized plans that take a specific toll on a school board's staff requirements. Gaspard is expected as a matter of routine to extend himself on his clients' behalf and, at least in theory, explore options that may run counter to the school board's fiscal and administrative interests. This conflict not only undermines Gaspard's individual professional relationships with clients, but also it reflects an overall problem in the design of school social worker responsibilities that makes the consistent provision of reasonable client services impossible.

Just as the performance of counseling services by a child welfare agency social worker or patient advocacy by a hospital employee may be inherently inconsistent with clients' best interests, the offering of school social work services by the employee of a financially strapped school district may create an analogous conflict. Consequently, behavioral health professionals concerned with public policy governing educational systems should be prepared to take extensive action in the protection of client interests. First, a long-range solution would require advocacy services offered to clients and their families to be assumed by public agencies equipped to render such services. Public health agencies and community mental health centers offer the desired independent judgment necessary to ensure competent representation of client interests respecting educational services. Short of this step, a more immediate alternative is to remove the school based professional entirely from administrative responsibility to the school system, and to ensure independent funding of the professional's job. Either of these suggested steps would go a long way to safeguard the independence of school based behavioral health professions and minimize the economic and administrative influences on them.

6

The Duty to Treat Clients and Co-workers With Due Process and Equal Protection

The U.S. Constitution can be regarded as a contract between the people and their government. It contains a basic set of general principles that serve as a foundation for all lawmaking at the federal and state levels. One of the Constitution's primary objects is the protection of individual citizens against oppressive and encroaching legislatures and public officials.

Through the court opinions that have interpreted the Constitution throughout U.S. history, a body of law has developed that describes the rights of citizens and the responsibilities of government servants toward them. Much of this law has come into existence as a result of the actions of behavioral health professionals, whose constitutional obligations to their clients and co-workers have been defined by many reviewing courts. A thorough review of constitutional law is beyond the scope of this book; indeed, the subject is most aptly addressed in an academic course of a year or more duration. At the same time, however, there are several fundamental constitutional principles that have had such a profound and permanent impact on behavioral health professionals and their clients that a basic understanding of them is essential for every provider.

The constitutional principles that have the most impact on behavioral health professionals can be summarized simply as *due process* and *equal protection*; both have a critical role in influencing the choices made by public and private sector professionals on a daily basis. Despite the monumental impact they have on the professional relationship, these legal principles are not significantly addressed in professional ethical codes. For this reason, behavioral health professionals who understand their meaning and application have a ready tool in addressing practice dilemmas that involve the interaction between health and human service agencies, their employees, and their clients.

A summary of various courts' historical interpretation of due process and equal protection is presented here in a format that emphasizes their use in making professional decisions. Although these principles primarily affect the relationship between publicly employed professionals and their clients, through recent civil rights legislation their influence has been extended to private agencies as well. Therefore, it is suggested that, along with other fundamental legal principles, the decision maker consider the duty to treat clients and co-workers with due process and equal protection as a first step in the consideration of any practice dilemma.

Introduction to Due Process and Equal Protection

The Fifth Amendment to the U.S. Constitution, ratified in 1791, protects among other things the right of all persons to be free from deprivations of "life, liberty, or property, without due process of law." This so-called *due process clause* is intended to protect citizens from intrusions upon basic rights by the federal government, although the precise scope of the protection offered is not specifically explained.

A similar due process clause is contained in the Fourteenth Amendment, ratified shortly after the Civil War in 1868. At the time of its ratification, the Fourteenth Amendment was primarily intended to grant rights to newly freed slaves, and to extend a host of protections to citizens against oppressive practices by state governments. The Fourteenth Amendment's due process clause is identical in language to the Fifth Amendment's, except that it applies to the actions of state governments and public officials.

The Fourteenth Amendment adds another layer of protection to state citizens by shielding them from the denial of "equal protection of the laws." This *equal protection clause* serves to protect individuals from discriminatory acts by state governments based on race, national origin, and other classifications. Note that, although the Fifth Amendment contains no equal protection clause, courts have ruled that its due process clause also extends equal protection to citizens from the discriminatory acts of the federal government (*Rodriguez-Silva v. Immigration and Naturalization Serv.,* 2001).

In addition to granting substantive rights to all persons, the Fourteenth Amendment conveys to Congress the power to enforce these rights through appropriate legislation. Congress has enacted much legislation protecting individuals from unfair and discriminatory practices, although its authority to do so has been limited in recent years by various courts.

The Fifth and Fourteenth Amendment have much in common. They both safeguard persons from unfair and discriminatory government practices, and each grants Congress the authority to enforce its provisions through legislation. However, because so many of the basic public health, welfare, and safety services provided in this country are administered by state and local governments, the Fourteenth Amendment's due process and equal protection clauses have become the dominant weapons relied upon by citizens to combat government misconduct. For that reason, there is an ever-growing body of common law that interprets the language contained in these provisions.

The Meaning of *Person* and *State Action*

At the heart of the Fourteenth Amendment is the protection afforded to every individual person from state actions. In order to understand the scope of this protection, each of these terms, as they are interpreted by courts, must be explained individually.

Who is a *person* for the purposes of the Fourteenth Amendment? Explaining the answer to this question is more problematic than it seems. A person, courts have noted, is any individual who has been deprived of life, liberty, or property at the hands of the government (*Crumpton v. Gates,* 1991). Because nonhuman entities can own property, it should not be surprising that corporations and other businesses are considered "persons" under the Fourteenth Amendment (*Northeast Ga. Radiological Assocs. v. Tidwell,* 1982). Because government action can affect a host of people besides the direct object of the action, the families and survivors of someone injured by the government are also regarded as persons entitled to constitutional protection.

Aside from the more traditional meanings imparted by the term *person*, newer interpretations have become more controversial in recent years. For example, if an unborn child fails to mature because of the actions of the government—perhaps a police beating resulting in the mother's death, or an accident involving the gross negligence of a public bus driver—might the fetus be a "person" entitled to constitutional coverage? Courts have repeatedly answered "no" to this question (see, e.g., *Lewis v. Thompson,* 2001), although this claim continues to be pressed in a variety of jurisdictions, sometimes with the vocal support of conservative and fundamentalist religious groups. The reason for their support may be obvious. A court willing to recognize the rights of a fetus to constitutional protection in a relatively uncontroversial case might ultimately open the door to a reconsideration of abortion rights recognized in the landmark case *Roe v. Wade* (1973).

What types of conduct should the government reasonably be answerable for? According to the Fourteenth Amendment, the answer is conduct that rises to the level of *state action*. State action can be described as any conduct by the government, its agents, officers, or employees that can be "fairly attributed" to the state, and that governs, limits, or affects a person's right to life, liberty, or property (*Lansing v. City of Memphis,* 2000).

The most obvious and formal type of state action is the enactment of a law or promulgation of a regulation by a state legislature or government agency (*Denver Area Educ. Telecommunications Consortium, Inc. v. Federal Communications Comm'n,* 1996). State action, as the definition implies, also refers to the acts of individual government officers and employees. This has usually been interpreted to mean that an officer or employee is performing a state action only if the action is made possible by specific authority granted under the law (*Griffin v. City of Opa-Locka,* 2001). For example, a police officer who places a child in protective custody is performing a state action; a police officer who sexually harasses a co-worker while off duty is committing a private action. As another example, a state child welfare worker who investigates suspected abuse and neglect is performing a state action; if the same social worker makes defamatory statements to friends about the family being investigated, a private action is being committed. A public employee who takes a state action while performing in an official capacity, or exercising responsibilities granted under the law, is sometimes described as acting *under color of law* (*Griffin v. City of Opa-Locka,* 2001).

Note specifically that a state action does not arise unless it intrudes upon a person's right to life, liberty, or property. For example, a police officer who places a suspect under arrest clearly restrains the individual's liberty. If the same police officer interviews the suspect about a crime in a noncoercive way and without arresting the person, then no interference with liberty has occurred, and therefore no state action has occurred.

A state-employed psychologist who is fired for insubordination may be losing a property right. If the same psychologist is verbally reprimanded instead of fired, then arguably no state action has occurred. Similarly, a police officer who tells a member of a minority involved in a street altercation that he should "stay in his own neighborhood" is probably not committing a state action, despite the toxicity of the statement.

Local governments, such as county commissions, city councils, and other public bodies are also included within the definition of "state." The reason is that these governmental forms are organized under state law, with state legislatures maintaining supervisory authority over the manner in which these local governments conduct their business. Therefore, a town constable who rounds up homeless persons and detains them pursuant to the town's antivagrancy ordinance is performing a state action. Likewise, a city planning and zoning commission that rejects an applicant's request for a residential group home permit is performing a state action.

In their strict interpretation of state action, recent courts have limited the power of Congress to enact social welfare legislation controlling the conduct of private parties. A notable example is the U.S. Supreme Court's recent invalidation of important aspects of the Violence Against Women Act of 1994 (VAWA) (*United States v. Morrison,* 2000). VAWA, which would guarantee the rights of persons to be free from violence motivated by gender, such as rape, sexual harassment, and stalking, includes a provision, 42 U.S.C. §13981(c), allowing victims to sue and collect civil damages from their assailants. In finding this remedy to violate the Fourteenth Amendment, the *Morrison* Court noted that VAWA exceeded Congress's power to regulate the behavior of state governments and their employees and agents.

A final word is in order about the terminology used here to describe government behavior: The term *state action* is used most often here because of this chapter's primary focus on the Fourteenth Amendment, which is concerned expressly with the conduct of state and local government activities. Indeed, the vast majority of publicly employed behavioral health professionals work for state and local government agencies, and therefore need to be concerned primarily about state and local agency conduct. Consequently, most of the examples cited hereafter involve actions by state and local government officials. The discussion presented, however, applies equally to the conduct of the federal government and its agencies and employees, which is regulated under the Fifth Amendment's due process clause. The term *government action*, when used here, refers generically to the behavior of the federal and state governments and their agencies and employees.

Consequences of Performing a State Action

Public Employees. Behavioral health professionals who work for the government as mental health personnel, child protective service workers, public agency administrators, teachers, public hospital employees, prison counselors, and public school based providers all need to be aware that their decisions involving clients are often state actions taken under color of law. Thus, placing an abused youngster in the protective custody of a child welfare agency, conducting a forensic interview and assessment, participating in the design of an individual educational plan for an educationally disabled child, and offering mental health services to prison inmates all fall within this category.

Professionals who provide these and numerous other public services are plainly representing governmental interests. Therefore, due process and equal protection principles have a special significance for them. Both of these constitutional doctrines govern the manner in which services should be provided and offer important protections to individuals whose rights are affected by them. Failure to honor due process and equal protection can result in civil and even criminal liability for the professional and the agency involved in misconduct. For example, §1983 of the Civil Rights Act of 1871 offers money damages and injunctive relief for the violation of constitutional rights.

Private Employees. Due process and equal protection also have significance for some privately employed professionals whose services are performed for agencies that work closely with the government in the delivery of behavioral health and human services to the public. For example, when a state agency delegates its authority to a private individual or company to provide compulsory services, or services that the government requires be used by a particular group of consumers, the private provider assumes the constitutional responsibilities ordinarily reserved to the state (*West v. Atkins,* 1988). As an illustration, if a state corrections agency contracts with a private prison to house inmates, the actions of prison officials and employees—including providers hired to perform medical and mental health services—are fairly attributable to the state (*West v. Atkins,* 1988). This is true because the services are mandatory, the inmates have no choice in the clinician from whom they receive services, and therefore the state must assume responsibility for the private agency's actions. In this circumstance, both the government and the private agency ordinarily are said to be acting under color of law.

In other situations in which the state contracts with private agencies to provide more limited mental health, child care, and other services to the public, the constitutional responsibilities of these private providers are far less certain. The present reluctance of courts to extend constitutional protections to the clients and employees of private agencies that provide services under state contracts may leave millions of persons with little or no recourse against the government for agency misconduct. With the increasing trend toward privatization of essential governmental functions, this important problem is certain to be revisited by future courts. A brief review of the law relating to private agencies and the state action doctrine is therefore timely.

Privatization and the State Action Doctrine. Privatization of services refers to a management strategy by which the government shifts the delivery of public health, human service, and other functions to the private sector, including both profit and nonprofit agencies, in order to improve service delivery and save money (Ewoh, 1999). Important benefits of privatization claimed by proponents include reduction of government size, expansion of individual freedom, and more efficient and inexpensive delivery of services (Ewoh, 1999). Privatization is accomplished in two essential ways: First, it occurs when federal, state, and local governments entirely delegate to a private vendor their responsibility for providing an important public service. This is occurring at present most notably in the areas of state corrections and prison support services. It is also taking place in the provision of such diverse public services as air traffic control, garbage collection, police and fire protection, public landscaping, and vehicle maintenance (Ewoh, 1999). Second, it occurs when governments contract out human services, and community health and mental health programs. Thus, purchase-of-service (POS) contracts with private vendors are used significantly by governments at all levels to provide services in such areas as child welfare, child day care, outpatient mental health counseling, substance abuse and alcoholism treatment, nursing care, homeless shelters, group homes for the chronically mentally ill, school psychological and counseling programs, and long-term care for the developmentally disabled (Gibelman & Demone, 1998). A national political debate focuses at present on additional proposals to extend government support to religious charitable institutions, or faith based services, and to offer vouchers to parents who wish to enroll their children in private schools.

Regardless of whether privatization actually accomplishes what its proponents allege it does, it has a very specific impact on the legal relationship between the public and the government, and particularly the constitutional recourse that historically has been available to citizens for inadequate service delivery. In legal terms, contemporary courts regard government vendors as private parties, and have disallowed constitutional claims against them (*Blum v. Yaretsky,* 1982; *Lansing v. City of Memphis,* 2000; *Simescu v. Emmet County Dep't of Human Servs.,* 1991; *Wolotsky v. Huhn,* 1992).

As the above-referenced cases reveal, even when the government subsidizes client costs, provides a substantial part of program funding, regulates vendor practices, is responsible for referring clients, leases space to an agency, or otherwise takes an active role in helping a private provider to deliver services to the public, courts have been unwilling to regard conduct by private agencies and their employees as state action. For example, courts have denied constitutional claims arising from the sexual abuse of children by a welfare-to-work participant at a privatized *workfare* program (*Simescu v. Emmet County Dep't of Human Servs.,* 1991), and the firing of a social worker by a private, nonprofit mental health agency responsible for providing all of the direct clinical services for an Ohio county (*Wolotsky v. Huhn,* 1992). In explaining their decisions, courts have noted that unless the government encourages, coerces, or actually conspires with the private actor in the commission of misconduct, there is no state action (*Lansing v. City of Memphis,* 2000; *Simescu v. Emmet County Dep't of Human Servs.,* 1991; *Wolotsky v. Huhn,* 1992). In other words, say the courts, unless the government actively participates in the vendors' misconduct, it is not fairly attributable to the government (but see contrasting opinions in *Hammons v. Norfolk S. Corp.,* 1998; *Jensen v. Lane County,* 2000).

The practical impact of the courts' present hostility to constitutional claims involving private government vendors is profound. It suggests that clients and employees of these providers have recourse for their misconduct only through private civil lawsuits against offending individuals and agencies. The courts have reacted favorably to the idea that these vendors and their personnel should be responsive primarily to market factors that influence their conduct, and that the threat of economic loss arising from their misconduct is one such market factor that should promote appropriate agency practice. Even the U.S. Supreme Court has expressed its approval of the concept that market factors alone should govern the conduct of government contractors (*Richardson v. McKnight,* 1997). Vendors therefore must be required pursuant to their government contracts to carry insurance that protects their clients from agency misconduct, and client and employee recourse against private agencies is often limited to lawsuits founded upon traditional liability theories, including tort actions, civil rights suits, and private contract actions.

Regardless of whether market factors actually do promote proper agency practices, the present discussion omits the simple point that the government has become increasingly insulated from any responsibility for its contractors' conduct. In effect, a government agency that hires a private contractor to provide services may be immune from responsibility for the contractor's physical and sexual abuse of, or racial and gender discrimination against, the contractor's clients and employees, among other offenses. The broad relief available to victims under §1983 lawsuits may therefore be unavailable from the government. The policy implications of this disturbing fact should be recognized by every public and private behavioral health professional concerned with the government's accountability to its citizens. To the extent that voucher systems, faith based service proposals, and other forms of privatized health and human service delivery remain on the agenda of Congress and state legislatures, policy decision makers must be aware that the use of the Constitution in safeguarding government accountability may become more and more removed from those persons reliant on private providers.

A Constitutional Strategy for Private Professionals. The present constitutional analysis should not dissuade privately employed behavioral health professionals from understanding and applying the principles discussed here. Even though constitutional protections extend primarily against state actions and acts committed under color of law by public agency professionals, the principles should be used by all behavioral health providers.

Two practical reasons compel the use of constitutional standards by private sector behavioral health professionals. First, many of the tasks associated with due process and equal protection are enforceable against private agencies and their employees as a result of federal and state legislation such as the Civil Rights Act of 1964. Many states have additional civil rights protections that require equitable procedures and nondiscrimination policies in the delivery of services to the public, and these should be understood and consulted as part of the constitutional strategy suggested here. Just as importantly, this approach ensures compliance with the duty to practice reasonably competently. Second, as noted earlier, private agencies that provide services to the government under contract may in limited circumstances be regarded as government agents, and their activities may be subject to enforcement through the same mechanisms that historically have been used against public agencies, the most notable being the §1983 action. Consequently, the duty to treat clients and co-workers with due process and equal protection is a useful tool for all behavioral health professionals in the consideration of practice dilemmas.

Using Due Process and Equal Protection Cases in Decision Making

A key aim in using due process and equal protection in decision making is to acquire the ability to predict the way in which courts are likely to interpret the constitutional aspects of a practice dilemma. On occasion, a problem may arise in practice that is comparable to a factual scenario that has already been assessed by a court. Reference to the summary of court decisions presented here may therefore be helpful to the decision maker for this purpose. Unfortunately, as the cases identified in subsequent sections demonstrate, courts are not always consistent in the way they interpret due process and equal protection law in individual decisions. Moreover, common law interpretations of due process and equal protection are in a state of constant evolution. For these reasons, it is probably more advantageous for the decision maker to understand the overall reasoning process that courts use in analyzing all due process and equal protection cases, rather than to memorize outcomes in individual cases. The streamlined strategies for handling due process and equal protection cases presented later may be especially helpful for the decision maker wishing to apply these principles in the consideration of practice problems.

Due Process

The body of common law defining due process is rich and extensive. Over the course of centuries of constitutional history, courts have interpreted due process as containing two basic components: *procedural due process*, which guarantees basic fairness in state and federal government actions, and *substantive due process*, which defines a set of fundamental rights specially protected from government invasion. Each of these components is addressed in the sections that follow.

Procedural Due Process

When the federal or state government, or a county or municipal council or commission, through its agencies and employees, seeks to interfere with a citizen's right to *life*, *liberty*, or *property*, it must do so with procedural fairness. Procedural fairness generally requires that the affected person have notice of the government's intent to interfere with the right and an opportunity to be heard (*Martin v. Commissioner,* 2000; *Mills v. New Mexico Bd. of Psychologist Examiners,* 1997). Each of these terms must be addressed individually.

Life, Liberty, and Property Rights. There are numerous instances in which a governmental body can interfere with the right of its citizens to life, liberty, or property. When the government executes a convicted murderer, it is quite literally depriving the convict of continuing life. Similarly, when the government seeks to incarcerate someone accused of a crime, it intrudes upon the person's freedom. Courts have extended the definition of liberty to include a variety of situations that probably were not contemplated by the framers of the Constitution. An oft-quoted statement by the U.S. Supreme Court describes liberty as

> not merely freedom from bodily restraint, but also the right of the individual to contract, to engage in any of the common occupations of life, to acquire useful knowledge, to marry, establish a home and bring up children, to worship God according to the dictates of his own conscience, and generally to enjoy those privileges long recognized as essential to the orderly pursuit of happiness by free men. (*Meyer v. Nebraska,* 1923, p. 399)

Under this expansive definition of liberty, courts have interpreted its coverage in varied ways. Indeed, its meaning depends on state and regional interpretations and is sometimes defined more liberally under state law (*Wolff v. McDonnell,* 1974). Thus, the right to liberty has been recognized by courts in a variety of contexts of particular concern to behavioral health professionals. For example, a child welfare agency seeking to obtain custody of an endangered child affects both the child's and the parents' family privacy, a recognized element of liberty in contemporary society (*Tenenbaum v. Williams,* 1999). In developing this *family privacy doctrine*, courts have indicated their intention to protect the right of a family to raise its children in the manner seen fit by the parents without fear of governmental intrusion (*Brokaw v. Mercer County,* 2000).

Additional interpretations of the meaning of liberty include the following: A juvenile proceeding that leads to an adjudication of delinquency and detention literally affects the child's continuing liberty (*In re R. G.,* 1996). A disabled child's right to attend class regularly is grounded in the liberty to attend public school (*W. B. v. Matula,* 1995). The right of a patient in a long-term care facility to be free from physical restraints is also an aspect of liberty (*Kansas v. Hendricks,* 1997). A state mental health agency that wishes to confine a mentally ill person exhibiting signs of dangerousness seeks to control the person's personal liberty (*Kansas v. Hendricks,* 1997). The right of a prison inmate to be free from the forced administration of antipsychotic medication also describes a liberty-related right (*Riggins v. Nevada,* 1992), as does the privilege of children in foster care either to be reunited with their natural parents or placed in permanent adoptive homes (*Joseph A. v. New Mexico Dep't of Human Servs.,* 1983). The right of a government employee or public school student to continue to work at a job or attend classes free from physical or sexual harassment is a freedom inspired by modern notions of everyday liberty and personal privacy (*Doe v. Claiborne County,* 1996; *Griffin v. City of Opa-Locka,* 2001). Finally, the right to vote is a significant component of liberty in a free society (*Olagues v. Russoniello,* 1986).

Courts have defined the meaning of property as used in the due process clause expansively. In addition to *tangible* property, such as personal belongings and real estate, a person's rights extend to *intangible* property, such as a job, a professional practice, a checking account, the expectation of future earnings from a contract, retirement and medical benefits, public assistance and other welfare privileges, and a public school education (*Board of Regents v. Roth,* 1972; *Doe v. Gates,* 1993; *Goss v. Lopez,* 1975). Additionally, one has a property right attached to any professional license one holds (*Mills v. New Mexico Bd. of Psychologist Examiners,* 1997).

In order to prove that an intangible property right exists, a person must be able to point to some law, regulation, contract, or other evidence that demonstrates the person's "legitimate claim of entitlement to it," and cannot rely merely on a "unilateral expectation of it" (*Board of Regents v. Roth,* 1972, p. 577). For example, a state agency employee on probationary or temporary status has no reasonable expectation this tentative job will continue indefinitely; in contrast, a permanent or tenured state employee does have such an expectation.

Property rights are often at the heart of civil litigation. When one is sued in court for money damages, one's property ownership is affected literally by the outcome. When one seeks compensation for the loss of a job or reinstatement to a former position, a property right is similarly at stake.

As with liberty rights, some property ownership claims may be created under state law, and their definition may therefore vary in different jurisdictions. For example, under the New Mexico Constitution (article VII, §3 and article XII, §10), the right of Spanish speakers to hold public office, to serve on juries, to vote, and to be educated together with their English-speaking neighbors is protected. Because of this explicit definition of the rights of minorities, a compelling argument can be made that the right to speak Spanish while holding a public job, or even while being educated in a public classroom, represents a liberty or property right (*Yniguez v. Arizonans for Official English,* 1994).

Notice and the Opportunity to Be Heard. As noted, persons facing the government's effort to interfere with a life, liberty, or property right are entitled to notice and an opportunity to be heard. The nature and quality of these protections are defined under federal and state laws, and courts are often called upon to evaluate the government's compliance with these laws in individual cases. On occasion, courts are asked to assess the consistency of the laws themselves with the Constitution's due process clause.

In general, courts evaluate governmental conduct according to the following rule: The amount of notice that one is entitled to from the government, and the opportunity that one has to be heard, both depend upon the importance of the life, liberty, or property right that is being invaded, the significance of the government's authority to invade it, and the risks imposed by loss of the threatened right (*Mills v. New Mexico Bd. of Psychologist Examiners,* 1997).

Most courts have defined adequate notice as anything that is reasonably calculated to alert a person that the government seeks to interfere with a protected right (*Martin v. Commissioner,* 2000). Under different circumstances, notice can be provided through the publication of a law, the serving of a subpoena requiring attendance in court, or a letter from a government agency advising that it seeks to terminate a person's public benefit.

When an individual is sued in court, a liberty or property right is almost invariably threatened. Procedural due process requires that the individual receive notice of the lawsuit's filing; this is commonly obtained through *service of process* by a sheriff or private process server. Most often, this involves personal delivery to the individual affected of a *summons*, which advises the individual that a lawsuit has been filed requiring a response within a limited number of days, and a copy of the lawsuit. Under some circumstances—most commonly where an individual's whereabouts are unknown—process may be obtained by *substituted service*, which often involves mailing notice of the lawsuit or publishing it in a newspaper.

Adequate notice also requires that legislation, ordinances, administrative regulations, and other binding expressions of law be made available to the public by publication. Additionally, the laws themselves must be tailored to reasonably identify the life, liberty, or property right they purport to affect. When law fails to reasonably identify its purpose because it is overbroad, vague, or otherwise unclear, it violates procedural due process (*United Food & Commercial Worker Union v. Southwest Ohio Reg'l Transit Auth.,* 1998).

In light of the preceding definition of procedural due process, consider the case of a social work licensing statute that defines community organization as "a conscious process of social interaction and method of social work concerned with the meeting of broad needs and bringing about [*sic*] and maintaining adjustment between needs and resources" (Social Work Practice Act, 1978/1999, §61-31-6(B)(3)). This law requires social workers practicing as community organizers to be licensed and unlicensed persons to refrain from engaging in this practice. Moreover, the law imposes criminal sanctions for its violation. Despite the apparent authority of the Social Work Practice Act, unless social workers reading the above provision have a reasonable understanding of what it is they are expected to do or refrain from doing, due process is violated. Arguably, this legislative definition of community organizing may fail the procedural due process test.

Some laws are acceptably vague in the protection of an important government interest. For example, legislation defining child abuse and neglect is often intentionally broad with the purpose of covering as many potential instances of child endangerment as possible. For example, a fairly typical legislative definition of an "abused child" is one "who has suffered or who is at risk of suffering serious harm because of the action or inaction of the child's parent, guardian or custodian" (Abuse and Neglect Act, 1978/1999, §32A-4-2(B)(1)). Courts have upheld this type of legislation as consistent with due process on the basis of the balancing test described above (see, e.g., *In re J. A. & L. A.,* 1991). With respect to child abuse codes, the government's interest in protecting vulnerable youngsters is stronger than the need for specificity. Additionally, courts have noted that the consequences for invoking a child abuse provision amount to the potential for loss of custody of a child, rather than the more invasive loss of freedom resulting from incarceration.

An opportunity to be heard usually refers to a hearing, which can range from an informal administrative proceeding to a formal jury trial. Courts suggest that the nature and time of the hearing depend upon the extent of the right interfered with and the importance of the government's interest in invading it. For example, when a state welfare bureau seeks to terminate the public assistance benefits of a client it suspects of defrauding the government, the person is entitled to prior notice of the proposed termination of benefits and a hearing to challenge the factual circumstances underlying the termination (*Goldberg v. Kelly,* 1970). This type of proceeding is often referred to as a *predeprivation hearing*, so named because the subject faces the loss of a potentially life-sustaining property right. As another example, a predeprivation hearing is called for in the case of a public school teacher facing termination because of a charge that the teacher has physically abused a student (*Winegar v. Des Moines Indep. Community Sch. Dist.,* 1994).

In contrast to the preceding examples, if a public child welfare agency wishes to obtain a temporary custody order involving a child whom the authority suspects is presently endangered by abuse or neglect, it may ordinarily do so without prior notice to the child's parents or an opportunity for them to have a hearing (*Tenenbaum v. Williams,* 1999). The parents are entitled to a hearing, but it may come some days after the child has already been removed from the parents' physical custody. In the case of the welfare recipient whose benefits are being suspended, the importance of the public assistance in ensuring the person's survival is deemed to be more significant than the government's interest in terminating benefits. Therefore, the right to a prior hearing is justified. On the contrary, in the case of the parents whose child is being removed temporarily from their home, the government's interest in protecting the vulnerable child from harm is greater than the parents' liberty-related right to privacy; consequently the opportunity for a prior hearing does not exist (*Tenenbaum v. Williams,* 1999).

Federal and state laws govern the quality of notice and the nature of the hearing that an individual facing deprivation of an important right is entitled to. As already noted, these laws vary widely in their definition of the nature, scope, and time of the notice and hearing. Generally, however, they have several basic aspects: Notice must be reasonably calculated to advise the person facing a loss of the reason for the government's assertion of its interest (*New York State Nat'l Org. for Women v. Pataki,* 2001). It must give the person facing a deprivation the chance to request an opportunity to confront the evidence that the government is relying on to assert its interest (*Ortez v. Washington County,* 1996).

As examples of instances giving rise to due process rights, consider the following: Parents challenging a proposed individual educational plan for their educationally disabled child may request an administrative proceeding presided over by a hearing officer (*Weber v. Cranston Sch. Comm.,* 2000). Although some of the essential elements of due process must be provided in this type of case, the administrative hearing itself lacks the more formal procedural safeguards available in some law courts, such as the right to a jury trial. Similarly, parents facing the removal of a child from their home because of the suspicion of child abuse may discover that the amount of evidence required for the state to justify the child's removal may not be as great as in a criminal case (*K. J. v. Pennsylvania Dep't of Pub. Welfare,* 2001). In contrast, a criminal suspect facing incarceration is entitled to a formal jury trial in which strict procedural safeguards and heightened evidentiary rules serve as a protection against the state's arbitrary interference with the defendant's right to liberty.

Hearings that satisfy procedural due process must include several important elements: First, they must be fundamentally fair under the circumstances. Second, they must allow for the person whose right is implicated to confront evidence and adverse witnesses that the state may rely upon to support its case. Third, judges or hearing officers charged with deciding the facts and outcome of each hearing must be fair and unbiased (*State v. Kelly,* 2001).

The more important the right that the government wishes to invade, the more formal the hearing that is required in order to be consistent with procedural due process. The most significant deprivation that can occur to any individual is the loss of personal freedom; thus, it should not be surprising that the most formal hearings are reserved for criminal defendants facing incarceration. Such individuals are entitled to a trial, the characteristics of which include the rigid collection and presentation of evidence, the examination and cross-examination of witnesses, and the creation of a permanent record of the trial. Basic procedural rules for the conduct of trials have been established over centuries of English and U.S. jurisprudential practice, and these principles vary greatly within the federal and state court systems. All of the rules, however, have the same essential purpose of protecting the right to procedural due process of the criminal defendant, and therefore a number of them are largely universal:

- Direct Testimony: Witnesses must appear in court and may testify only as to factual information of which they have firsthand knowledge.
- Expert Testimony: Witnesses may offer opinions when facts require scientific or technical interpretation, and where a judge requires their assistance in the assessment of complex factual information.
- The Hearsay Rule: It requires that direct testimony avoid the repetition of out-of-court statements that are used in court to prove their truth; such statements are often unreliable and cannot be subjected to cross-examination in court.
- Heightened Evidentiary Standard: It requires criminal prosecutors to prove that a crime has occurred *beyond a reasonable doubt*. This standard has been interpreted as meaning that the judge or jury deciding a criminal case must have "an abiding conviction, to a moral certainty, of the truth of the charge" (*Victor v. Nebraska,* 1994, p. 8). The procedural due process protections recognized in criminal trials have been extended to other types of hearings in which individuals face substantial deprivations of liberty-related rights. For example, many of these safeguards apply in juvenile delinquency adjudications, in which a child's custody may be transferred to a state authority for a lengthy period (*In re Gault,* 1967).

Substantive Due Process

An additional and more controversial definition of due process has evolved in a number of court decisions. It provokes debate in that a significant number of jurists believe it extends the meaning of the Constitution's due process clause well beyond the express terminology of the clause and therefore beyond the range intended by its framers. According to this definition, some rights involving life, liberty, or property are so important that they must be considered *fundamental*. According to this definition, fundamental rights not only must be procedurally safeguarded, but also are to be protected from any invasion at all by the government or its employees unless a *compelling interest* in doing so is demonstrated (*Branch v. Turner,* 1994). Each of the terms associated with substantive due process is best approached individually.

Fundamental Rights. Fundamental rights have been defined by courts over the years on a case-by-case basis. Although courts have recently become reluctant to expand this list of privileges, they generally agree that it includes, at the least, all of the protections contained in the U.S. Constitution's Bill of Rights, which consists of the following basic protections:

- First Amendment: freedom of speech, religion, press, and assembly
- Second Amendment: the right of organized militias to bear arms
- Third Amendment: protection from the forced quartering of soldiers by private citizens
- Fourth Amendment: the right to be free from unreasonable searches and seizures
- Fifth Amendment: the freedom from double jeopardy and self-incrimination in criminal proceedings
- Sixth Amendment: the right to an attorney and a speedy trial in criminal proceedings
- Seventh Amendment: the privilege of a jury trial in criminal proceedings
- Eighth Amendment: the freedom from cruel and unusual punishment
- Ninth Amendment: the protection granted to the people to identify new rights not already established
- Tenth Amendment: the freedom of states from federal interference in local concerns—the so-called *States' Rights* Amendment

A variety of additional fundamental rights have been identified in a string of important U.S. Supreme Court decisions. Although nowhere suggested by the express language of the due process clause, the Court has recognized these rights to be implied by the language of the Constitution, most notably by the guarantee of liberty offered in the due process clause and the broad protections offered in the Bill of Rights. Among these *penumbral* rights, or rights existing within the shadow of the Constitution, that the Court has defined are the following:

- The right to marry, have a family life, and bring up children (*M. L. B. v. S. L. J.,* 1996) (also known as the *family privacy doctrine*)
- The right to share a house with one's extended family (*Moore v. City of E. Cleveland,* 1977)
- The right of a competent person to consent to medical treatment and to enjoy a confidential relationship with a health care practitioner (*In re Columbia Valley Reg'l Med. Ctr.,* 2001)
- The right to bodily privacy, including the freedom from forced medication (*Riggins v. Nevada,* 1992)
- A woman's right to have an abortion (*Roe v. Wade,* 1973)
- The right to have access to contraceptives (*Griswold v. Connecticut,* 1965)
- The right to vote (*Harper v. Virginia Bd. of Elections,* 1966)

In addition to the fundamental rights included in the above list, some states have expanded their own constitutions to create special protections for citizens not recognized under federal law. For example, virtually all states have declared public education for children to be a constitutional right worthy of special protection (*Davis v. Monroe County Bd. of Educ.,* 1999). In the *Davis* case, the Supreme Court suggested that where a state constitution protects the right of access to public schools, the right ought to be considered fundamental. This point remains, however, unsettled, and many courts continue to reject the notion that educational access is a fundamental right (*Seal v. Morgan,* 2000). Note additionally that the right to attend public schools ordinarily is interpreted to extend strictly to primary and secondary education, i.e., grade school through high school (see, e.g., *Claremont Sch. Dist. v. Governor,* 1997; *Sheff v. O'Neill,* 1996).

Compelling Interests. As already noted, neither the government nor its subdivisions or employees may ever interfere with a fundamental right unless a compelling interest in doing so is demonstrated. What specifically is a compelling interest? Over the years, courts have often described it as a reasonable justification related to the government's responsibility to accomplish its constitutional and legislative responsibilities and objectives (*County of Sacramento v. Lewis,* 1998). At their most basic, these responsibilities and objectives include maintaining the public health and safety of citizens and protecting the property rights of individuals and businesses. It is also helpful to understand compelling interests as reasons grounded in the government's need to provide services reasonably competently and to protect vulnerable members of society. When the government can demonstrate a compelling interest in interfering with a fundamental right, it must do so using the *least restrictive means*, or the minimum possible invasion of the right (*In re D. W., M. B., and D. B.*, 2001; *Open Door Baptist Church v. Clark County,* 2000).

As an example of the interplay between fundamental citizen rights, compelling government interests, and the least restrictive means rule, consider the government's important role in protecting the welfare of vulnerable children based on the doctrine of *parens patriae* (*In re Kendall J. and Darris P.*, 2000). When a state official such as a child welfare social worker has a reasonable suspicion that a youngster is in danger, the child may be placed in protective custody without the parents' consent (*Tenenbaum v. Williams,* 1999). Despite the acknowledged concern of the parents in making decisions regarding the child's best interests, the law recognizes a balance between this right and the state's interest in the child's protection (*Tenenbaum v. Williams,* 1999). Therefore, the reason for placing the child in protective custody is compelling. While the child's best interests and ultimate custody are being considered and investigated by the child welfare agency, the least restrictive means requirement obligates the bureau to take every reasonable step to minimize the necessity to remove the child from home. This requires, for example, that child welfare personnel demonstrate they have made a good faith effort both to rehabilitate the parents and reunite the family through the design of an appropriate treatment plan (*In re D. W., M. B., and D. B.*, 2001).

Even while their fundamental right to family privacy is interfered with, parents still have a right to procedural due process. This requires that they be provided with notice—in this case, advisement by the welfare agency that their child has been placed in custody. It also necessitates that they be granted an opportunity to be heard, meaning here most likely a custody hearing as soon as possible after the child has been placed in protective custody, at which time the parents may respond to allegations that the child has been abused (*Tenenbaum v. Williams,* 1999).

Other examples of compelling circumstances justifying the government's interference with a person's fundamental right involve instances in which the government's authority to maintain public health and welfare supersedes individual freedoms. For example, the government can regulate the conduct of elections, including the enactment of voting registration and campaign laws, in the interest of maintaining their integrity (*Seymour v. Elections Enforcement Comm'n,* 2000). A city can require demonstrators who wish to stage a parade to obtain a permit so that public safety is protected (*Cox v. New Hampshire,* 1941). A state legislature can regulate lobbying activities for the purpose of combating corruption (*Associated Indus. v. Commonwealth,* 1996). A state prison can deny the request of a death row inmate to undergo a Native American sweat lodge ceremony, a religious cleansing ritual involving a dome-like structure heated by hot rocks or coals (Colmant & Merta, 1999), because of the potential the practice has for interfering with the prison's maintenance of discipline (*Rich v. Woodford,* 2000). (However, in a scathing dissent by two judges, the *Rich* court's majority position was attacked on the ground that "human decency (does not deny) a condemned man his last rights based on . . . implausible security concerns" (*Rich v. Woodford,* 2000, p. 965)).

Additional examples of compelling circumstances include the following: A high school can censor a student newspaper whose printed discussion of sexual activity, pregnancy, and divorce interferes with the school's educational mission, including the maintenance of classroom discipline (*Hazelwood Sch. Dist. v. Kuhlmeier,* 1988). A county zoning authority can deny a permit to a church because it conflicts with the residential ambiance of a rural neighborhood (*Open Door Baptist Church v. Clark County,* 2000). A court can require a convicted rapist to register as a sex offender (*State v. Kelly,* 2001). A state prison can deny the request of a Native American inmate from the Lakota Nation to grow his hair long in accordance with religious beliefs in the interest of maintaining prison discipline, including the "quick identification" of prisoners and the "removal of a place to hide small contraband" (*Pollack v. Marshall,* 1988, p. 659). (However, on the basis of a more recent case, *Flagner v. Wilkinson* (2001), involving a comparable claim by an Orthodox Hasidic Jew, the authority of prison officials to curtail religious practices, including grooming customs, now appears to be highly questionable.))

The arguments offered by government agencies for interfering with fundamental rights are not always successful. For example, a state prison that refuses to honor the religious dietary requests of an inmate improperly interferes with the fundamental First Amendment right to practice religion (*Besh v. Bradley,* 1995). Similarly, a prison cannot refuse inmates' requests for religious counseling or, in the case of Native Americans, deny reasonable access to medicine bags and other religious items (*McKinney v. Maynard,* 1991). A public school that refuses to allow students to use a recreation room for after-hours religious club activities similarly interferes with free speech, assembly, and the practice of religion (*Good News Club v. Milford Cent. Sch.,* 2001). In the *Good News Club* case, the U.S. Supreme Court rejected the school's claim that it had a compelling interest based on enforcement of the separation between church and state. Prison officials who require an inmate to complete an Alcoholics Anonymous program as a condition of parole interfere unjustifiably with the inmate's religious freedom, because AA advocates belief in a "supreme being" (*Rauser v. Horn,* 2001). Parents facing child abuse proceedings cannot be ordered to undergo mandatory psychological testing (*In re T. R., J. M., C. R., & C. R.,* 1999). A college professor cannot be fired for the occasional use of profanity and discussion of sexual topics in class (*Vanderhurst v. Colorado Mountain College Dist.,* 2000). The Immigration and Naturalization Service cannot detain indefinitely an "undesirable" Cuban national on the simple ground that it has been unable to effect deportation because of a lack of cooperation by the detainee's country of origin (*Rosales-Garcia v. Holland,* 2001).

Other practices by public agencies that affect fundamental rights may prove in the near future to violate substantive due process standards. For example, the imposition of dress codes on public school students, a practice often justified on the basis of maintaining school discipline, may limit without compelling justification students' right to privacy and self-expression (see, e.g., *Pyle v. School Comm.,* 1996). Similarly, schools that rely excessively upon alternative teaching strategies emphasizing morality training, affective techniques, self-revelation and role-playing, group counseling, and other pseudo-psychological methods may violate privacy. In a recent case, *Altman v. Bedford Central School District* (2001), parents successfully challenged these teaching practices at the trial level, although their victory was ultimately overturned on appeal, leaving open the possibility of future substantive due process challenges.

Currently, interpretations of fundamental citizen rights and compelling government interests are being reconsidered in two notable court cases. In a decision almost certain to be appealed to the U.S. Supreme Court, Wisconsin's highest court has upheld a probation order in the prosecution of a man for failing to pay child support; the terms of probation included the condition that the man refrain from having additional children (*State v. Oakley,* 2001). The compelling reason offered by the state for the invasion of the fundamental right to procreate is Wisconsin's interest in ensuring that "parents support their children" (*State v. Oakley,* 2001, p. 1).

Whether the *Oakley* court's decision is consistent with the least restrictive means principle will be a significant question for future courts. *Oakley* may represent the latest example of the judiciary's increasing willingness to define parenthood, and particularly fatherhood, in terms of economic and moralistic precepts. Thus, courts have redefined fatherhood as something more than "the mere existence of a biological link," recognizing instead that, from a legal perspective, it comes into existence only when a father agrees to develop a supportive financial and social relationship with a child (*Lehr v. Roberston,* 1983, p. 261). By thus limiting the characterization of fatherhood as a fundamental right, courts and legislatures have controlled the procedural privileges formerly available to the absent fathers of out-of-wedlock children, such as the right to consent to adoptions (*Lehr v. Robertson,* 1983).

In New Mexico, a trial court denied a Navajo prisoner the right to participate in a sweat lodge after prison officials claimed the ceremony would require hundreds of additional support personnel to oversee and was motivated by the prisoner's intent to disrupt prison functioning (*Chavez v. Lemaster,* 2001). This decision notwithstanding, Native American leaders point to the demonstrable success of sweat lodges in leading convicts to address long-term alcohol abuse and antisocial conduct, and enhancing the spiritual growth and rehabilitation of participants (Colmant & Merta, 1999). According to New Mexico's corrections secretary, prisoners at high-security facilities are presently "allowed to keep only a minimum number of religious items in their cells," which may include no more than "an eagle feather and a medicine bag" (Terrell, 2001).

Note that in those instances in which a fundamental right is involved, a government agency seeking to impinge on the right must still satisfy the procedural due process privileges of the person affected. For example, the imposition of long-term discipline upon a public school student, the firing of a public employee, the termination of parental rights of an abusive parent, and the promulgation of zoning ordinances in a city all require procedures, rules, and regulations to be adopted that guarantee the right to notice and an opportunity to be heard of the individual facing the deprivation.

Handling Due Process Dilemmas: The Duty to Treat Clients and Co-workers With Due Process

As revealed by many of the cases already cited, the duty to implement due process principles does not only apply in relationships with a primary client, but also in interactions with other members of the public, including agency co-workers, to whom behavioral health providers owe professional obligations. Thus, applying the duty not only tends to enhance the best interests of clients, but also maximizes broader societal interests, such as the promotion of diversity. Therefore, the prudent professional should identify its application in all practice dilemmas that involve agency responsibilities to clients, employment disputes, disciplinary actions against agency subordinates, professional relationships (including conflicts of interest) with clients and co-workers, and other areas involving individual liberty or property rights.

Consistent with the strategy outlined in the decision making framework, the duty to treat clients and co-workers with due process should be considered together with other basic legal principles as a *first* step in the consideration of professional decisions. Remember that this duty is not ordinarily articulated within ethical codes, despite its enormous impact on basic human rights defined by society. This point underscores the importance of addressing due process considerations as an initial step in decision making.

Before discussing a suggested approach to handling due process dilemmas, a few words are in order about the complexities presented by constitutional law. The review of cases presented here is intended to provide the decision maker with a general sense of the manner in which the principles of procedural and substantive due process have been interpreted by a variety of courts. The cautious professional should not feel overwhelmed by the broad scope of the factual situations that courts have been called upon to consider; they are presented mainly as a rough guide offering an overarching definition of due process and its components. However, under the common law system, these definitions tend to change over time. Therefore, one is better off obtaining a general sense of the letter and spirit of due process rather than attempting to master the names, dates, and holdings of individual court opinions.

The procedural and substantive due process rules outlined above present a strategy for recognizing and addressing due process issues in practice. They can be summarized in the following steps:

- Identify specifically the life, liberty, or property right affected
- Identify whether the right is fundamental
- If the right is fundamental, substantive due process requires that the interest not be violated unless a compelling interest is demonstrated
- Identify any state action that might interfere with the right:

  - If the actor is a public agency, or an employee of a public agency, the actor's conduct is a state action if it affects the life, liberty, or property right identified above
  - If the actor is a private agency that has contracted with the government to provide services to the public, the actor's conduct may be a state action in limited circumstances (see text)
  - If the actor is a private agency providing services independently of the government, there is no state action and the agency alone is responsible for its conduct according to the duty to practice reasonably competently and federal and state civil rights legislation
- Identify the person whose life, liberty, or property right is affected
- If a life, liberty, or property right is affected, procedural due process requires that the person receive reasonable notice and an opportunity to be heard
- Identify remedies for violations of due process:
  - If the actor is a state agency, §1983 relief is available
  - If the actor is a state contractor, §1983 relief is available only in limited circumstances
  - If the actor is a private agency, relief is available under applicable civil rights legislation and through civil lawsuits

These steps can be demonstrated using two professional scenarios previously discussed: vignette 1, "The Bigoted Client," and case example 14, "The School Social Worker." In "The Bigoted Client," a Hispanic individual receiving mental health services makes disparaging remarks about Anglo clients and their preferential treatment at a clinic. Using the steps highlighted above, the client's personal privacy and speech, as well as his interest in receiving quality mental health care, can be identified readily as liberty-related rights. He may also have a property related right to receive government-sponsored health care.

Proceeding to the next step, the client's personal privacy and speech can be identified as fundamental rights. The client's statements, however obnoxious they may be to the therapist, enjoy protection. Unless the therapist can demonstrate a compelling reason, usually defined as some important public safety concern, the therapist should avoid any important treatment decision, i.e., a state action, that hinges on the content of the client's remarks or is either directly or indirectly punitive.

Identifying the state action requires first that the clinic's affiliation be considered. In the original case example, the agency is described as "public." Assume for the sake of this discussion that state government is directly involved in the administration of the agency. Any action taken by the therapist that might affect the quality of services received by this client, or threaten his right to receive services in the future, potentially interferes with his liberty and property rights. Should the therapist reassign the client, a major treatment decision may be made perilously on the basis of protected speech. If the well-meaning therapist attempts to "correct the client's mistaken impression," or confronts the client's racism in a way that unduly entangles the client's personal beliefs with the course of therapy, the provider may mistakenly use the therapeutic relationship in a manner that compromises the client's personal privacy. Even the therapist's diagnosis may be influenced inappropriately by the client's utterances.

Are there any compelling interests that justify the therapist's intervention? In considering this question, it is instructive to review the agency's duties to the client and to the public in general. For this purpose, it is helpful to reconsider the discussion of the duties to practice reasonably competently and to identify the primary client. The agency's essential legal obligation is to provide reasonably competent mental health services. Unless the client's activities interfere with that mission, the client's statements remain protected. Were the client to threaten the therapist, disrupt the agency's functioning, complain about the provider's or agency's services to a clinical supervisor, or in some other way interfere with the agency's ability to meet its obligations to the public, the therapist and the agency would have compelling reasons to respond appropriately. No indication, however, is provided in this dilemma that the client has engaged in any such conduct.

What, then, is an appropriate response to the client's statements? Arguably nothing. Unless the therapist can reasonably identify a relevant mental health issue arising from the statements uttered by the client, the therapist's response may do more clinical harm than good. Although this point may not seem terribly pressing in the context of a routine outpatient professional relationship, consider its significance to the institutionalized. Persons receiving long-term care in public mental health facilities and nursing homes, as well as inmates in penal institutions, often risk differential treatment based on their demeanor and receptivity to services. When the provider allows the client's "attitude," personality, political beliefs, or other expressed opinions to affect the professional relationship, the risk to the client is great. If a psychotherapist allows the client's verbal provocations to compel the treatment delivered, the effect may be not unlike the plot of Ken Kesey's classic novel, *One Flew Over the Cuckoo's Nest*.

In "The School Social Worker," Amalia's claim to a free and appropriate public education grants her a property right recognized under federal law and supported by state legislation and administrative regulations governing the design and implementation of IEPs. Even though educational opportunity has not yet been declared to be a fundamental right in New Mexico (*Trujillo v. Taos Mun. Sch.*, 1996), the right to a free public school education is given at least some protection by New Mexico's Constitution (article XII, §1), a fact that places a special burden on the IEP team to design an appropriate education for Amalia. Construction of the IEP by the school and its professional staff is plainly a state action, granting Amalia and her family the right to procedural due process.

The social worker is an intimate part of the creation of the IEP, and, as the case example notes, may be called upon to testify in the event the plan's contents are challenged by the parents. The fact that the parents have the authority to challenge a plan with which they are dissatisfied stems from the property right connected to their daughter's education. The IEP, by its specification of the services to be offered the girl, greatly affects that property right. If, for example, the IEP denies her the right to be mainstreamed with her peers, her parents may object to this deprivation. For this reason, the school's formulation of the IEP must comply with procedural due process. In this case, the parents have a right to notice, meaning that they must have the chance to see the plan itself and receive information about how they can object to the plan's contents. Additionally, they are entitled to an opportunity to be heard; here, it means the right to request an administrative hearing.

In order to satisfy the procedural due process obligations presented by "The School Social Worker," the full and open participation of the social worker is required. If, for example, the social worker denies parents an opportunity to participate fully, as might be done in this case by failing to provide adequate Spanish interpretation and an appropriate number of preparatory meetings, the social worker may become an active agent in the denial of procedural due process to the parents. Even the inadequate communication of the IEP's contents, suggested in the case example by the parents' apparent confusion and request for an additional meeting, represents a violation of procedural due process.

Procedural due process also plays an important role in the design of the administrative hearing the parents have the right to request. Until fairly recently, such hearings were often conducted with an employee of the school board serving as the hearing officer responsible for presiding over the hearing. Consistent with procedural due process, IDEA (§1415(b)(2)) requires that any hearing officer considering an IEP appeal must be independent from the local school district, and neither employed by or affiliated with the school system, in the interest of guaranteeing the officer's impartiality.

Due process also entitles the parents an opportunity to hear specific information concerning the educational assessment and expert participation of psychologists, counselors, teachers, and other professional members of the IEP team that have been involved in its construction. Note that, consistent with the purposes of the administrative hearing, the adversarial climate and formal procedural and evidentiary rules associated with complex civil and criminal trials is not present.

Important questions concerning the sufficiency of procedural due process in the creation of IEPs should be raised by social policy proponents familiar with constitutional guidelines. Specifically, champions of the disabled must be concerned with the quality of the advocacy that parents and children receive in the formulation of IEPs. For example, parents involved in the design of an IEP, particularly those for whom language presents a roadblock, may require extensive assistance in order to participate fully in the process. Aside from the social worker, whose advocacy role is limited—as "The School Social Worker" demonstrates—parents may not receive the aid of an attorney unless they can afford it. Neither state nor federal law grants the right to subsidized legal assistance in the formulation and contest of IEPs, despite the monumental importance of this process in the life of an educational disabled child.

The right to the assistance of an attorney is an important procedural protection that courts and legislatures have been willing to extend only to those individuals facing an extreme deprivation, such as the loss of liberty that occurs from criminal prosecutions or delinquency proceedings (*In re Gault,* 1967; *Lassiter v. Department of Soc. Servs.,* 1981; *United States v. Deninno,* 1996). State legislatures have also protected the right of indigent respondents in child abuse and neglect proceedings to obtain the free assistance of counsel (Abuse and Neglect Act, 1978/1999, §32A-4-10(B)), based on the impact that a threatened change in child custody has on the fundamental right to parent. The right has not, however, been similarly expanded to cover other types of civil proceedings.

In child welfare, child custody, and other types of litigation involving the right of families and minor children, courts may be required, or they may voluntarily choose to appoint, a guardian *ad litem*, or legal guardian, to represent the interests of a minor or incapacitated person in court. The need for a guardian *ad litem* often arises when a young person is faced with a significant threat to a liberty or property right, such as may occur when custody is considered in a child abuse or divorce proceeding. The appointment of the guardian *ad litem* is a means of honoring the child's due process right to be heard in court concerning the issues that are the subject of the litigation.

The failure by legislatures and courts to extend due process protections to other types of cases can in part be blamed on the financial cost of providing expanded procedural safeguards. Thus, granting a right to legal assistance and other significant due process rights ordinarily provided in more formal trial settings is a prohibitively expensive and immediate public cost, and, as already noted, reserved only for cases involving the most significant government deprivations. Therefore, the behavioral health lobbyist who can demonstrate the enormous indirect expense resulting from the failure to provide formal due process protections to IEP contestants and others forced to litigate their right to participate in important government programs, such as Supplemental Security Income (SSI), veterans' benefits, and workers' compensation may be able to convince future legislatures to reconsider this question.

The foregoing discussion of procedural and substantive due process can provide only a brief overview of the diversity and complexity of these important constitutional principles. However, decision makers who understand the overall role these principles play in the protection of essential human rights have a useful aid in the evaluation of important practice dilemmas.

Equal Protection

This second of two fundamental safeguards provided by the Fourteenth Amendment limits the extent to which the government can classify or categorize its citizens. As the *equal protection clause* reads, no state shall "deny to any person . . . the equal protection of the laws." The basic purpose of this provision is to direct state governments "that all persons similarly situated should be treated alike" (*City of Cleburne v. Cleburne Living Center,* 1985, p. 439). Note that this direction also applies to the federal government and its agencies and employees. Courts have explained this by reasoning that equal protection is implied by the Fifth Amendment's due process clause (*Bolling v. Sharpe,* 1954). This point notwithstanding, most behavioral health professionals are employed by state government agencies; for this reason, the review of equal protection law presented here focuses on the actions of state and local governments, agencies, and employees.

A review of interpretive court decisions helps to define equal protection, explain the extent to which the government can identify and group its citizens, and distinguish several classifications, such as those based on race, religion, gender, and disability that the government is especially discouraged from using in defining legal rights. Although a complete review of equal protection court decisions is beyond the scope of this book, it is imperative for every behavioral health professional to acquire a basic knowledge of its boundaries. With this in mind, this section presents a basic historical overview of the parameters of the equal protection clause.

As noted above, the Fourteenth Amendment was initially intended to protect newly freed slaves from oppressive and discriminatory practices by state governments, and it therefore targets state actions specifically. As with the due process clause, the influence of equal protection as interpreted by a multitude of courts has expanded over the years, so that the coverage initially offered solely to African Americans has broadened to include other vulnerable groups.

Governments need to categorize and classify citizens in a variety of ways, and courts have noted that the equal protection clause does not forbid states when necessary from treating "different classes of persons in different ways" (*Reed v. Reed,* 1971, p. 75). In fact, most economic, social, health, and public safety laws and regulations must define the groups that are to benefit from or be burdened by their impact. It is therefore inevitable that, as some groups benefit from government classifications, others may be disadvantaged (*Greenville Women's Clinic v. Bryant,* 2000). For example, states may wish to base eligibility for public assistance on family income, or enforce mandatory retirement ages in certain types of employment. States also need to classify children as "abused" or "delinquent" in order to establish treatment systems and determine eligibility for services. They must designate some persons as "mentally ill" and others as "incapacitated" in order to establish standards for protective interventions and to remove some persons from the threat of criminal prosecution for their violent behavior.

Through years of interpretive decisions, courts have developed an analytic system for identifying and restricting certain types of classifications that violate the letter and spirit of the equal protection clause. This three-tiered system examines government classifications by rank ordering them according to the harm they threaten to members of a classified group. Under this system, the more serious the threat of harm presented by the classification, the more suspect the classification is. This point is clarified by a review of each tier of equal protection analysis.

The first tier of equal protection analysis defines certain types of classifications that courts regard as *suspect,* meaning that they are presumed to have an invidious and harmful impact on the people they categorize. Under this definition, when the government attempts to classify persons on the basis of certain protected characteristics, such as race, religion, national origin, or ethnicity, or, if the classification burdens a fundamental constitutional right, the purpose of the classification is considered extremely objectionable (*Ball v. Massanari,* 2001; *Greenville Women's Clinic v. Bryant,* 2000).

Perhaps the most notorious historical example of a suspect classification is the *de jure,* or legalized, segregation of African American citizens through Jim Crow legislation that persisted for years in the U.S. One such instance of segregation, involving African American students in the Topeka, Kansas, school system, was successfully challenged in the landmark case *Brown v. Board of Education* (1954).

The denial of a woman's right to an abortion stands as a classic example of a government classification that burdens a fundamental right (*Roe v. Wade,* 1973). Specifically, the *Roe* Court found that the absolute denial to women of abortion services interferes with the right to personal privacy guaranteed by substantive due process.

Under the analysis used in *Brown, Roe,* and other cases in which suspect classifications have been identified, courts have subjected these classifications to *strict scrutiny.* Strict scrutiny means that courts must examine whether the classification is "narrowly tailored to serve a compelling governmental interest" (*Adarand Constructors, Inc. v. Pena,* 1995, p. 219). Under this test, the vast majority of state and federal government actions that classify on the basis of suspect criteria or interfere with fundamental rights have been invalidated as discriminatory under the equal protection clause.

Strict scrutiny of state actions that classify on the basis of a suspect grouping has had an important influence in the forging of social policy. For example, courts have found government affirmative action programs that for years had used racial and gender criteria to enhance the qualification of minority and women applicants for government jobs and public school education to violate the equal protection clause (*Hopwood v. Texas,* 1996). In the *Hopwood* case, a federal appeals court was unimpressed by the University of Texas law school's argument that its affirmative action program was intended to heighten the representation of Latino and African American candidates in the school. Rather, the court found that the school's state action—the granting of preferential application points to minority candidates—could not survive the strict scrutiny test. Although the law school claimed that its program was intended to be ameliorative, or a positive effort to correct the historical effects of past discrimination, the state's claim that this represented a compelling interest was not accepted by the court. Remember that a compelling interest has been defined as a reason motivated by the government's direct public responsibilities. Courts such as *Hopwood* have become increasingly hostile to the notion that the correction of past injustices constitutes an immediate governmental concern. Nevertheless, continuing inconsistency in court opinions regarding the acceptability of race based affirmative action (see, e.g., *Grutter v. Bollinger,* 2002) makes it highly probable that the Supreme Court will resolve this matter finally.

The *Hopwood* Court went on to suggest that the use of race in an ameliorative manner itself tends to stigmatize racial minorities, by reinforcing the view that they are unable to succeed without government assistance. The present effect of the *Hopwood* decision is to raise substantial doubt about the acceptability of race based affirmative action programs in public employment and education. Indeed, on the basis of *Hopwood* and more recent court decisions, many such programs have been terminated or drastically restructured. In the wake of these court cases, alternatives to race based affirmative action are being considered by major government employers and state-supported educational institutions.

Notice that equal protection claims such as those raised in *Hopwood* often assert many of the same protections offered by substantive due process. Thus, if one is classified on the basis of a suspect category or a fundamental right, one may challenge it either as a violation of equal protection or of substantive due process; each claim is subject to essentially the same judicial review, i.e., strict scrutiny.

Another impact of strict scrutiny review has been to expand the scope of religious freedom in state-administered institutions. As noted earlier, prisoners have successfully pressed their requests to receive religious counseling and to have dietary requests honored. Except where state penal institutions have been able to demonstrate compelling reasons for the denial of such requests—usually based on the prison's need to maintain discipline and security, as in the refusal of access to sweat lodge ceremonies—strict scrutiny review often has upheld prisoners' assertions that limiting religious practice is a discriminatory prohibition that interferes with a fundamental right. Additionally, it represents a suspect classification to the extent that is distinguishes some religious practices—often Native American traditions—from other spiritual pursuits. Consistent with this point, corrective legislation such as the religious freedom provision of New Mexico's Native

American Counseling Act (1978/1993, §33-10-4) has been enacted as a means of reinforcing the equal protection and substantive due process rights recognized by courts.

A second tier of equal protection analysis defines some state classifications as *quasi-suspect.* Quasi-suspect classifications include gender and "illegitimacy" (*Ball v. Massanari,* 2001; *Kazmier v. Widmann,* 2000). The standard of review that courts are required to apply in gender classification cases is sometimes described as *intermediate scrutiny* or *heightened review,* according to which quasi-suspect classifications will only be upheld if they are "substantially related to an important governmental interest" (*Ball v. Massanari,* 2001, p. 823; see also *Kazmier v. Widmann,* 2000). What is the effective difference between strict scrutiny and intermediate scrutiny? The simple answer is, not very much, and in truth virtually all discrimination on the basis of gender has been declared to be unconstitutional by reviewing courts. Under intermediate scrutiny, for example, the Supreme Court struck down the Virginia Military Institute's overt discrimination against female applicants to this formerly all-male academy (*United States v. Virginia,* 1996). In its decision, the Court indicated that any gender based classification would need an "exceedingly persuasive justification," and that, although gender is not a proscribed classification, categorization by sex "may not be used . . . to create or perpetuate the legal, social, and economic inferiority of women" (*United States v. Virginia,* pp. 534).

Because state constitutions have been amended to include equal rights provisions guaranteeing the equality of the sexes, gender discrimination in state social and welfare legislation is virtually always impermissible. The failure of courts to recognize gender as a suspect classification can be based on several reasons: First, the nation has failed to adopt a federal equal rights amendment, a step that would settle the question nationally. Second, a factually appropriate case has not yet been appealed to the Supreme Court that would offer an opportunity for the recognition of gender as a suspect classification, although the *Virginia* case has come close to accomplishing this task. In view of the deep ideological divisions within the Court, it would be unlikely for a consensus to emerge on the issue of gender classification in the foreseeable future. Third, the prospect of absolute equality of the sexes may continue to raise the specter in some judicial minds of unisex bathrooms and women fighting alongside men in combat situations. Indeed, present federal selective service registration policies that target solely young men who have reached the age of 18 can be blamed on this point. Fourth, ameliorative legislation, including affirmative action and other protective policies that promote the interests of women may be easier to justify when removed, at least in part, from the microscope of equal protection. Recent court decisions both support and contradict this conclusion. Following an intermediate standard of review, these cases have both affirmed (*Danskine v. Miami Dade Fire Dep't,* 2001) and struck down (*Engineering Contractors Ass'n v. Metropolitan Dade County,* 1997) gender based affirmative action programs.

A third tier of classification recognized by courts is defined as *nonsuspect*. Classifications that are nonsuspect are regarded, in effect, as presumptively valid (*Kaplan v. United States,* 1998). Courts called upon to review nonsuspect classifications require the government merely to point to some rational purpose for using a particular categorization. This is ordinarily a fairly easy standard for the government to satisfy because virtually all legislation has at least some logical basis.

The vast majority of classifications that governments are required to make fall into the nonsuspect category. Categorizations based on class, family income, and age are three of the most often used classifications, and, in light of the role that governments play in administering public welfare and employment programs, it is fairly easy to understand why these particular groupings of people are considered permissible. Public assistance, Medicare, and Social Security all would be impossible without means testing or age based eligibility requirements imposed by law.

The status of class and family income as nonsuspect classifications presents an interesting possibility for the revitalization of affirmative action. Government employers and educational institutions that design fair and rational but race neutral systems for granting reasonable preferences to job applicants and students from lower economic strata may well achieve many of the earlier aims of race based affirmative action; at the same time, however, dependence on suspect criteria will have been avoided. Reliance upon class, income, and other categories in the design of such programs can therefore be expected to increase in the near future.

Although the courts' definition of nonsuspect classification makes the enactment of major social welfare legislation possible, it also has effectively limited Congress's power to enact civil rights legislation that protects the interests of citizens falling within nonsuspect categories. For example, Congress attempted to address age based discrimination in the workplace by enacting the Age Discrimination in Employment Act of 1967 (ADEA), the purpose of which was to end the practice of arbitrary age discrimination in hiring and firing within the public and private sectors. In embracing this law, Congress intended to express its belief that certain forms of age discrimination have been committed on the basis of "inaccurate and stigmatizing stereotypes" (*Hazen Paper Co. v. Biggins,* 1993, p. 610), and that no rational explanation could ever justify this practice. Despite Congress's arguably good intentions, the Supreme Court has found that the requirements ADEA imposes on state and local governments "are disproportionate to any unconstitutional conduct that conceivably could be targeted" (*Kimel v. Florida Bd. of Regents,* 2000). Thus, says the Supreme Court, state governments may continue to use age as a measuring stick for other qualifications that are relevant to their legitimate interests. Mandatory retirement in certain employment, for example, has been upheld on the presumptively rational basis that it ensures the quality of services offered the public and the health of older workers, enforces the state's interest in incorporating new, younger workers into the work force and tax base, and makes the orderly administration of pension plans possible (*Breck v. Michigan,* 2000). With the constitutionality of ADEA in doubt, the reinstatement of age-related classifications in public employment is a real possibility.

As another example of the limitation that nonsuspect status imposes on the enactment of social welfare legislation, courts continue to consider physical and mental disability to be nonsuspect classifications (*Lavia v. Pennsylvania,* 2000). This fact notwithstanding, Congress enacted the Americans With Disabilities Act (ADA) in 1990. Among other things, ADA in 42 U.S.C. §12112a prohibits government and private employers from discriminating against qualified disabled individuals in any aspect of employment, including the right to be hired. Additionally, ADA imposes requirements on public and private employers to make "reasonable accommodation" to disabled employees in assisting them to qualify for employment and meet their job responsibilities. In placing this burden on employers, courts have noted that ADA unconstitutionally forces upon employers greater restrictions than are warranted under the equal protection clause (*Lavia v. Pennsylvania,* 2000). The courts have suggested instead that in the case of disability—a nonsuspect classification—equal protection should permit the employer's "rational" consideration of disability in hiring and accommodating the disabled (*Lavia v. Pennsylvania,* 2000).

In light of court decisions restricting Congress's power to enact remedial legislation under the Fourteenth Amendment, the federal government reasonably can be expected in the immediate future to amend some of its civil rights policies, including the laws mentioned above. The present attitude of judiciary favoring the strict construction of the Constitution would appear to require legislation to be more narrowly tailored to outlaw specific, discriminatory practices proven to have occurred in the recent past, and to remedy their present-day effects.

It might be anticipated that the limitations placed by courts on legislation benefitting members of nonsuspect groups would inspire an effort to demonstrate that such groups actually should enjoy suspect or quasi-suspect status. Given the historical evidence of human suffering among the aged, the physically and mentally disabled, persons mired in alcohol and substance abuse, the developmentally disabled, and other vulnerable groups, suspect status would appear to have been richly earned. However, courts in recent years have largely refused to include additional classifications within the scope of suspect or quasi-suspect status, despite frequent court challenges seeking this recognition. For example, categorizations based on disability and mental retardation have both been identified recently as nonsuspect, despite the intense and articulate efforts of the claimants to demonstrate the "negative attitudes, "fear," and "irrational biases" associated with the treatment of the disabled (*Board of Trustees of Univ. of Ala. v. Garrett,* 2001, p. 367). Similar results have been obtained in the case of persons suffering from alcoholism (*Ball v. Massanari,* 2001).

Gay and lesbian persons have been unable to persuade courts that homosexuality is anything but a nonsuspect classification (see, e.g., *Equality Foundation v. City of Cincinnati,* 1997; *Lofton v. Kearney,* 2001; *Thomasson v. Perry,* 1996). In cases brought by gay servicemen, courts have upheld legislation requiring military discharge under the federal government's "Don't Ask, Don't Tell" policy, enacted under the National Defense Authorization Act for Fiscal Year 1994, on the basis that the policy is rationally related to the military's need to maintain troop morale, discipline, and unit cohesion (*Richenberg v. Perry,* 1996; *Thomasson v. Perry,* 1996).

The status of homosexuality as a nonsuspect classification has more widespread impact closer to home. Specifically, this categorization has continued to permit the gay lifestyle to be cited by courts as a decisional factor in child custody determinations. In 1995, the Virginia Supreme Court upheld the award of custody to a child's grandmother on the basis that the natural mother's "active lesbianism" could burden a child living under such "conditions" by reason of the "'social condemnation' attached to such an arrangement" (*Bottoms v. Bottoms,* 1995, p. 108). More recently, the authority of states to enact legislation restricting the rights of gays to adopt and provide foster care has been directly upheld (*Lofton v. Kearney,* 2001).

In an unusually restrictive interpretation of the purposes of the Fourteenth Amendment, a divided U.S. Supreme Court has expressed its unwillingness to expand the coverage of suspect and quasi-suspect status to additional vulnerable groups, suggesting that the presence of "negative attitudes" and "fear" concerning these persons "alone does not a constitutional violation make" (*Board of Trustees of Univ. of Ala. v. Garrett,* 2001, p. 367). With this philosophy strongly in place in the minds of some of the Court's justices, it is unlikely than any expansion of the definition of suspect and quasi-suspect classification will be witnessed in the years to come, at least in the absence of a demonstration that a group has experienced systematic historical discrimination having a discernible, immediate impact.

Defining some classifications as nonsuspect may actually support Congress's authority to enact legislation that benefits historically victimized populations. For example, categorizations associated with legislation that advances Native American interests have been regarded as nonsuspect (*Narragansett Indian Tribe v. National Indian Gaming Comm'n,* 1998). The Supreme Court has suggested that Indian classifications must be considered unique from other suspect racial classifications because of the federal government's regulation of tribes, which is "rooted in the unique status of Indians as a 'separate people' with their own political institutions" (*United States v. Antelope,* 1977, p. 646).

Without the nonsuspect status that Indian classifications enjoy, much of the national and state legislation promoting the sovereign interests of Native American nations would be all but unconstitutional under a heightened equal protection review. Examples of such legislation include the Indian Child Welfare Act of 1978 (ICWA). This law guarantees the authority of tribes to decide the custody of American Indian children in child welfare cases. The Indian Civil Rights Act of 1968 extends most Bill of Rights and Fourteenth Amendment principles, including equal protection and due process, to Indian tribes. Finally, the Indian Gaming Regulatory Act (IGRA) (1988/2001) permits and regulates gambling on Indian reservations for the purpose of promoting tribal economic survival and self-determination.

It must be noted that classifications based on Native American profiling only protects the government's right to enact *ameliorative* legislation that benefits its trust obligation toward Indians. It does not give the government a license to enact prejudicial, racially discriminatory legislation. However, many would argue that the very maintenance of the trust relationship stigmatizes Native Americans by ensuring the federal dominance over Indian people and the perennial dependency of tribes.

The refusal of courts to expand the scope of equal protection to other historically disadvantaged groups may result in an increased role for the states in this area. Numerous state legislatures have enacted legal protections defining the rights of various classes of citizens, including the institutionalized, those in nursing and other long-term care facilities, and the mentally ill. Almost every state has adopted legislation guaranteeing the right of access of physically disabled persons to public facilities and government employment (see, e.g., White Cane Law, 1978). An oft-quoted priority of Congress's legislative agenda is the passage of a bill of rights for health care patients, a law that would guarantee certain protections to HMO consumers, and, in effect, would recognize medical patients as a discrete class of citizens.

In addition to enacting civil rights legislation, some states and federal territories have amended their own constitutions in an effort to expand the scope of the federal equal protection clause. Many states, for example, have ratified an equal rights amendment guaranteeing the equality of both genders. As already noted, the majority of state constitutions offer a level of protection to public educational access, a point that makes it incumbent upon state governments to avoid classifications interfering with students' school attendance. The Commonwealth of Puerto Rico has taken the additional step of ratifying a territorial equal protection clause that forbids classification on the basis of "social origin or condition"; in doing so, Puerto Ricans have declared their intent to prohibit discrimination on account of poverty (*Nieves v. University of Puerto Rico,* 1993). Whether these innovative constitutional approaches will have a substantial effect in addressing the targeted social problems remains to be seen.

Handling Equal Protection Dilemmas: The Duty to Treat Clients and Co-workers With Equal Protection

The outline of equal protection principles presented can be applied practically by behavioral health professionals in their consideration of practice dilemmas. As noted earlier, constitutional law is always undergoing change. One's success using equal protection principles in making practice decisions depends not so much on having an encylopedic memory of individual case decisions as on a grounded understanding of the meaning of acceptable and suspect classifications. In pragmatic terms, this requires that one acquire the ability to recognize a practice dilemma as presenting an equal protection problem. Whenever one faces a decisional conflict involving the classification of a client, co-worker, or some other member of the public with whom the professional comes into contact, an equal protection analysis may be helpful in the assessment of the parties' rights. In such situations, the steps that should be observed can be summarized as follows:

- Identify the person being classified
- Identify the right affected by the classification—life, liberty, or property

- Identify the type of classification:
  - Suspect/quasi-suspect: race, religion, national origin, ethnicity, gender, and classifications that affect fundamental rights
  - Nonsuspect: all other classifications, including class, income, age, and the use of Native American categorizations to support tribal interests
- Identify any state action that might create a suspect or quasi-suspect classification:
  - If the actor is a public agency, or an employee of a public agency, the actor's conduct is a state action if it affects the life, liberty, or property right identified above
  - If the actor is a private agency that has contracted with the government to provide services to the public, the actor's conduct may be a state action in limited circumstances (see text)
  - If the actor is a private agency providing services independently of the government, there is no state action and the agency alone is responsible for its conduct according to the duty to practice reasonably competently and federal and state civil rights legislation
- Determine whether the classification is justified:
  - Suspect/quasi-suspect classifications must be narrowly tailored and serve a compelling interest
  - Nonsuspect classifications must serve a rational government purpose;
- Identify remedies for violations of equal protection:
  - If the actor is a state agency, §1983 relief is available
  - If the actor is a state contractor, §1983 relief is available only in limited circumstances
  - If the actor is a private agency, relief is available under applicable civil rights legislation and through civil lawsuits

To demonstrate the application of these steps in equal protection cases, consider the following scenario: A school of social work affiliated with a public university is revising its admissions standards. The committee in charge of this task has decided to recommend that applicants be graded on, among other things, their "narrative statement of personal history and philosophy." Suggested criteria for grading this statement would require raters to evaluate each applicant's "political activism in the pursuit of social justice," "advocacy on behalf of progressive social welfare policies," and "demonstrable commitment to diversity."

Following the steps suggested above, each candidate assessed under the proposed system can readily be identified as a person classified by the school's selection process. There is a property right involved, because access to education fits this definition. The classification may very well be suspect, because it grades potential students on the basis of written expressions that may involve political ideology and preferences that arguably fall within the individual's zone of privacy protected under the First Amendment. This freedom involves a fundamental right, which the government ought not to be invading under the pretext of evaluating academic ability.

There is state action in the school's proposed use of the narrative statement as part of its gatekeeping role in determining admission to the social work program. There is probably no compelling interest that justifies this broad request for a statement of personal philosophy; it does not sufficiently confine its area of questioning to points reasonably related to the school's interest in seeking the most qualified applicants for a university social work education. If it were more narrowly tailored to assess the specific academic skill levels of prospective applicants without treading on personal political ideology, it is possible the grading criteria could be revised appropriately. If not, applicants denied admission on the basis of their narrative statements might conceivably have a civil rights action against the state university and its school of social work.

Consider the following additional example: A mental health bureau affiliated with an Indian nation wishes to promote the education of its tribal employees. Toward this end, it will finance scholarships for students who enroll in a master's level counseling program. Successful applicants must be enrolled members of the tribe.

Equal protection analysis of this scenario focuses on the classification of applicants for a scholarship—a potential property right—based on tribal membership. In effect, non-Indian applicants that hold positions within the mental health bureau are excluded from eligibility for the scholarship. The government action (recall that Native American tribes are involved in a trust relationship with the federal government) limits the right of access of potential non-Native applicants to the scholarship. Under current law, this classification should be regarded as nonsuspect because it supports an affirmative action program that justifiably promotes the interests of tribal members. It is arguably based on a rational motive, namely, to promote the training of qualified Native American professional counselors to provide culturally competent services to tribal members.

Legislative Enforcement of Equal Protection Rights

Congress's power to seek compliance with the Fourteenth Amendment stems from Section 5, which authorizes it to "enforce, by appropriate legislation" the Amendment's protections. Under this authority, Congress and many state governments throughout history have enacted remedial legislation intended to accomplish two objectives: first, to outlaw discrimination against individuals protected by the equal protection clause, and second, to equalize access of protected persons to major social institutions, including education and employment.

Congress has approved much legislation protecting members of suspect and quasi-suspect classes from discrimination in public employment, educational access, public housing, and other areas regulated directly by the federal and state governments. The best known and most comprehensive law in this category remains the Civil Rights Act of 1964. More recently, Congress has enacted legislation, including ADA and ADEA, that extends federal protection against discrimination to nonsuspect classes, including the disabled and aged. As noted earlier, laws offering expansive protections to nonsuspect groups have frequently been the focus of successful court challenges, based on the argument that Congress has exceeded its authority under the equal protection clause.

Governmental policies creating affirmative action and other measures intended to equalize access to education, employment, public transportation, and housing have all been grounded in the legislative authority granted by the Fourteenth Amendment. However, courts often have expressed open hostility to these policies, frequently because they violate the heightened scrutiny standard imposed on suspect classifications. In the alternative, some courts have offered the view that the equal protection clause authorizes Congress solely to forbid present discrimination, not to enact corrective legislation intended to address the impact of past discrimination. Thus, race based affirmative action measures in public education, public employment, and the awarding of public contracts have all been invalidated on the basis of this limited interpretation of equal protection's coverage.

Civil Rights Act of 1964. In light of the restrictive interpretation of the equal protection clause many courts have adopted, the Civil Rights Act of 1964 remains the major piece of social legislation relied upon by private individuals to enforce Fourteenth Amendment protections. The reason for this lies in the Act's sweeping and comprehensive coverage outlawing all forms of discrimination based on race, religion, gender, and national origin. Additionally, the drafters of the Act extended its coverage to private agencies and businesses through the authority of the Constitution's *commerce clause* (art. I, §8, cl. 3), which empowers Congress to regulate private businesses engaged in activities whose impact extends across state boundaries.

Among other protections, the Act and its amendments ensure equal access to voting registration procedures (Title I), require desegregation of public schools (Title V), and mandate equal access to federal assistance programs (Title VI).

Additional provisions of the Act prohibit discrimination by private organizations and businesses, including educational institutions, public accommodations, transportation systems, and other employers involved in interstate commerce (Titles II and VII). For the purposes of the Act, a business is involved in interstate commerce if it employs at least 15 persons.

At the heart of the Act lies Title VII's extensive prohibition against discrimination in the public and private sector based on race, religion, and gender. Title VII additionally creates an enforcement mechanism, the Equal Employment Opportunity Commission (EEOC), through which meritorious claims of discrimination by government and private agencies and employers can be addressed through a civil enforcement process.

EEOC functions as a civil investigatory agency that, upon the filing of a complaint, investigates and responds to any allegation of discrimination. If EEOC finds evidence of prejudicial conduct it has the authority to respond by initiating a civil lawsuit seeking cessation of the offending behavior and other forms of relief. If EEOC rejects the complaint on the basis of insufficient evidence, or otherwise chooses not to act further, the complainant is free to initiate a private lawsuit seeking damages and other remedies for the civil rights violations complained of. Such proceedings are often instituted through the authority of §1983, whose provisions are addressed below.

A variety of U.S. Supreme Court opinions have made it more difficult for aggrieved employees to sue offending employers by interpreting the 1964 Act to require proof of an employer's specific intent to discriminate on the basis of race, religion, or gender. Congress has addressed this issue by enacting the Civil Rights Act of 1991, which, among other things, allows employees to prevail in civil rights cases by demonstrating merely that discrimination has played at least some role in the workplace decisions giving rise to the complaint. Additionally, the 1991 Act restricts the use of quotas and other race based measures used by public and private employers in the recruitment and selection of prospective personnel.

Remedies for Governmental Violations of Constitutional Rights

Because the Constitution is intended primarily to limit the power of the federal and state governments over the people, virtually all constitutional violations occur when the government itself commits them. Consequently, the ability of citizens to challenge governments directly when they abuse constitutional principles is a critically important safeguard. Toward that end, Congress has created an important enforcement mechanism for persons who have been deprived of their rights under the due process and equal protection clauses, as well as other basic constitutional guarantees. The most important of these, the Civil Rights Act of 1871, creates a means through which persons who have suffered constitutional losses can seek redress from the responsible governmental agent. It is the subject of the next section.

Section 1983 of the Civil Rights Act of 1871

In enacting the Civil Rights Act of 1871, Congress intended to create a format for persons aggrieved by governmental misconduct—including violations of due process and equal protection—to challenge the wrongdoing in court and seek redress for its consequences (*Crawford-El v. Britton,* 1998). As with the Fourteenth Amendment itself, the 1871 Act was originally intended to address Jim Crow legislation adopted in the post–Civil War South targeting African Americans. Just as courts have expanded their interpretation of the Fourteenth Amendment's coverage to include many other persons besides African Americans, so too have judicial interpretations of the 1871 Act extended its protections to additional groups.

The most significant enforcement mechanism under the 1871 Act is §1983, which has become the most used legal tool for the assertion of constitutional rights against the government. Under §1983, a person may bring a civil lawsuit against the government requesting relief from its misconduct if the following circumstances exist:

- A constitutional violation has been committed
- The violation has been caused directly by a "state actor," meaning a person performing a state action or acting under color of law (*Shrum v. Kluck,* 2001)

Lawsuits filed under §1983, commonly known as *civil rights actions*, permit aggrieved parties to seek money damages and other forms of relief from courts. Their usefulness lies in the wide latitude they offer judges to fashion appropriate remedies in individual cases.

Note that §1983 actions are intended to protect persons mainly from the power of the government, and involve individual defendants only to the extent that they enforce or violate some government policy (*Crawford-El v. Britton,* 1998). Consequently, lawsuits filed under §1983 commonly name as defendants the government agencies accountable for misconduct and the individuals, acting in their official capacities, that have facilitated it.

Under §1983, actions may be brought against several parties. Most importantly, they may be instituted against the government itself—including federal, state, and local agencies—whenever a law, ordinance, regulation, or agency policy causes a constitutional violation (*Lanigan v. Village of E. Hazel Crest,* 1997). Typically this occurs when laws enacted by legislatures are administered or enforced by government agencies, resulting in harm to a member of the public.

As an example of the strategy §1983 offers to the victims of an unconstitutional law, consider the following scenario: A state child welfare statute provides that parents suspected of child abuse must undergo a mandatory psychological examination, even if they are unwilling to consent to it. The requirement is enforced by a child welfare agency, whose administrator appoints personnel to perform investigations and provide services to families in crisis. The administrator assigns agency staff, including social workers, counselors, and psychologists, to assess for suspected abuse. Because the legislative requirement pertaining to psychological examinations appears to violate due process, families who experience emotional or other harm as a result of the law can challenge it by instituting a §1983 suit against those responsible for carrying out the mandatory exams, such as the agency administrator and staff members. The lawsuit thereby serves as a vehicle for testing the constitutionality of questionable legislation.

As an additional example of the relief offered by §1983, consider the case of a county sheriff who forcibly removes children from their home when a social worker requests police assistance, based on reports suggesting that the youngsters are endangered by their surroundings. In this situation, the sheriff's assistance is founded on a customary law enforcement practice that requires police intervention in the transportation of children to the child welfare agency's custody. Assume further that the practice is not required by law, nor is it mandated by agency regulation; rather, it is based on a regional tradition that some argue police have been inadequately trained to carry out. The constitutional sufficiency of this policy and its implementation may be challenged by a §1983 action naming the county and the sheriff (*Brokaw v. Mercer County,* 2000).

Section 1983 actions of the type described above often seek court rulings holding a law, regulation, or policy to be unconstitutional, together with an order restraining the responsible government agency from enforcing it. In this respect, §1983 is often useful in identifying unconstitutional laws and policies while at the same time insulating from personal responsibility the individual government officials responsible for their enforcement.

Interestingly, state and local legislators responsible for the enactment of invalid or unconstitutional laws are themselves immune from personal liability, and cannot ordinarily be sued under §1983 (*Bogan v. Scott-Harris,* 1998). The reason for the layer of insulation provided to legislators is that public policy supports the concept that elected officials must enjoy the freedom to consider legislative proposals without the undue pressure that would inevitably result from fear of litigation.

The use of §1983 actions to protect the public from unconstitutional administrative practices can have a profound effect on the manner in which important public services are administered. For example, if a child welfare bureau fails to provide adequate supervision of children within its foster care system, resulting in deprivation of the children's liberty rights and the denial of due process, the bureau can be sued under §1983 (*Joseph A. v. New Mexico Dep't of Human Servs.,* 1983).

Even when laws, regulations, and government policies are not unconstitutional, §1983 offers a remedy against the wrongful conduct of government employees if the behavior deprives persons of their constitutional rights. This occurs most often when a public servant violates a federal or state law, regulation, or administrative policy, or acts in a manner that a reasonable person would understand to violate established constitutional principles (*Lanigan v. Village of E. Hazel Crest,* 1997). As an example, a school teacher who sexually abuses a student violates the child's constitutional right to privacy and bodily integrity—both liberty-related rights protected by substantive due process (*Maldonado v. Josey,* 1992; *Shrum v. Kluck,* 2001). Consequently, the teacher faces liability under §1983 for these acts.

In order for government employees to be vulnerable to a lawsuit under §1983, their conduct must have directly caused an injury to a complaining party through an act committed under color of law. As an example, unprofessional conduct by child welfare bureau employees has prompted §1983 actions in a variety of situations. Most notable among these is the case of a social worker who falsely advised the natural mother of a purportedly neglected child that a state welfare agency had obtained permanent custody of the woman's child (*Holloway v. Brush,* 2000). The act was perpetrated in an apparent effort to discourage the mother from contesting the agency's formal action to terminate her parental rights. In another instance of social worker misconduct, several child welfare bureau employees used speculation, conjecture, and other false information to get a court order permitting forced entry into a foster home in order to investigate suspicions that children were being abused (*Snell v. Tunnell,* 1990). In this case, §1983 was found to be an appropriate response to the deliberate manufacture of evidence. Similarly, when a child welfare social worker refused to remove the name of a man suspected of child abuse from a central registry, even after an investigation failed to uncover evidence of any child abuse, §1983 provided appropriate redress for this unconstitutional conduct (*Achterhof v. Selvaggio,* 1989).

Note that although individual government employees may be liable for damages under §1983, their agencies are not responsible for personnel misconduct unless supervisors or administrators have knowingly permitted or authorized it to occur, or otherwise have been indifferent to the conduct in a way that "shocks the conscience" (*Shrum v. Kluck,* 2001, p. 779–780). As an illustration, an adult protective service bureau social worker who failed to investigate suspected elder abuse because of personal incompetence might be liable for damages under §1983. The worker's agency would not also be liable under §1983 unless the agency's supervisory staff were aware of the conduct, encouraged or contributed to it in some fashion, or allowed it to continue after it began to occur. This situation occasionally emerges in agencies that have inadequate staff or budgetary resources to meet their legal responsibilities to the public. In an era in which curtailment of resources for social programs, including public assistance, education, and health services is a fact of life, §1983 actions may remain virtually the only vehicle by which the inadequacy of service provision may be argued before the courts. In New Mexico alone, §1983 actions have successfully challenged the unsatisfactory provision of services to children in foster care (*Joseph A. v. New Mexico Dep't of Human Servs.,* 1983), state penitentiary inmates (*Duran v. Apodaca,* 1980), and the developmentally disabled (*Jackson v. Fort Stanton Hosp. & Training Sch.,* 1990).

The above examples demonstrate §1983's dominant use in protecting the public from misconduct by the government and its agencies. Courts have been most reluctant, however, to extend its coverage to occasional individual acts of misconduct that can best be addressed through simple malpractice actions. In other words, behavior of public employees that violates the duty to practice reasonably competently, but does not rise to the level of constitutional deprivation, is most appropriately remedied through civil lawsuits, criminal prosecutions, and other remedies available under state and federal law.

In limited circumstances the government may be responsible under §1983 for the actions of private agencies and individuals, particularly when the government assumes responsibility for the care and custody of a class of persons, but contracts with a private vendor to provide these services on its behalf. Thus, when the government houses prisoners in privately managed prisons or provides long-term mental health services and nursing care through privatized systems, §1983 may impose governmental liability for the misconduct of agency employees (*Conner v. Donnelly,* 1994; *Richardson v. McKnight,* 1997; *West v. Atkins*, 1988). The most often-cited rationale for this liability is that, in the case of persons for whom services are provided under duress, the government cannot escape responsibility for the quality of these mandatory services by delegating it wholesale to a private contractor (*Conner v. Donnelly,* 1994; *Richardson v. McKnight,* 1997; *West v. Atkins*, 1988). Instead, both the contractor and the government are expected to uphold constitutional standards in service delivery.

As noted previously, §1983 provides for two main types of relief to claimants who are able to demonstrate constitutional deprivations. First, money damages are available from individual defendants and the government. Second, injunctions may be issued by a judge when a public agency or employee threatens to continue a pattern of conduct resulting in a constitutional violation. Temporary restraining orders and preliminary injunctions may enjoin government agencies and individuals from enforcing a law, regulation, or policy that violates due process or equal protection. Temporary restraining orders typically are issued only upon a showing that a course of conduct, if not halted at once, endangers a person immediately and irreparably.

In addition to the more common forms of relief, courts on occasion have fashioned extraordinary remedies for alleviating the effects of constitutional deprivations when continuing harm threatens a large segment of the population. In the case of *Joseph A. v. New Mexico Department of Human Services* (1983), a federal court in New Mexico approved a *consent decree*—a judicial order fashioned by the parties and submitted to the court for its approval—mandating the reorganization of foster care and adoption services conducted by the state's child welfare bureau. In a decree unprecedented in its breadth, the New Mexico Human Services Department was directed to put in place a comprehensive system for service provision to the many children in state custody. Among other things, the court ordered the department to plan, supervise, and maintain oversight on a sequential timetable of all of the services provided from first intake to final discharge.

In agreeing to the unusual relief requested by attorneys representing children in the department's foster care system, the *Joseph A.* court found that the department, which then was responsible under state law for the investigation and resolution of child abuse cases, had violated substantive due process and equal protection standards. Specifically, the court noted that the department had failed to honor the children's liberty-related right to family privacy by neglecting to promulgate regulations ensuring the quality of services provided to children placed in its custody. Among other problems, youngsters in foster care had often been consigned to an unstable life in multiple foster care settings, with insufficient planning by the department either for the reunification of families or for the placement of children in permanent adoptive homes. So inadequate was the department's supervision of these children that in many cases records identifying their whereabouts either were nonexistent or could not be located. The department lacked an adequate computer system to assist in maintaining records and had insufficient social work staff—particularly in the area of adoption and permanency planning—to satisfy its constitutional obligations to children in its custody. The novel and expansive relief fashioned by the court required the department to budget sufficiently for the training, hiring, and retention of social workers, and further mandated the creation and maintenance of a computerized system for the ready identification of children and families served statewide.

A roadblock in the assessment of §1983 liability against government officials and employees is the concept of *sovereign immunity*. As granted in the Eleventh Amendment to the U.S. Constitution, immunity insulates the government, its agencies, and employees from liability in the interest of safeguarding the provision of important public services from the threat of litigation. Immunity is ordinarily waived by Congress and by state governments when important public considerations warrant suits by members of the public. This happens most often when government employees commit acts of negligence and engage in other forms of tortious conduct. In such cases, federal and state tort claims legislation governs the extent to which these professionals may be answerable to the public in court for their misconduct. Behavioral health providers serving in child welfare, mental health, and other areas of public sector practice most often find themselves defendants in civil rights cases when they violate the duty to practice reasonably competently and/or the duty to seek informed consent.

Constitutional violations present a special ground for the removal of the immunity shield from public officials. When §1983 actions are founded upon a claim that a law or agency regulation is unconstitutional, in most cases the government agency responsible for enforcing the policy will waive its own immunity in order to allow a court to evaluate the legitimacy of the provision in question. More routinely, however, §1983 claims are founded on an accusation of wrongdoing by a public agency and its employees resulting from their failure to comply with constitutional or other legal standards. In such circumstances, the doctrine of *qualified immunity* often shields employees from personal liability for damages under §1983. With qualified immunity, government officials will ordinarily be protected from liability if they reasonably believe that their conduct has been lawful and constitutional according to established standards (*Mabe v. San Bernardino County Dep't of Soc. Servs.,* 2001).

To demonstrate the application of qualified immunity, consider the following dilemma: A child welfare agency in Santa Fe, New Mexico, receives a phone report from a public school teacher that a child has come to school with several bruises and a swollen arm. The agency's follow-up investigation results in the child's placement in protective custody by a social worker and police officer. Assume further that the teacher has failed to advise the social worker and police officer that the child presents disciplinary problems, has been suspended in the past for fighting in the schoolyard, and was disciplined for fighting before school on the morning of the phone referral.

A brief review of law governing the above scenario lends context to the significant constitutional issues involved. In all states, legislation requires the reporting of suspected child abuse by behavioral health professionals, medical personnel, teachers, and other providers. In some states, including New Mexico, this burden is placed additionally upon every member of the public. Moreover, laws in every state require that child welfare agencies investigate instances of suspected child abuse. The same legislation usually requires that these agencies place into protective custody—often under the direction of police—children reasonably suspected of being abused or neglected. Note also that due process protects the right of parents to maintain custody of their children unless an emergency—such as the threat of child abuse—justifies immediate action by the state.

If the social worker and police officer in the above example place the child under a reasonable but mistaken assumption that the youngster has been abused, they both enjoy qualified immunity from any claim of wrongdoing (*Mabe v. San Bernardino County Dep't of Soc. Servs.,* 2001). The teacher most probably would not similarly be protected, because a professional's failure to share important contextual information violates clear legal responsibilities connected with the reporting of suspected child abuse. For this reason, the teacher might well be subject to §1983 liability in the event the child's parents seek compensation for the violation of their civil rights.

As an alternative example, suppose that a child protective service social worker coerces a parent to allow her to examine a child for signs of physical abuse without any reasonable, prior suspicion that abuse has occurred. This is an extreme, although not unheard-of example of the overzealous investigation of suspected child abuse by state employees. In this scenario, the social worker knowingly violates state law, and therefore would not be entitled to immunity for any resulting §1983 action (*Mabe v. San Bernardino County Dep't of Soc. Servs.*, 2001).

Most elected officials and political appointees enjoy a much greater degree of protection from liability for damages under §1983 than do other government employees. Under the doctrine of *absolute immunity*, these individuals provide particularly important public services connected with the creation and enforcement of public policy, and therefore are shielded completely from the threat of civil rights lawsuits. As an example, legislators enjoy absolute immunity for their lawmaking activities. Additionally, judges, prosecutors, children's court attorneys, and state social workers acting in a *quasi-judicial* role enjoy the same absolute immunity. A quasi-judicial role refers to the assistance state social workers provide to courts considering abuse, neglect, and other child welfare cases. This includes helping in the preparation and filing of petitions, making recommendations to the court on child custody, and testifying (*Ernst v. Child and Youth Servs.*, 1997).

Using Due Process and Equal Protection as a Vehicle to Make Professional Decisions: Case Examples

The case examples that follow offer an overview of diverse, everyday behavioral health scenarios that raise significant constitutional questions. They are offered with the aim of demonstrating the usefulness of applying constitutional analysis in making professional decisions. For this purpose, the outlines for identifying and handling due process and equal protection dilemmas are helpful in sorting out each of the constitutional issues presented in the case examples.

Case Example 15: Due Process and the Problem Student

Phillip Yazzie is a freshman at a public high school in Farmington, New Mexico. He and his family have relocated recently from Shiprock, New Mexico, on the Navajo reservation, so that his mother could find work as a secretary. An average student, Phillip has found himself in trouble at school repeatedly since the beginning of the academic year. Frequently involved in fights, his most recent altercation resulted in another student's sustaining a fractured rib. Phillip faces several alternative disciplinary measures; these are to be considered during a conference involving Elizabeth Ray, the school principal, and Tom Muti, the school guidance counselor. Elizabeth favors expulsion. Tom favors Phillip's referral to an in-school suspension program, which is a disciplinary method that ordinarily combines a traditional deterrent strategy with a preventive approach intended to address the root causes of students' behavioral problems (Haley & Watson, 2000; Sheets, 1996).

In-school suspension programs typically require participating students to be removed from their regular classes in order to take part in counseling and remedial courses that emphasize learning fundamentals, including the improvement of reading and writing skills. The in-school suspension program presently in place at Phillip's high school is a work in progress. Neither the funds nor the staff have been available to provide extensive personal counseling. Nevertheless, the program offers students individual attention with their schoolwork, and Tom regards the one-on-one approach to be a step in the right direction. Phillip's suspension will no doubt result in a delay in his fulfillment of core academic requirements, and he is unlikely to graduate together with his peers.

Elizabeth's and Tom's consideration of Phillip's discipline benefits from a thorough review of due process principles. The decision makers must assess the nature of any life, liberty, or property right that may be affected by a decision, and must also identify whether the right is fundamental. With respect to education, Phillip plainly has a property right. As noted earlier, New Mexico is one of many states that have supplemented basic rights recognized in the U.S. Constitution by guaranteeing access to public education in their state constitutions (*Davis v. Monroe County Bd. of Educ.*, 1999). Some courts have suggested that the effect of doing this is to elevate public education to a fundamental right, thus placing upon state agencies the burden of demonstrating a compelling interest when limitation of educational access is sought (*Davis v. Monroe County Bd. of Educ.*, 1999; *Phillip Leon M. v. Greenbrier County Bd. of Educ.*, 1996).

Regardless of whether Phillip's right to attend school should be considered fundamental, it is protected under the New Mexico Constitution (article XII, §1). This fact has important significance for the decision makers in this scenario. For one thing, it suggests that they cannot deprive Phillip of an education and that they must be prepared to offer him essentially the same services offered to all other students (*Phillip Leon M. v. Greenbrier*

County Bd. of Educ., 1996). This issue places a special burden on those considering student discipline; specifically, it presents a powerful constitutional argument in favor of an appropriately designed in-school suspension program.

When school administrators contemplate the creation of in-school suspension programs, they often face the sobering reality of a limited budget and insufficient personnel. This lack of resources may result in an in-school suspension program that serves mainly as a means of removing a troublesome student like Phillip from his environment, with the emphasis placed more on punishment than alternative education. The constitutional principles already discussed suggest that this design may well violate students' substantive due process rights. Moreover, a hastily structured in-school suspension program that relegates counseling to an afterthought may give insufficient attention to cultural issues, thus threatening the competence of the intervention. With these points in mind, Tom may be in a position to recommend implementation of a program that offers an alternative educational approach. A good model for this is the peer-driven counseling program offered to Navajo students at Window Rock High School, Window Rock, New Mexico, which offers a balance of culturally competent academic and support services, such as "staying straight" groups, for students facing substance abuse, and "insight" groups, for students with scholastic and personal problems, among others (Edwards & Edwards, 1998).

Note also the potential problems in this scenario raised by the Individuals With Disabilities Education Act (IDEA) (1975/2001). If Phillip has a diagnosable educational disability connected with his behavior, then his isolation may deprive him of his right to mainstreaming with his peers. This deprivation may rise to constitutional proportions as an interference with Phillip's liberty rights under the Fourteenth Amendment. Given this reality, it is appropriate to reconsider case example 14, "The School Social Worker," in light of the constitutional analysis presented here.

Phillip's dilemma introduces an important point regarding the usefulness of state constitutions in supplementing fundamental rights created under the U.S. Constitution. It also suggests the need for behavioral health professionals to be acquainted both with federal constitutional protections and those offered at the state level. Specifically, in order to perform completely the due process and equal protection analyses suggested here, professionals must understand and apply not only fundamental rights created under the U.S. Constitution, including family privacy and all of the freedoms created by the Bill of Rights, but also supplemental privileges conferred by state constitutions.

Case Example 16: "Counseling Out" Wanda Romero

Dr. Dolores Hickey teaches psychology at a public university in New Mexico. At a monthly faculty meeting with her colleagues, she "staffs" students, meaning that she identifies those who appear to be having major academic issues, personal problems interfering with their educational progress, or other difficulties. Dolores, a licensed clinical psychologist, has much experience in the diagnosis and treatment of mental disorders and brings this knowledge to her classroom interactions with students. Her classes tend to be interactive and "hands-on," with students encouraged to achieve self-awareness by sharing personal issues with the class. She regards this classroom exercise as an important aspect of the use of reflective insight in psychology, a task encouraged by some professional educators.

At the most recent student staffing, Dolores discusses Wanda Romero, a second-year master's student and Santa Clara Pueblo member. Wanda, according to Dolores's description, is a C student and has looked "overwhelmed" in class for the last four weeks. She sits silently, never participating in class discussions, and, additionally, she looks "withdrawn and depressed." Although her class papers have been submitted on time, they are sparsely written and lack self-disclosure, a specific requirement described in the course syllabus. Wanda has declined all of Dolores's requests for a meeting to discuss these observations, and Dolores now seriously questions Wanda's emotional maturity and appropriateness for psychology practice. She seeks her colleagues' advice on whether Wanda should be "counseled out," a process by which university faculty and administration deliver a strong, personal recommendation to a student to withdraw voluntarily from classes and, perhaps, seek readmission at a later date.

This scenario presents a classic and unfortunate example of a threatened interference with fundamental rights by a state actor under color of law. The fundamental rights involved here concern Wanda's personal privacy and self-expression, both liberty-related privileges recognized under the First and Fourteenth Amendments. Wanda's personality, her manner of personal expression, and her attitude toward Dolores are her own business until such time as the state actors—school administration and faculty—can present a compelling reason for interfering with them. A compelling reason here would need to be grounded in the school's public responsibility, which includes the training of competent psychologists, the maintenance of academic standards for that purpose, and the creation of an orderly environment in which to perform both tasks. Pending the moment that Wanda's behavior either violates the school's established academic standards or compromises the rights of other students and faculty, no compelling reason exists to address Wanda's behavior. Even assuming that Wanda's behavior suggests clinical issues—a conclusion that is as yet highly suspect—the evaluation that Dolores appears to be offering is not reasonably related to her role as a psychology educator. Rather, it threatens to use the power differential between professor and student to impose clinical "treatment" on an involuntary client. In this respect, the scenario raises clear informed consent issues. In constitutional terms, Wanda has a plain, liberty-related right to remaining free from arbitrary counseling.

This case example can be understood alternatively as an equal protection dilemma. The school's counseling out of Wanda—the state action performed by Dolores and her colleagues—can be regarded as a classification on the basis of Wanda's fundamental right to privacy and self-expression, as discussed earlier.

The foregoing constitutional review of Wanda's case is not intended to suggest that a student's communication can never be interfered with or classified by a university. The grading of examinations and papers is one such example of a classification. In contrast to the categorization attempted by Dolores, however, grading is reasonably related to the school's essential purpose, and uses uniform standards that keep students more or less on an equal footing. Students' performances in field practicum and clinical training placements may also require faculty evaluations that grade students on the basis of their communications with clients and co-workers. Here again, however, such evaluations must be narrowly defined to serve the limited purpose of evaluating student competence objectively in specific tasks.

The use of due process and equal protection analyses was described earlier as a means of promoting diversity. The present case example offers a compelling demonstration of this point. In cross-cultural professional relationships, diverse communication styles may sometimes be inappropriately labeled as a failure—often by a minority student—to conform to expectations. By strongly discouraging this type of labeling, the duty to treat clients with due process and equal protection offers specific protections to the recipients of government services, including students. Moreover, recognizing the applicability of due process and equal protection can help to discourage the use of speech based classifications as a proxy for even more noxious categorizations, such as those based on race and religion.

The present case example also raises interesting procedural due process concerns. In the scenario, Wanda plainly has a property right associated with her education. It cannot be regarded as fundamental, because no constitutional protections—either federal of state—have yet been recognized to grant a person the right to an advanced professional education. Wanda's property right is protected, however, by procedural due process. In her situation, the counseling out process may be used—either intentionally or not—as an informal, less confrontational form of gatekeeping, i.e., the process of determining the eligibility of entrants into the behavioral health professions. When it is practiced in the manner described in the present case example, it serves to eliminate the procedural rights that a public university student has, including notice of the reasons justifying formal disciplinary action and an opportunity for a hearing. The faculty's "request" that a student withdraw from classes under the circumstances presented is not much different from a police officer's "request" to enter the home of a person having a loud party. Both appeals take advantage of authority, and both may be intended to accomplish a specific end without formal process.

Wanda's dilemma offers vital guidance for decision makers considering the impact of constitutional protections on practice problems. As the case example suggests, mastery of the principles underlying due process and equal protection offers decision makers practical assistance in the consideration of critical practice decisions. Moreover, Wanda's case demonstrates that a client's right to life, liberty, and property has concrete implications for every professional relationship.

Case Example 17: The Reprimand

Carlita Dominguez, a social worker at a county adult protective services office in northern New Mexico, has a caseload of 40 clients. She is required to investigate and assess instances of suspected elder abuse within one county. As part of her employment responsibilities, she must prepare case notes, maintain client records, perform intakes and assessments, and design treatment plans. A capable verbal communicator, she has good rapport with staff and clients alike. Carlita has worked at the office for three years and has "permanent" status as a state employee. Permanency in this context means a type of tenure offered after a probationary period by many state employment systems. It gives employees such as Carlita a vested interest in continued employment.

Carlita unfortunately is not used to the copious record keeping required in state government. An internal audit has revealed Carlita's failure to use appropriate administrative forms and to include comprehensive case notes in client files. Her supervisor, Abe Chen, has verbally admonished her on two previous occasions for this conduct, and on the basis of the internal audit has now issued a written reprimand that he has directed be included in Carlita's permanent personnel file. Carlita, upset, has fired off a letter to Abe complaining that the letter is unfair, unfounded, and will surely "have an impact on my ability to get promoted in the future." What is more, she complains, it has been issued without prior warning and without an opportunity for her to address whatever "minor paperwork issues" were the object of the reprimand. As Carlita puts it, "the long-term damage to me will be much greater than the trivia you're complaining of." Therefore, Carlita makes it known that she intends to file a grievance on the issuance of the reprimand.

Although department policies and procedures must guide Abe in his issuance of a written reprimand, the actions he takes should also be based on a review of due process concepts. If Abe surveys the due process principles under discussion here, he would conclude that there are no substantive or even procedural due process issues implicated in this scenario. Carlita does have a property right connected with her job; however, this entitlement is not directly threatened by the reprimand. A property right must be based on an expectancy founded on some contract, such as an employment agreement. The fact that Carlita's future ability to get promoted or hired by another agency may be indirectly affected by the reprimand is too tenuous a connection to suggest any property deprivation. Furthermore, Carlita has no liberty based right to be free from discipline, including written reprimands (see, e.g., *Haynie v. Bass,* 1990; *Paul v. Davis,* 1976; *Stanton v. City of W. Sacramento,* 1991). Consistent with the deference to agency administrators that is necessary for effective and efficient agency practice, Abe's responsibilities to Carlita in connection with the issuance of the reprimand are minimal and certainly do not rise to the level of notice and a hearing.

An additional note about the property rights of government employees and clients is appropriate here. As has already been demonstrated, a right must attain some threshold level of significance before it will be considered a property claim subject to procedural due process protections. In the case of government employment, this usually means some deprivation of pay and benefits (*Stanton v. City of W. Sacramento,* 1991). Thus, when a public employee faces demotion, suspension without pay, or dismissal, procedural notice and a hearing are ordinarily required. As already noted, this right does not extend to all employees, but rather only to personnel whose permanent or tenured status within a public agency allows them to assume a continuing expectation of employment.

The foregoing analysis of property rights also has application in case example 16, "'Counseling Out' Wanda Romero." Specifically, Wanda's property interest in a graduate education is not affected until such time as the university takes some action that significantly impairs it. Verbal and written reprimands by faculty and other disciplinary measures do not rise to this level of interference. Indeed, anything short of suspension or expulsion will not invoke protections afforded to property rights under due process principles (*Goss v. Lopez,* 1975). As noted, the counseling out procedure represents an immediate threat to this interest.

Case Example 18: The Job Announcement

The posted employment notice for a state human service position in Santa Fe, New Mexico, advertises that there will be a preference in favor of applicants who are "bilingual and bicultural." The successful applicant will perform intake services for a public agency that serves a densely Hispanic region in northern New Mexico. Yolie Manzanares, the agency's deputy administrator, has received a complaint from a job applicant who feels that she has not received an invitation to interview for the position because she is not Hispanic, and, as her resume indicates, has only a working knowledge of Spanish. On the basis of the complaint, Yolie has decided to take a fresh look at the job announcement, which apparently has been approved by the agency's equal opportunity officer. She is prepared to bring her knowledge of the Fourteenth Amendment, together with state and local laws pertaining to equal employment, to this examination of the job notice.

Yolie's review of the announcement should include a careful equal protection analysis. First, she must assess whether any persons are being classified improperly and whether any constitutional right is being affected by the classification. Yolie should quickly decide that a job posting for a state position represents a classification of applicants, whose access to employment should be considered a property interest.

In this scenario, the state action—the hiring process that will result in the acceptance of one applicant and the denial of many others—is in part based upon applicants' language and ethnic qualifications. Yolie can safely decide that at least one of the two criteria under review—bicultural status—appears to suggest a suspect classification of applicants. Applying her duty to treat clients with equal protection, Yolie must identify a compelling reason for this classification. She may point to community need, which is likely to include the assistance of a fluent Spanish communicator.

Clearly, the agency's performance of its legal responsibilities to the public in part depends on its ability to communicate with its clients. However, to address this need by creating an ethnic preference in job applicants is likely to be interpreted by a court as an overbroad classification in the sense that it assumes cultural identification is necessary for competent communication. Given the present intolerance of courts for any suspect classification, especially one based on race, this one is unlikely to survive a §1983 action.

In contrast, the second criterion, which bases qualification for the position on bilingual ability, appears to address the same need in a manner that is more narrowly tailored to the agency's interests. Moreover, it is skill based, as opposed to identity based, and does not necessarily suggest a racial preference. Viewed in this light, it is a less suspect classification—perhaps a nonsuspect one—and can be rationalized on the basis of client need. Indeed, the agency cannot be expected to provide reasonably competent services to its clients and to seek informed consent from them without a sufficient number of bilingual staff members. Based on this consideration, Yolie may wish to rephrase the position announcement in a way that satisfies the letter and spirit of equal protection.

Case Example 19: The Consent Decree

Monica Castillo faces the loss of her children. Based upon a school guidance counselor's report to the county office of the Children, Youth, and Families Department (CYFD) in Clovis, New Mexico, Monica's two children, Felicity, 8, and Antonia, 6, have been placed in protective custody. Both children had reported to their guidance counselor that they had been physically abused by Monica's live-in boyfriend, Angel Montoya. Upon receiving the report from the guidance counselor, police officers, with the assistance of Rita Constant, CYFD social worker, brought both children to a "safe house" where the youngsters were interviewed and evaluated by a trained clinical specialist. On the basis of the safe house interview, the children were then placed in protective custody, whereupon Rita, in accordance with her legal responsibility, notified Monica immediately.

CYFD has obtained temporary custody of the children, and the agency has begun the process of investigating the case in preparation for an adjudicatory hearing. The adjudicatory hearing is the trial stage of a child abuse proceeding, at which time a children's court judge will consider evidence presented by a children's court attorney, representing CYFD, demonstrating that the youngsters have been abused and remain in danger because of Monica's relationship with Angel. The evidence presented will suggest additionally that, because Monica has failed to protect the children from this abuse, their best interests warrant a permanent change in their custody to CYFD. The evidence will include teachers' statements, the safe house interview, and forensic evidence demonstrating that the children were abused. Additionally, videotaped interviews of the children will be reviewed by the judge. The judge's decision will include a factual finding as to whether the abuse actually occurred, and also a disposition as to the children's permanent custody.

Monica, together with her court-appointed attorney, has taken part in interviews with Rita. During these discussions, Monica has expressed shock and disbelief at the allegations involving Angel. Rita empathizes with Monica, although the social worker also believes that Monica's position regarding her boyfriend is naive and dangerous to the children's best interests. Aware of the fact that Monica was not directly responsible for the abuse apparently inflicted on the children, Rita, her supervisors, and the children's court attorney would like to devise an outcome that would ensure the children's safety, minimize the continuing trauma to the children, avoid a costly adjudicatory hearing, and also allow some opportunity for the children to remain with their mother. Toward that end, Rita and the children's court attorney propose a consent decree. In the consent decree, Monica would concede that the children have been abused and that they require protection. Supervised custody of the children would remain with Monica under certain conditions.

A key condition that Rita wants in the consent decree is that Monica leave her residence, not reside with Angel, not have contact with Angel, and not allow any interaction between Angel and the children. Should she agree to these terms, the proposed consent decree would be submitted to the children's court judge for approval. During her initial discussions with Rita and the children's court attorney, Monica has expressed some consternation that Angel's rights are being ignored in the ongoing negotiations.

The choices that Rita and the children's court attorney must make with respect to the contents of the consent decree are driven largely by constitutional considerations. Indeed, substantive and procedural due process are the operative issues in the analysis of Monica's and Angel's rights. The removal of Monica's children represents a state action that affects her liberty-related right to family privacy. In this case, CYFD's initiation of a court action has been undertaken with the contention that Monica has allowed the children to be endangered by permitting Angel to reside with the children. Should she wish to contest CYFD's petition and refuse the offer of a consent decree, Monica and her attorney would no doubt hope to demonstrate at the adjudicatory hearing that Monica has not been aware of her boyfriend's conduct and that she has already addressed the situation by terminating her relationship with Angel.

Can the judge approve CYFD's request to limit Monica's freedom to have a continuing relationship with Angel? CYFD plainly has a compelling interest in protecting the children, and this concern supersedes Monica's fundamental right to family privacy. At the same time, however, the state wishes to impose this requirement on Monica without granting her the opportunity to respond to the accusation that her children are threatened by the relationship with Angel. Is this a denial of procedural due process? Arguably not, because procedural due process only guarantees the right of an *opportunity* to be heard. It can be waived by a party where there is a fair reason for doing so, or if the party does not disagree with the facts that are being alleged by the opposing party. In Monica's situation, she would still have the opportunity to be heard at an adjudicatory hearing if she does not consent to the state's offer to settle the case.

Note that the consent decree must be entered into by Monica with informed consent, meaning that she must understand the risks and benefits it provides. Her own attorney is the professional primarily charged with explaining this information, although Rita and the children's court attorney also have the responsibility of communicating fully with Monica and her attorney concerning their expectations surrounding the consent decree. This discussion is fortified by a full explanation of any supportive family services CYFD has to offer. Unless Monica first attains an informed understanding of the consent decree's potential impact on her, she cannot approve it. Moreover, if Monica were to sign a consent decree without understanding it, the resulting elimination of the adjudicatory hearing would violate her right to procedural due process.

What about the impact of the state's proposed consent decree on Monica's relationship with Angel? The decree may be overbroad in the sense that it places a permanent restriction on Monica's personal relationship with Angel, rather than confining itself to the protection of the children. In this respect, it may violate Monica's fundamental right to personal privacy, regardless of the facially reasonable grounds that seem to justify it. Furthermore, unlike the waiver of procedural due process rights associated with consent decrees, courts are not willing generally to allow people to waive their substantive due process rights (but see also *State v. Oakley* (2001), in which a judge's award of probation in a criminal case involving a man's nonpayment of child support was linked specifically to the man's pledge to refrain from fathering more children).

The importance of recognizing Monica's fundamental due process rights in this case example is not purely an academic point. Placing restrictions on Monica's personal relationship with Angel is not far removed from placing other, more onerous provisions on her. Imagine, for example, that the consent decree were to require Monica to hold a full-time job, get married, avoid extramarital sexual relationships, or take other measures ostensibly intended to benefit the children's best interests. Here, the imposition of the state's value system on Monica's personal life would become more obvious and even less reasonably related to the youngsters' welfare. For this reason, the protections offered by substantive due process are real and tangible.

What are Angel's due process rights in this scenario? He faces no interference with a property or liberty right because he has no constitutional claim to a personal relationship with Monica's children. Regardless of whether he feels a need for personal vindication in court, any aspersions on his character that he believes the state has caused do not rise to the level of a property right. He faces neither a monetary penalty nor the loss of employment and therefore is not entitled to any notice of the state proceedings.

As already suggested, should Monica be unable to reach an agreement with the state concerning the consent decree, she would be entitled to an adjudicatory hearing, at which time a judge would decide an important factual issue: whether the children have been abused as defined by law. At this hearing, some, but not all of the procedural due process protections afforded to criminal defendants at more formal trials would be present, consistent with the state's interest and Monica's deprivation. For example, Monica would be entitled to hear and respond to evidence suggesting that the children have been abused. Evidentiary rules would require the omission of hearsay, unless the judge were to find a compelling reason for admitting it. Monica would not be entitled to a jury trial. The factual determination as to whether the children have been abused would be made by the children's court judge. Moreover, Monica's attorney might not have an opportunity to cross-examine the children; their statements could be offered by videotape.

All of the rules associated with procedural due process in this scenario are consistent with the state's interest in protecting the children from abuse. These rules are not as extensive as those applied in criminal cases because Monica's deprivation—the loss of custody of her children—is not considered to be as invasive as the loss of her own liberty through incarceration.

Finally, the conduct giving rise to the child abuse proceeding in this case example might also result in the institution of another action: the criminal prosecution of Angel and possibly Monica for the physical abuse and/or neglect of the children. If this were to occur, the guilt or innocence of the defendants would be established in a formal trial separate from the children's court proceeding. During this criminal trial, more extensive protections would be available, including the right to a jury and a heightened, i.e., "beyond a reasonable doubt," evidentiary standard.

Case Example 20: The Forest Fire Revisited

Case example 5, "The Forest Fire," presented the case of Peter Baca, a San Ildefonso Pueblo member suffering the aftereffects of the Cerro Grande fire, which devastated lands within several New Mexico counties in 2000. As reported by the national media, the forest fire was the result of a controlled burn started by the staff at Bandelier National Monument as part of a forest management program intended to reduce the possibility of forest fires through the clearance of highly flammable brush on federal lands. The fire came out of control apparently as the result of unpredictably high winds, a problem that may have been exacerbated by incomplete communication concerning weather conditions between Bandelier and the National Weather Service. The fire destroyed both public and privately owned property, with hundreds of families and businesses displaced.

Admitting the federal government's responsibility for the fire and its results, Congress has enacted legislation, the Cerro Grande Fire Assistance Act (CGFAA) (2000), providing compensation for those who have suffered damages as a result of the fire. Eligibility for benefits depends on the filing of an application with the Office of Cerro Grande Fire Claims, a bureau organized under the Federal Emergency Management Agency (FEMA). Information concerning eligibility requirements has been published in local newspapers and mailed to residents with home addresses in the vicinity. Additionally, benefit claim forms have been mailed to residents of Los Alamos County, which has borne the brunt of the personal property losses, including many primary family residences.

As noted in case example 5, Peter resides at San Ildefonso Pueblo, and commutes approximately 18 miles to his job at the Los Alamos National Laboratory. Peter's symptoms are similar to those being reported by other persons who have lived through, and have been evacuated from the fire. Indeed, the effects of the evacuation, together with the government's response to it, are the subject of several major research studies presently in progress (see, e.g., Villa, 2001).

As with all natural disasters, the fire's long-term effects may ultimately be experienced most acutely by the poor, the elderly, and those lacking the resources to support themselves without government intervention. However, the government regulations promulgated in connection with the administration of the claims bureau have focused on the documentation of claims relating to land and business losses. A time limit has been imposed on the filing of claims, and documentation requirements have been mandated for those filing requests for compensation.

Peter is bearing part of the burden of the costs for his treatment with the psychotherapist, Noel Patrick. Peter's insurance benefits cover only some of the expenses of therapy and pay merely for a limited number of sessions. Noel's position as Peter's psychotherapist does not render him qualified to offer legal advice to Peter concerning any right to compensation from the government. Noel's understanding of constitutional principles may, however, assist him in directing Peter to a source for funding his continued treatment and thereby allow sufficient services to meet Peter's needs. It may also encourage Noel to suggest Peter's solicitation of an attorney's services. Moreover, awareness of constitutional standards may place Noel in a unique position to advocate publicly on behalf of other clients similarly situated to Peter. This type of client advocacy is consistent with the ethical aspirations of the behavioral health professions, including social work, counseling, and psychology.

In the present case example, Noel's recall of due process standards may offer the best help in his client advocacy. Specifically, these guidelines should prompt Noel to use due process analysis in a deliberate way. If he does so, Noel should arrive at the following conclusions: Although the property interests of home and business owners have been the most immediately impacted by the fire, Peter and others in his situation have also suffered health damage. The cost of mental health services has a measurable economic value directly attributable to the fire; therefore, Peter has experienced a property loss stemming from the blaze. Furthermore, there is a reasonable likelihood that psychotherapy has been made necessary at least in part because of government action in connection with the controlled burn. Also, Congress's enactment of the compensation package represents an additional government action because the law defines both the level of compensation and the procedures that must be used in order to obtain financial relief. Procedural due process therefore requires that the compensation law carry with it reasonable notice that advises potential claimants of their rights and the opportunity for a hearing. A due process hearing is most likely to be necessary in the event the government disagrees with any losses claimed by victims such as Peter.

The strict requirements of procedural due process suggest that CGFAA may have created a disparity among the different classes of victims affected by the government's actions. For example, the notice that the government has provided to victims has been delivered through the media and in mailings directed to residential addresses. This suggests the primary targeting of permanent residents of the Los Alamos town site, and the government's dominant interest in compensating the real estate and business losses of local denizens. Have the rights of other victims, including those of renters, transients, and workers from surrounding communities been comparably protected? Has the government acknowledged responsibility for all compensatory damages that reasonably have occurred as a result of its conduct?

Even more to the point, has it designed a comprehensive claims system that adequately allows for long-range and unanticipated costs to be calculated, summarized, and reimbursed? As to all of these questions, the answer arguably is no, a fact that may tend to limit the number of claims brought against the government for incidental and health-related problems that are likely to manifest themselves in the years to come. When such claims ultimately are made, and then denied by the government as untimely, the full impact of procedural due process on the claims process may be argued in future litigation.

Noel's tasks in assisting Peter and other clients should include advocacy and claims processing. Given these clients' precarious situations, Noel may be the best equipped professional to provide them with important public information concerning financial recovery and other community services available for fire victims. For example, Noel can facilitate access to government claims processes, legal assistance, community support groups, and other sources of assistance that may be invaluable in allowing clients to receive the long-term care they may require.

Note finally how §1983 might offer a reasonable legal response by the class of victims afflicted by the government actions outlined in this case example. At first glance, the government's conduct might seem to fall more into the realm of isolated incidents of negligence than constitutional violations, and therefore might be inappropriate as the subject of a §1983 action. Because the behavior of the government and its agents seems initially to have violated no specific law or administrative regulation, the liability of government officials under §1983 for constitutional deprivations is not immediately apparent. A credible argument might be made, however, that the government's policies and customary practices in connection with land management place the public at unnecessary risk of personal harm and property damage, thus interfering with the fundamental right to personal privacy and bodily integrity. Whether such a strategy will be used to address the Cerro Grande disaster remains to be seen. However, there is a precedent for the successful use of civil damage actions against the federal government for its failure to maintain controlled burns on public forest land (*Anderson v. United States,* 1995). Of more immediate interest to most social workers, counselors, and psychologists, the usefulness of §1983 actions to challenge the government's inadequate management of public health and human services remains limitless.

7

The Duty to Maintain Confidentiality

Comparable to the duty to seek informed consent, the duty to maintain the confidentiality of clients' statements describes one of the essential characteristic elements of every professional relationship. Even though all ethical codes to some extent impose the requirement of confidentiality on behavioral health professionals, this duty is a legal responsibility first, and its parameters are defined by legislation in every state. This point is important to understand because recognizing the broad significance of confidentiality in advancing public policy encourages its appropriate application, together with other basic legal principles, in the resolution of practice dilemmas.

The decision making framework encourages the use of law as a first step in the consideration of practice choices in the behavioral health professions. Considering the duty to maintain confidentiality is an especially useful aid in addressing practice situations that challenge the limits of the professional relationship. Often, these circumstances occur when a client has revealed provocative information that may compromise the rights either of the client or of a third party. The boundaries of confidentiality in these instances are examined in the case examples described later.

The legal doctrine supporting confidentiality in professional relationships promotes an important public interest favoring the encouragement of persons to seek the appropriate professional assistance they may need. As the "bank robber" example in chapter 1 indicates, this policy may not be immediately apparent when a provider is forced to consider a difficult practice choice that stretches the professional relationship to the breaking point. Put differently, the need to maintain confidentiality is not always intuitive, nor does it inevitably appear to serve the immediate interests of parties to a professional dilemma. Given this reality, it is all the more important to understand fully the legal considerations favoring confidentiality in professional relationships.

The principle supporting confidentiality in professional relationships is centuries old. Its application, however, has been limited until comparatively recently only to certain established professions, such as law, medicine, and the clergy, to which the public right of access has been deemed an urgent necessity. With the expansion of behavioral health professions in the last century, legislatures have understood the importance of broadening the duty of confidentiality to cover providers in these fields. As a result, the duty of confidentiality has been extended to psychotherapists, including social workers, counselors, and clinical psychologists (although, as will be seen, the imposition of this responsibility remains controversial). The rule of confidentiality now also applies to licensed social workers engaged in child welfare investigations and other forms of public sector practice.

Of all the areas in which confidentiality applies, it is perhaps most important—and creates the most problems—in the delivery of mental health services. Given the prevalence of mental illness within contemporary society and the invasive nature of psychotherapy, confidentiality helps to ensure the access of clients to behavioral health professionals. This point was effectively communicated in the recent case *Jaffee v. Redmond* (1996), in which the Supreme Court expansively reviewed the present state of mental health services in this country and the need to ensure public access to appropriate treatment.

Although all 50 states had already adopted rules protecting confidentiality in clinical psychology and social work at the time the *Jaffee* case was decided (the *Jaffee* decision merely extended the rule of confidentiality to behavioral health professionals testifying within the federal court system), the *Jaffee* court used the opportunity to review the compelling public policy grounds for confidentiality in psychotherapy. With specific reference to clinical social workers, the *Jaffee* Court noted that these professionals have become the most significant providers of mental health services to the poor, and that confidentiality has helped to equalize the right of access of all economic strata to care. This point has relevance for psychologists and counselors as well; confidentiality in mental health care promotes diversity and equal access in each of these service areas.

Given the spotty record of community mental health centers in promoting service use by some minority populations (U.S. Department of Health and Human Services, Office of the Surgeon General, 2001), heightening public awareness of the right to confidentiality may prove to be an important part of future public outreach efforts. Additionally, with the increasingly prominent role that mental health counseling has attained in contemporary society, the recognition by courts of new confidentiality protections serves as a reminder of its importance in each community.

In fact, a federal court has recognized for the first time a rule of confidentiality covering participants in twelve-step groups, specifically Alcoholics Anonymous (AA) (*Cox v. Miller,* 2001). In this case, the court's recognition of the public policy favoring confidentiality led to the exclusion of self-incriminating statements concerning a homicide made by an AA member during a program meeting. Noting the spiritual and religious tenets of the AA program, the court felt justified in extending the confidentiality duty imposed on religious communications to program participants (*Cox v. Miller,* 2001).

Elements of Confidentiality

The rules governing professional confidentiality are different in all states, and the reader is cautioned to examine specific licensing and other legislation applicable to the reader's area of practice. For the purposes of the decision making framework, however, a general discussion of the elements of confidentiality that are common to virtually all jurisdictions helps to demonstrate this duty's usefulness in addressing behavioral health practice dilemmas.

Principles applicable to confidentiality are usually organized by profession; they can ordinarily be found in each state's licensing legislation governing the practice of social work, counseling, psychology, and other behavioral health services. Sometimes, these standards are also contained in legislation regulating the use of evidence in court proceedings, as well as in other areas, such as law governing the reporting, investigation, and resolution of child abuse cases. As might be expected, this makes for a great number and variety of laws governing confidentiality in each profession. They all have some common elements, however, and these can be summarized in several basic principles:

First, confidentiality is both a *duty* and a *privilege*. It is a duty in the sense that it binds each professional to maintain the client's verbal and written confidences in secret, and not to reveal them to anyone else, including other clients, families of the client, additional providers, insurance companies, attorneys, courts, police, and government officials, without the client's express consent. Adherence to this obligation is an important aspect of the duty to practice reasonably competently. Violating confidences, where no exception permits it, is malpractice (*Eckhardt v. Charter Hosp.,* 1997; *Pierce v. Caday,* 1992). It may subject the professional to civil liability and is often defined as a criminal act under professional licensing legislation. Confidentiality also extends a privilege to the client, meaning that the client enjoys the right either to enforce it or to waive it. Waiving the right to confidentiality often happens as a matter of course when a client authorizes the filing of an insurance claim, joins a therapy group, or brings a malpractice action against a therapist.

Second, maintaining confidentiality and explaining its limitations to the client are integral aspects of the duty to seek informed consent. The most essential reason for this is that clients' expectation of confidentiality is critical to their commitment to seek professional help. Given this fact, the privilege of confidentiality is coextensive with the client's right to grant informed consent for services, and each right supports the purposes of the other. Thus, confidentiality extends to the person or entity responsible for granting informed consent to enter into a professional relationship with a social worker, counselor, or psychologist. Understanding that the privilege belongs to the grantor of informed consent, but not necessarily to the client, makes it easier to understand why parents are entitled to know details of their child's surgery, but may not be authorized to receive similar information concerning their child's psychotherapy.

When clients seek services from a behavioral health or human service agency, informed consent is ordinarily granted to the agency to perform services that are then delivered by individual agency employees. This fact helps to explain why the agency has the primary responsibility to maintain the confidentiality of its professional relationship with each client, while individual employees may be free from a legal perspective to discuss aspects of a client's case among themselves.

The link between confidentiality and informed consent may be better understood by reconsidering case example 6, "The Guidance Counselor." In this scenario, Roscoe Manygoats's counseling session should be confidential because he alone has the right to grant informed consent for it. To the extent that his misconduct raises academic issues, however, his mother has the right to that limited information because, as Roscoe's guardian, she alone has the legal authority to make decisions about his education. In other words, she grants informed consent for him to attend public school and has a right of access to reports about his educational progress. This information remains confidential as to all other individuals and agencies outside the school.

As an alternative example highlighting the association between informed consent and confidentiality, consider the rights of persons experiencing family violence involving young children. In a fairly common situation, a social worker investigating suspected child abuse establishes a professional relationship with a vulnerable child in need of protection. The child lacks legal capacity to provide informed consent in this circumstance, and it is instead provided by the agency charged with representing the child's best interests. Consequently, statements made by the child concerning the abuse are confidential, but statements made by the child's mother, a focus of the child abuse investigation, are not.

The foregoing example underscores another important issue concerning confidentiality: The right to confidentiality usually extends to primary clients but not to secondary clients of public agencies. This important point is a reminder that services to secondary clients are only provided appropriately under limited circumstances. As an illustration of this point, consider the responsibilities of a government psychologist assigned to conduct a forensic examination of a criminal suspect for the purpose of evaluating the suspect's propensity for violence. In this situation, the psychologist's primary legal responsibility is to assess the suspect's dangerousness in order to protect the public. A court provides the consent necessary for the examination, and the suspect enjoys no right to confidentiality with respect to the psychologist's delivery of a clinical report to the court.

Third, confidentiality supports the public policy encouraging the promotion of public access to professional services. This policy is expressed variously in court opinions, legislation, and professional ethics codes, and all may differ somewhat in their technical definitions of confidentiality and its exceptions. These relatively minor differences confuse rather than support the process of resolving practice dilemmas involving client privacy issues. Moreover, they tend to cause the misperception that confidentiality supports different purposes, depending on the special character of each professional relationship. Therefore, although the cautious professional is encouraged to be aware of legislative differences, more assistance in professional decision making is probably gained by understanding the broader context of the public purpose served by confidentiality. Thus, the prudent decision maker should understand that confidentiality serves the same purpose when a psychologist maintains it as it does when a social worker or counselor honors it.

Fourth, the duty to maintain confidentiality may apply even where no formal professional relationship with a primary client is created. This is particularly true in the conduct of research involving human subjects. Thus, federal policy imposes strict confidentiality standards on educational institutions and hospitals involved in human testing (U.S. Department of Health and Human Services Rules Governing the Protection of Human Subjects, 1991/1994).

Fifth, confidentiality standards frequently require government agencies to maintain the privacy of important public functions, such as child abuse investigations and the storage of adoption records. Indeed, children's court proceedings in which child custody, abuse and neglect, and other juvenile issues are litigated are ordinarily sequestered for the protection of the children and families involved. Other legislative policies may impact both public and private providers. For example, federal law mandates strict confidentiality in the maintenance of records pertaining to persons who seek treatment for alcoholism and substance abuse (Public Health Service Act, 1992/2000). In light of the wide diversity in rules governing confidentiality in the delivery of various behavioral health services, the provider practicing in any of these speciality areas is urged to consult applicable federal and state legislation for more specific guidance.

Sixth, there are some generally recognized exceptions to the rule of confidentiality, and all of these are related to important public policy favoring the limited disclosure of information. The exceptions have usually arisen as the result of court opinions, such as *Tarasoff*, interpreting the definition of reasonably competent practice, and have only later found their way into federal and state legislation and professional ethics codes. These exceptions usually include:

- The client's threat to commit a future act of violence against himself or others
- A reasonable suspicion of child or elder abuse or neglect
- The client's waiver of the right to confidentiality
- The client's charge of malpractice against the professional

Note that the exceptions to confidentiality are "risks" that should be made known to the client in the course of seeking informed consent. Each of these exceptions is addressed individually.

Threat of Future Criminal Conduct or Harm

Behavioral health professionals have the legal duty to practice reasonably competently. Among other things, this includes the obligation to promote their clients' best interests and to avoid conduct that causes foreseeable harm. In psychotherapy and counseling relationships, a client frequently shares information that reflects highly personal and emotional content, together with the client's future plans and aspirations. Because the professional relationship itself plays an important role in the revelation of this information, it is appropriate to impose on the provider a responsibility to manage this material in a reasonable manner. If, in the course of the professional relationship, clients reveal information or engage in conduct that raises a reasonable possibility that they might harm themselves, then professionals have the legal duty to take appropriate steps to forestall injury, including alerting others, such as the police. Here, competent practice reasonably demands that confidentiality give way to protect the health of clients and third parties.

Most behavioral health professionals have become familiar with the case of *Tarasoff v. Regents of University of California* (1976), which, as it has been interpreted, appears to impose upon psychotherapists a newly created duty to take reasonable action to protect not only the client, but also other persons to whom harm has been threatened. In reality, as the *Tarasoff* court itself explained, the duty is not new, but simply a more expansive interpretation of the common law definition of reasonably competent practice that extends the responsibility of the professional for managing information that may cause foreseeable harm. Understanding this bridge between the *Tarasoff* rule and the time-honored common law standard governing the behavioral health professions helps to alleviate much of the confusion surrounding *Tarasoff* and subsequent cases that have both embraced and rejected it.

The *Tarasoff* court reasoned that, if a professional knows, or "under applicable professional standards reasonably should have determined" that a client intends to commit a violent act against an identified person, the professional has a duty to take reasonable steps to protect the intended victim (*Tarasoff v. Regents of Univ. of Cal.,* 1976, p. 440). If the duty is violated, the professional faces a negligence lawsuit by the victim's family seeking civil damages. In effect, the burden imposed on providers by *Tarasoff* specifically authorizes the violation of confidentiality by warning the victim and taking other appropriate steps to prevent foreseeable harm. By suggesting that mental health professionals might incur civil liability for failing to interpret correctly their clients' more ambiguous statements and conduct, the *Tarasoff* decision has caused a panic among providers convinced that they now have a duty to predict violence, a skill most of them nevertheless lack. This is unfortunate to the extent that it may already have had a chilling effect on the willingness of some therapists to enter into professional relationships with clients who have had past episodes of violence, including spouse abusers and sexual offenders, many of whom are most in need of a trust relationship with a compassionate provider.

Tarasoff has become a household word to mental health professionals, who have incorporated it into their ethical codes, cited it in their agency policies, and continue to rely upon it when discussing informed consent and confidentiality issues with their clients. Thus, the NASW Code (Ethical Standard 1.07(c)) closely follows the *Tarasoff* theme by authorizing social workers to reveal information when "necessary to prevent serious, foreseeable, and imminent harm to a client or other identifiable person." Similarly, the NBCC Code (Section B4) advises counselors to "take reasonable action to inform potential victims and/or inform responsible authorities" when the client "indicates that there is a clear and imminent danger to the client or others." Finally, the APA Code (Ethical Standard 5.05(a)) permits psychologists to disclose confidential information when required "to protect the patient or client or others from harm."

Many states have enacted legislation that permits but does not require professionals to reveal confidences if they concern a threat of future violence or criminal conduct. Thus, in many jurisdictions it is flatly wrong to suggest that a "*Tarasoff* duty" exists, except to the extent it implies one faces a civil negligence lawsuit for failing to honor it.

Despite the presumed authority that *Tarasoff* continues to have, its application has been limited in many jurisdictions (including California) to situations in which the client actually reports a credible threat of immediate harm. This trend may lay to rest any implication that the therapist has any duty that extends to the interpretation of violent tendencies.

In other jurisdictions, *Tarasoff* has been further limited or even repudiated. Thus, the Tenth Circuit Court of Appeals in *United States v. Glass* (1998) has held that disclosure is only warranted where a client's threat is plainly serious when made and it is the only way to avert harm to the identified victim. In other words, the statement cannot be revealed or testified about for other purposes, such as a subsequent criminal prosecution of the client (*United States v. Glass,* 1998). More recently, the Fourth Circuit has adopted virtually the same rule (*United States v. Hayes,* 2000). The Tenth Circuit has further limited the *Tarasoff* doctrine by suggesting that it has no application unless the therapist has some ability to exert physical control over the threatening patient or client, as is the case with inpatients at a secure mental health facility (*Weitz v. Lovelace Health Sys., Inc.,* 2000). Moreover, the Tenth Circuit has found that the "duty to warn" does not apply when the intended victim of threats has independent knowledge of the existence of harm (*Weitz v. Lovelace Health Sys., Inc.,* 2000).

Even more interestingly, the Texas Supreme Court has rejected *Tarasoff* entirely, suggesting that imposing liability on mental health professionals would force them to "face a Catch-22," specifically, that "they either disclose a confidential communication that later proves to be an idle threat and incur liability to the patient, or they fail to disclose a confidential communication that later proves to be a truthful threat and incur liability to the victim and the victim's family" (*Thapar v. Zezulka,* 1999, p. 640). Rather, the

Texas court implied, professionals' decisions should lie within their own discretion, based upon a reasonable consideration of practice standards.

The *Thapar* decision has critical implications for any behavioral health professional who practices under state legislation or an ethical code permitting but not requiring revelation of confidences where a client has made threats of violence. This includes most states' professional licensing legislation governing the practice of social work, counseling, and psychology. It suggests that professionals should base a decision to reveal confidences on individual professional judgment and not on fear of a lawsuit.

The aforementioned cases all imply that the public policy favoring confidentiality must prevail over any other consideration except where the professional by revealing a confidence has a reasonable opportunity to prevent serious future harm. This interpretation is consistent with many of the common law principles governing behavioral health practice.

How should the *Thapar* case and other recent court definitions of confidentiality and its limitations be interpreted by behavioral health professionals? Because these cases are essentially grounded in the duty to practice reasonably competently, providers should make the choice to violate a confidence in a *Tarasoff*-like scenario only when they have a realistic opportunity to interview, assess, counsel, and protect their clients and other members of the public in a prudent manner. For example, a provider who prematurely and recklessly reveals information in an attempt to prevent an uncertain harm risks doing more damage than good (see, e.g., *Eckhardt v. Charter Hosp.,* 1997). The best interests of clients and third parties are usually better served by a therapist's cautious and complete assessment of the potential risk posed by a client. Furthermore, the *Glass*, *Thapar*, and *Hayes* cases reinforce the point that professionals should reveal confidences solely to prevent a future act of violence, and only to the extent necessary to avert the harm.

Because no behavioral health discipline has established any body of practice knowledge that includes the prediction of violent behavior, the reasonable competence standard does not require any provider to forecast a client's future violence. Rather, it requires solely that a professional act appropriately when a client expresses a credible and immediate threat to commit a specific violent act. The reasonable professional confronted with ambiguous client communications must take appropriate steps to ascertain the meaning of these statements. At the least, this includes using competent interviewing techniques that clarify the intended meaning of client speech.

Revelations of past misconduct, regardless of how horrendous, generally do not create a reason for revelation of this information that supersedes the important public policy favoring the encouragement of clients to seek mental health services (*United States v. Glass,* 1998; *United States v. Hayes,* 2000). The general thinking of courts, as described in the "bank robber" situation cited earlier, is that ensuring confidentiality offers the most effective way to encourage offenders to come forward to relate their past history, at least offering the chance that such conduct ultimately can be addressed appropriately.

Suspicion of Child or Elder Abuse or Neglect

Virtually all states have child and adult protective service legislation requiring medical, school, and behavioral health professionals to report to an appropriate public welfare or police authority any reasonable suspicion that the abuse, neglect, or exploitation of a child or vulnerable adult is taking place. As noted earlier, this duty is an aspect of reasonably competent practice imposed on behavioral health professionals. Moreover, if the suspicion of abuse arises in the context of a professional relationship with a client, the duty to report the information supersedes the client's right to confidentiality. A number of states have extended the responsibility to report suspected child abuse to all members of the public.

Waiver of Confidentiality

The right to confidentiality can be waived by clients in a variety of ways, many of which are defined individually under state and federal law. In general, however, clients waive their right to confidentiality either expressly, i.e., deliberately and in writing, or by a course of conduct that reflects a specific intent to do so. When they waive confidentiality expressly, clients must do so in a manner consistent with the rules pertaining to informed consent. In other words, only clients who possess the capacity to waive confidentiality, have an understanding of the risks and benefits of confidentiality, and do so voluntarily, may waive it legally. Unless confidentiality is waived under these circumstances, a client's waiver is invalid and the professional's disclosure of information violates the duty to practice reasonably competently and any applicable licensure and criminal laws.

The most obvious example highlighting an express waiver of confidentiality occurs when clients sign a written authorization to release medical records for the purpose of making a claim to an insurance or other third-party provider. The fact that an insurer is underwriting services does not give it the right to have medical information absent an express, written waiver from the client. Also note that a provider does not have the right to release treatment information that is not reasonably necessary for the establishment of a claim for payment. Thus, the release of client data other than a general statement of diagnosis and description of services rendered violates client privacy and is inconsistent with reasonably competent practice.

As discussed earlier, third-party providers are attempting novel ways to circumvent the privacy principles outlined above. Their continuing efforts to claim an ownership interest in client files and their maintenance of extensive computer database records of client information increasingly threaten well-established principles governing professional relationships. Federal and state policies protecting the privacy of client records, such as the U.S. Department of Health and Human Services Standards for Privacy of Individually Identifiable Health Information (2000), the Uniform Health-Care Information Act (1985) (adopted thus far in Washington and Montana), and the Model State Public Health Privacy Act (1999), may offer new assistance in the preservation of client privacy rights.

In view of complex and ever-changing problems involving client privacy, it is necessary to emphasize the importance of reviewing the confidentiality law principles outlined above before resorting to ethical codes for guidance. As already noted, these codes offer guidance that is on occasion aspirational and overbroad in its coverage. This is true particularly in the management of confidentiality issues, as the case examples demonstrate. For example, the APA Code (Ethical Standard (5.05(a)) directs psychologists that they may disclose confidential information "where permitted by law for a valid purpose, such as . . . to obtain payment for services." This statement perhaps unintentionally appears to give license to psychologists to take liberties with confidential records in a manner at odds with basic legal standards governing confidentiality. The NASW Code (Ethical Standard 1.07(h)) more accurately directs that social workers "not disclose confidential information to third-party payers unless clients have authorized such disclosure." Note, however, that even this statement merely restates an essential legal principle.

It may be appropriate for a provider to request a client's express waiver of confidentiality in circumstances where it facilitates the professional relationship. Providers who undertake services with clients who are at-risk in the sense that they have a history of depression or self-destructive conduct may contract with a client to allow limited disclosure of information, for example, to family members or other professionals wherever there exists a reasonable apprehension that the client may be in trouble again. This type of waiver can be designed to suit the needs of the professional relationship. As an illustration, a provider wishing to offer services to a client who has reported a history of sexual misconduct may contract with the client to permit the professional's open communication with other family members in order to ensure their safety. The same waiver may permit the professional to violate confidentiality under circumstances that fall short of conditions requiring a legal disclosure. For example, the waiver might specify that if the client manifests depression, fails to maintain employment, or engages in other conduct that, in the professional's reasonable judgment, creates a risk of harm to the client or others, confidentiality may be violated to the extent necessary to forestall the risk. Used in this fashion, the contractual waiver is an effective way to manage professional relationships with difficult clients.

As might be imagined, seeking an express waiver of confidentiality creates problems when clients who lack capacity or are involuntary receive professional services. In these instances, the rules of informed consent provide helpful guidance. In the case of clients who lack mental capacity to grant informed consent, their surrogates, including parents, guardians, and courts exercise informed consent on their behalf. Similarly, clients who lack legal capacity, typically children and adults upon whom services have been court-imposed, in many instances have their right to confidentiality, together with the right to waive it, enforced by surrogates, most often parents or judges. The same can be said for involuntary clients, whose services are often court-ordered. With respect to all clients who lack capacity or are involuntary, although the right to confidentiality is limited, it should be honored consistent with the aim of respecting human dignity and, to the extent possible, supporting the principle of self-determination.

Some waivers of confidentiality are implied by circumstances. For example, a client who joins a psychotherapy group reasonably understands that the group is an open forum for the discussion of confidential matters. Although the leader may contract with group members to maintain confidences outside of formal meetings, these agreements are effectively unenforceable against individual members who choose to share disclosures with the outside world. Maintenance of therapeutically effective group dynamics is therefore the best way for a group facilitator to encourage members to respect each other's privacy. The decision maker should be reminded that, despite the partial waiver of confidentiality implied by most group settings, facilitators still owe a duty of confidentiality to each group member, at least with respect to the barrier of privacy that protects the group from external intrusion.

Charge of Malpractice

In all jurisdictions, licensing legislation or common law protects the right of all professionals to defend themselves from a client's charge of professional malpractice. Such charges may often necessitate that a behavioral health provider share confidential information with licensing officials, attorneys, and judges as a means of demonstrating the nature and scope of the services provided to a client. The waiver recognized by law in these circumstance extends solely to the revelation of information reasonably necessary for the professional to conduct a defense in disciplinary proceedings, civil lawsuits, or criminal prosecutions. It does not, however, grant further license to reveal information to other third parties.

Using Legal and Ethical Principles to Address Technology-Related and Other Problems Involving Privacy

The law generally offers a more effective starting point for professional decision making than ethical codes. Although they are important in the interpretation of legal standards pertaining to individual professions, ethical codes tend to be more general in their discussion of practice parameters, and often defer to appertaining legal principles in important professional areas. The treatment of confidentiality in ethical codes bears this point out.

All ethical codes recognize that the confidentiality doctrine is essentially a legal principle that promotes the seeking out of professional services by potential clients. This point is aptly expressed in the APA Code (Ethical Standard 5.02), which notes that "confidentiality may be established by law, institutional rules, or professional or scientific relationships." Consequently, psychologists are directed to look to law governing individual situations in the consideration of practice decisions involving confidentiality and privacy. The NASW Code (Ethical Standard 1.07) and NBCC Code (Section B16) contain comparable provisions.

The NASW, NBCC, and APA Codes each contain ethical standards requiring professionals to maintain the confidentiality of clients' verbal and written statements. These provisions are intended primarily to explain and enhance basic legal precepts governing client privacy. For example, the NASW Code (Ethical Standard 1.07(c)) suggests that confidentiality covers "all information obtained in the course of professional service," and that it may be violated only "for compelling professional reasons." The NBCC Code (Section B16) mandates simply that counselors keep "the counseling relationship and information resulting from it . . . confidential." Lastly, the

APA Code (Ethical Standard 5.02) suggests that confidentiality is a "primary obligation" and that it involves the taking of "reasonable precautions" by psychologists.

The complexities of contemporary behavioral health practice make the design and enforcement of ethical rules pertaining to confidentiality ever more problematic. With the increasing tendency of public and private agencies and health maintenance organizations to maintain copious, computerized databases of client information, and with the consistent use of e-mail, fax, and other electronic transmission methods, access to these data has become increasingly and dangerously easy to obtain. Professionals who offer clinical and consulting services via the Internet face an even greater challenge in ensuring the privacy of their distant clients.

Given the growing use of technological advancements to maintain records and communicate with clients, the ethical codes of the behavioral health professions have expanded in size and complexity as part of an effort by their framers to keep abreast of scientific progress. Thus, the NASW Code (Ethical Standard 1.07(m)) advises social workers to properly use "computers, electronic mail, facsimile machines, telephones, and telephone answering machines." The NBCC Code (Section B14) requires counselors to acquire a "facilitation level of knowledge with any (electronic) system" and (Section B6) asks them to "ensure that data maintained in electronic storage are secure." Similarly, the APA Code (Ethical Standards 5.04 and 5.07) directs psychologists to maintain confidentiality in the management of client information, both in written form and in computer databases.

Despite the best intentions of ethical code drafters, lengthier codes do not necessarily make more ethical practitioners, nor do they offer many specific, enforceable standards that guide decisions related to the electronic storage and transmission of client information. However, technology related issues in the immediate future are likely to pose major challenges to the maintenance of confidentiality in professional relationships. Given the convolution of many privacy-related practice dilemmas, the best initial guidance in addressing them is obtained by the consideration and application of the duties to practice reasonably competently and seek informed consent.

Consistent with the decision making framework, the prudent behavioral health professional is urged to examine all confidentiality and client privacy dilemmas by reviewing their legal aspects. Specifically, the following steps are encouraged:

- Identify clearly the participants in the professional relationship, including the behavioral health provider and primary client

- If services are provided in an agency setting, the duty to maintain confidentiality is owed to each client by the agency as a whole
- Identify the confidentiality interest affected
- Apply the following general legal principle:
    - Maintain confidentiality unless a specific legal reason justifies its violation
- Where it is debatable whether any specific legal reason justifies the breach of confidentiality, the following rule helps to resolve any question:
    - Manage privacy and confidentiality issues by practicing reasonably competently and with informed consent, with special regard to community standards and characteristics
- If technology is involved in the dilemma,
    - Identify the technology used in the communication to or about the client, or in the transfer or maintenance of information about the client
    - Consider whether the technology as used reasonably guarantees the confidentiality and privacy of the client
    - Consider whether, in light of community standards, the technology employed is used consistently with the duty to practice reasonably competently and the duty to seek informed consent

As an example of how this system might be applied in a confidentiality dilemma, consider the following situation: A counselor specializing in the treatment of drug addiction offers an on-line seminar using Web based technology. Participants who pay the entry fee will be able to hear the live audio feed delivered by the counselor, and will also be able to participate in a weekly "chat session" intended to serve as a support group. The chat session will be facilitated by the counselor.

In this scenario, each of the seminar and chat participants is a primary client, and each enjoys a right of privacy that is unmitigated by the use of Internet technology. The counselor may take great pains to ensure that the audio feed is encrypted and that only participants who pay a fee receive a password to access the audio feed and chat session. Nevertheless, no participant can actually have a reasonable expectation of privacy because the technology cannot account for the conduct of individual members at various sites who may invite others to sit in. The counselor may address the confidentiality problem by seeking informed consent from participating members and disclosing risks of participation. The provider may personally regard the use of Internet technology as the most feasible way to provide group support to members who are isolated or lack access to live programs. At the same time, however, the unrestrained access to personal information that this approach risks may so restrain individual participants from communicating openly as to render the effectiveness and appropriateness of the process suspect. Moreover, without the in-person assessment of clients, their responses to group therapy are virtually unknowable.

Consider the following scenario: A licensed social worker is employed by a nonprofit organization that administers a counseling and support program to the victims of sexual abuse. Services are funded in part by a state human service agency. Concerned that one of the social worker's clients may be attempting to defraud the government by claiming to be pregnant as the result of a rape, the agency director seeks to examine the client's files. The social worker refuses, claiming that ethical standards mandate the maintenance of confidentiality. Specifically, the social worker argues that the promotion of clients' well-being and self-determination—both aspirational principles advanced by the NASW Code—preclude revealing this information to anyone.

The foregoing example is inspired by a court case, *Smith-Bozarth v. Coalition Against Rape and Abuse, Inc.* (2000), in which a social worker's assertion of confidentiality was examined through the legal analysis outlined above. The *Smith-Bozarth* court attempted specifically to define the scope of the professional relationship between client and provider. It also examined both the agency's and social worker's duties to provide reasonably competent clinical services to the client.

Applying the steps highlighted earlier, it is reasonable to conclude that the woman seeking services for alleged sexual abuse is the primary client of the *agency*, and not of the social worker individually. In seeking services, the woman likely spoke first with the agency receptionist, was referred to an intake worker, granted informed consent to participate in the program, and was finally assigned an agency social worker for services. The social worker's denial of information to other agency members who need access to client data therefore obstructs the overall professional relationship between client and agency, including the many providers who jointly fulfill the agency's role. Examined differently, the social worker's duty to practice reasonably competently includes cooperation with agency co-workers in the performance of the agency's mission. Even though social work ethical principles might broadly support the social worker's claim of confidentiality in this instance, in reality no agency could perform its essential functions if such a literal interpretation of the right to privacy restricted internal communication of client information. In this situation, the reasonable fear of welfare fraud would of itself provide an adequate rationale for the agency director's request to review the client's file.

Note that the social worker in this scenario does owe an individual duty to the client to practice reasonably competently both as a social worker and an agency employee. In this regard, the professional must support the relationship between agency and client by protecting the privacy of records against access by the outside world.

In this scenario, the social worker's primary reliance on the social work code of ethics leads to an erroneous practice decision. The most important reason for this mistake is the failure of most ethical codes to define the legal parameters of the professional relationship, including the meaning of "client." The present example demonstrates dramatically that initial reliance on ethical codes in the resolution of confidentiality-related dilemmas may result in errors that compromise both the professional's legal position and the quality of services provided.

Another scenario offers an additional example of legal analysis in addressing client privacy dilemmas. Once again, it is inspired by a court case, *Proenza Sanfiel v. Department of Health* (1999): A man accidentally obtains a computer previously owned, then discarded by a large mental health facility. The man, who happens to be a licensed psychiatric nurse, quickly discovers that patient records have not been erased from the computer's hard drive. Aware that the hospital is already under investigation for patient abuses, and zealously intending to shed further light on the facility's carelessness, he contacts the media, and allows news reporters to see the computer. He is convinced that the risk of invading the former patient's privacy is more than offset by the need to protect the great many patients who remain threatened by the facility's recklessness. Therefore, he permits the reporters to film the computer screen, but also asks that identifying information be blurred by digital video technology. Unfortunately, the reporters disregard his request and use the data they have viewed to contact one of the patients. Understandably, this results in severe emotional distress to the patient after it becomes apparent that information concerning the person's hospitalization has been leaked to the public.

Following the same steps suggested earlier, one must conclude that all present and former patients of the psychiatric hospital are to be considered primary clients of the facility. Although they have never formed a professional relationship with the nurse, he has inadvertently obtained electronically preserved records of their treatment history, together with other confidential information. This information is still privileged, even though it has unintentionally come into the hands of a third party. Therefore, it is plain that the hospital has failed to take reasonable measures in its use of technology to ensure the confidentiality of its clients' records.

The nurse's individual responsibilities can also be analyzed by considering the duty to maintain confidentiality. As a licensed behavioral health professional, he is charged with knowledge of the same essential legal principles that any other provider is expected to understand. Although no formal professional relationship has ever existed between the nurse and any of the hospital's patients, a fair interpretation of the duty to practice reasonably competently would require the nurse to maintain the confidentiality of *other* professionals' relationships with their patients and clients. Indeed, this interpretation is consistent with the *Tarasoff*-inspired concept that a behavioral health provider should avoid any professional conduct that could cause foreseeable harm to a member of the public. The nurse has plainly violated this duty, regardless of his aspiration to acquaint the public with the hospital's wrongdoing. Examined in yet another light, by using confidential information without obtaining the consent of the patients involved, the nurse has made a practice decision without obtaining the informed consent of persons who might be affected by his actions.

Consequences for Breach of the Duty to Maintain Confidentiality

Violating the duty to maintain client confidences can occur through negligence, recklessness, or deliberate conduct. Depending on the severity and intentionality of the violation, civil, disciplinary, and even criminal consequences may ensue for the unwary behavioral health professional. Each of these potential consequences is addressed individually.

Civil Liability

Violating confidentiality without legal justification is incompetent practice. Whether done negligently or deliberately—the above examples demonstrate that each is possible—it is malpractice, and can subject the violator to civil liability and an award to the client of money damages as relief for all foreseeable harm caused by the violation (*Eckhardt v. Charter Hosp.,* 1997; *McCormick v. England*, 1997; *Saur v. Probes,* 1991). Typically, the damages claimed by clients include emotional suffering and invasion of privacy occurring as the result of the release of privileged information. This may include not only the immediate infliction of psychological distress caused by the violator's own conduct, but also other incidental harms. For example, in the "bank robber" example discussed earlier, the professional's release of information to police authorities might result in the client's in-custodial questioning, and further require the client to hire legal counsel. The costs of these consequential damages could be compensable.

Violating confidentiality can also cause physical harm. Such was the unfortunate case in New Mexico when a counseling center's clinical staff confronted a man with statements made about him by his wife during an individual therapy session (*Eckhardt v. Charter Hosp.,* 1997). Specifically, the man was told that his wife had stated in therapy that he was an "abusive alcoholic" whose emotional volatility and physical abusiveness were the result of his drinking problem. As might reasonably be expected, revelation of this information to the man resulted in his physical abuse becoming worse, and his wife ultimately brought a civil action against the center for its negligence in the handling of confidential information. The counseling center staff defended their action on the basis that release of information was supported by public policy favoring the protection of an at-risk client. This argument notwithstanding, the *Eckhardt* court found that a strict interpretation of confidentiality law—not to mention common sense—offered no excuse for revelation of the information shared by the client. The client had never suggested her husband posed an immediate threat to her. Rather, the statements made during counseling had suggested merely that the man had been abusive in the past. Moreover, the center's management of the information—specifically its forced showdown with the husband—was not performed in a manner consistent with the reasonable protection of the client's best interests. Indeed, it played a direct role in provoking the violence that followed.

Violating confidentiality can also be understood as a breach of contract, in which the professional's relationship with the client, undertaken in return for payment, has been wrongfully abandoned (*Eckhardt v. Charter Hosp.,* 1997). Moreover, revealing information that is inaccurate or derogatory may be regarded as defamatory by the client or some third party who is the subject of the advertised statements. The same conduct can subject the offender to civil liability based upon the resulting harm to either party. This fact demonstrates another danger to the imprudent professional who listens to client statements made in confidence, accepts them as factual without further investigation, and then reports the contents to a third party. The "bank robber" dilemma should be reconsidered in this light.

Criminal Liability

Licensing legislation governing the practice of each of the behavioral health professions contains criminal penalties for its violation. Because confidentiality is a duty ordinarily imposed upon licensees under state law, violating it can result in criminal prosecution. Prosecution is usually reserved for individuals who have broken confidentiality willfully, as opposed to negligently or unintentionally. Duties under individual state licensing statutes must be consulted in order to understand the extent of criminal liability.

Policy makers have been increasingly willing in recent years to view new legislative strategies as a valuable way to protect the privacy of certain classes of vulnerable clients, such as persons in drug rehabilitation and HIV/AIDS patients. In addition to federal law guaranteeing the privacy of those in treatment for substance abuse and alcoholism, most states have enacted legislation protecting the confidentiality of records pertaining to HIV/AIDS testing. Criminal penalties often apply to the violation of these statutory duties.

Note that the extension of privacy privileges to HIV/AIDS patients and substance abusers does not suggest that these rights are limitless. With respect to a client who engages in, or reports a credible plan to engage in dangerous health practices that are overtly threatening to the client or others, professionals have a duty to handle the matter with the same degree of competence owed when a client reveals a plan to commit a dangerous criminal act. As noted earlier, this ordinarily involves appropriate warnings and other actions that protect the well-being of any intended victim.

Disciplinary Action

Violation of the duty to maintain confidentiality is unethical in addition to being unlawful, and it may result in disciplinary action under the licensing legislation of each behavioral health profession. Given the significant public policy role that confidentiality plays, violations of client privacy are not easily tolerated, and severe disciplinary action is not unheard-of in cases in which a violation has been willful. Discipline may result even in instances in which a professional has had a heartfelt belief that revelation has provided some benefit to a third party, as in the case of the psychiatric nurse mentioned earlier.

As an additional example of the unlawful but possibly well-intended revelation of client confidences, the following case is instructive: A psychologist who provided marital counseling to a couple later proceeded to take an active professional role in the couple's eventual divorce (*Mississippi Bd. of Psychology Examiners v. Hosford,* 1987). Specifically, the psychologist offered the husband's attorney an unflattering opinion regarding the wife's parental fitness. Not surprisingly, the wife's consent was never obtained. The psychologist therefore was found to have violated the duty of confidentiality and suffered the suspension of his license. This result was mandated despite the psychologist's contention that rendering an opinion was reasonably necessary in order to promote the best interests of the couple's six-year-old son, the subject of a custody fight. The *Hosford* case underscores the point that confidentiality and loyalty to a client go hand in hand in that they both encourage the client to seek services as appropriate and reveal fully all information pertinent to the presenting problem.

The *Eckhardt* and *Hosford* cases both demonstrate the courts' reluctance to deviate from strict enforcement of a client's right to confidentiality. More than anything, these court decisions suggest that a legal analysis of confidentiality issues is the best *first* step in the consideration of any privacy-related practice choice in the behavioral health services. Indeed, the *Eckhardt* and *Hosford* courts have specifically repudiated broad exceptions to confidentiality of the type often described in ethical codes. It is especially helpful to remember this point in the subsequent case examples.

Using Confidentiality as a Vehicle to Make Professional Decisions: Case Examples

Professional choices involving confidentiality typically call upon the behavioral health professional to decide

- How to manage and protect a client's privacy
- Whether to reveal a client's confidences to a third party
- Whether to use technology in a way that presents a risk confidentiality will be violated accidentally

Professional ethical codes sometimes imply—probably without meaning to—that providers have more leeway to violate confidences than actually authorized under the law. Therefore, addressing confidentiality dilemmas, according to the system offered here, directs the professional's consideration in a way that appropriately emphasizes the public policy encouraging client privacy. Furthermore, it is suggested that the decision maker identify and apply the duty to maintain confidentiality, together with each of the other legal principles addressed elsewhere, as an initial step in the resolution of all behavioral health practice dilemmas. The case examples that follow illustrate this point with scenarios highlighting the Hispanic and Native American populations of New Mexico.

Case Example 21: An AIDS Patient From the North

Carlos Fulgenzi has been diagnosed with AIDS. From the rural town of Pecos, he has traveled the approximately 25 miles to Santa Fe to seek medical treatment as well as counseling for his recurrent depression. Carlos seeks out the assistance of Gregory Hartpence, a Santa Fe psychologist. Gregory advises Carlos that he has a therapy group for AIDS patients, whose members come from all around northern New Mexico. He encourages Carlos to join the group on a trial basis, during which time Carlos can determine whether group therapy works for him.

During his first session, Carlos advises the group that he is "going out in style." Specifically, he plans "to have as much sex with as many people as possible." Members of the group press him for more information, but Carlos throws up his hands, indicating that he has said all he wants to.

This scenario presents problems for Gregory involving the effective management of client privacy and exceptions to the general rule favoring confidentiality. With respect to the management of confidentiality, Gregory is well advised to consider the duty to practice reasonably competently; special consideration should be paid here to the influence of cultural and regional context. Were Gregory to review scholarly literature pertaining to AIDS in different geographic regions, he might familiarize himself with the special privacy issues faced by patients residing in these areas. Research suggests that rural AIDS sufferers, wary of the stigma this disease continues to cause, tend to avoid treatment in their own localities, preferring instead to seek support at distant sites or not to seek it at all (Goicoechea-Balbona, 1997). Carlos's trek to Santa Fe may already reflect this point. Gregory's competent handling of this issue might therefore reasonably lead him to rethink his earlier encouragement of the group setting until such time as he has explored fully Carlos's concerns about privacy. Gregory's failure to recognize confidentiality issues, together with culture-specific aspects of privacy, may literally drive Carlos from seeking any kind of health care, and even hasten his death (Goicoechea-Balbona, 1997).

Carlos's outrageous statement during the group may be less demonstrative of an actual intent to engage in unsafe sex than a reflection of denial, fear, panic, and a need to let off steam. Nevertheless, his outburst during the group session raises questions about his right to confidentiality. Even though he has not formally joined the group, Carlos is one of Gregory's primary clients, and enjoys confidentiality with respect to his participation. Gregory's competent handling of the situation requires that he explore its meaning privately with Carlos in order to ascertain whether there is disclosed any specific intent to engage in a sexual act with an identified person. Unless such an intent is revealed and is credible, the cases cited earlier suggest that a *Tarasoff*-like duty to warn others or to protect Carlos, perhaps through a mental health evaluation, is not yet invoked. Gregory has no reasonable recourse when the statement made is as vague and flamboyant as Carlos's. Here, the legal principle mandating the maintenance of confidentiality plainly supports Carlos's best therapeutic interests at the inception of treatment.

Case Example 22: The Recovering Sex Offender

Lorenzo Medina is a clinical social worker providing direct mental health services at a community program in Grants, New Mexico. His new client, Curtis Horse, is a 45-year-old Navajo man who seeks Lorenzo's services for treatment of recurrent depression. Sometime after the institution of weekly counseling sessions, Curtis advises Lorenzo that he was convicted in 1984 of the criminal sexual penetration of a 10-year-old girl. For that crime, Curtis served two and one half years in jail out of a five-year sentence, and was released on probation in 1987. He has satisfactorily completed his probation, stayed gainfully employed since his release, and had no subsequent criminal record. Curtis also advises Lorenzo that he wishes to move to an apartment in a house owned by his brother Max. Curtis's brother is a single parent and has three children under the age of 12 living with him. Max is aware of Curtis's history, but feels capable of managing the situation. Family support, Max believes, is the most important therapy for Curtis.

In this scenario, Lorenzo's practice decisions concern the nature of services he should offer Curtis, and the conditions under which he should offer them. Additionally, Lorenzo must examine the limits of confidentiality with specific respect to information about Curtis's criminal history and proposed living arrangement.

As with all problems that present client privacy issues, this practice dilemma is best analyzed by strict application of the rules governing confidentiality and its limitations. Furthermore, the principle mandating reasonably competent practice, including its cultural aspects, should determine how the privacy considerations raised must be managed.

In the present case, application of the duty to maintain confidentiality extends to the information revealed by Curtis, despite the admittedly worrisome impact that his past has on his proposed living situation. No specific, *Tarasoff*-driven duty to warn or protect is immediately evident here. Indeed, an early violation of the duty to maintain confidentiality in this instance could render permanent damage to a family that appears mutually supportive and willing to work through a difficult circumstance. Curtis is legally entitled to the same scope of protection as any other client, irrespective of his troubled history.

Curtis's revelations about his plans should raise sufficient concern in Lorenzo's mind as to suggest the need for a thorough assessment of the potential risk of harm to Curtis's family. Reasonably competent practice here would include Lorenzo's thorough evaluation of the presenting mental health problem. It is entirely possible that Curtis's initial description of the issue masks a reoccurrence of his sexual disorder, which is notoriously resistant to treatment. Lorenzo's interview must screen for this possibility without destroying the confidential bond between client and therapist and compromising the purposes of therapy. Questions concerning Curtis's present mental state and future plans must therefore be both specific and candid. Here again, however, Lorenzo's overly aggressive management of these issues may alienate Curtis and discourage him from placing full faith in his therapist.

At the completion of his interview and assessment, Lorenzo might feel sufficiently concerned about Curtis's home environment to enter into a therapeutic contract with Curtis at the commencement of services. Such a contract could ask Curtis to waive confidentiality with respect to Lorenzo's authority to share information with Max. More than that, the situation might call for Max to be intimately involved in the course of Curtis's therapy. From the standpoint of Lorenzo's duty to seek informed consent from Curtis, Max's potential participation in therapy is a treatment option that might be presented to Curtis at an appropriate time in the initial phase of services, together with the anticipated risks and benefits offered by this strategy.

An impressive body of research suggests that the use of family therapy with Native American clients facing serious mental health issues reflects culturally competent practice (Brucker & Perry, 1998). This point has a specific impact on Lorenzo's management of confidentiality. Given the general underusage of formal mental health services by Native Americans, appropriate confidentiality management may be a critical factor in offering Curtis and his family a sufficient incentive to assume the risks involved in therapy. Moreover, it suggests that Lorenzo's handling of privacy issues focus not simply on the individual legal duty owed to Curtis, but also upon the maintenance of the *family's* sense of unity and integrity.

In recent years, enactment of *Megan's Law* by state legislatures has authorized the mandatory registration of sex offenders as part of an effort to enhance the protection of persons, primarily young children, most vulnerable to recidivist conduct. In the present scenario, Curtis's conviction is too old to invoke the duty to register as a sex offender. Were Curtis under such a responsibility, however, Lorenzo might well allow this fact to influence the professional relationship, specifically with regard to the maintenance of confidentiality between therapist and client. This would be a mistake, because the duty to register as a sex offender serves a public policy need that is quite distinct from the purpose fulfilled by maintenance of confidentiality. The former policy is justified as an important aspect of the deterrent strategy embraced by the criminal justice system, whereas the latter is a technique used to enhance the full use of available mental health services by the public. Understanding this distinction may help Lorenzo to avoid the unnecessary estrangement of his client in the name of fulfilling a presumed public policy. Lorenzo must recall that it is highly unlikely he would have had the opportunity to intervene in Curtis's problem unless the expectation of confidentiality had contributed to Curtis's decision to seek therapy.

The preceding discussion notwithstanding, at least one significant court case has suggested that a professional therapist treating a self-acknowledged pedophile does have a duty to warn potential victims of the client's proclivities, at least where it is reasonably foreseeable that the client intends to place himself in a situation that will give him extraordinary access to children (*Almonte v. New York Med. College,* 1994). In the *Almonte* case, a resident psychiatrist disclosed to his therapist that he was a pedophile and that he planned to specialize in child psychiatry upon his completion of his residency. After the resident's molestation of a ten-year-old patient, the boy's parents sued the therapist for failing to disclose to them the resident's pedophilia. The *Almonte* Court agreed with the parents that the duty to disclose had existed.

The *Almonte* case differs from the previous case example in several important respects. First, the *Almonte* court plainly believed that the pedophilic patient's unusual disclosures to his therapist represented a specific plan to harm children, and that the revelations should have given the therapist reasonable cause to suspect that his patient intended purposefully to use his future practice as a means to gain access to children. Second, the therapist's responsibility to safeguard the medical profession against incompetent and impaired practitioners created an immediate duty to protect the future patients of a questionable doctor.

The *Almonte* opinion bucks the general trend represented by the majority of court decisions that require the disclosure of a specific plan to commit a violent criminal offense before a duty to disclose, warn, or take other protective action is imposed on a professional. As already noted, this policy is based on the courts' reluctance to instill a fear of lawsuit in the minds of clinicians whose professional decisions are best made through a careful deliberative process.

Case Example 23: Reconsidering the "Counseling Out" of Wanda Romero

Please reconsider the scenario discussed in case example 16 concerning the "staffing" and "counseling out" of a student in a public university's psychology program. The case example raises interesting questions concerning the extent to which confidentiality should be afforded generally to students. These questions are most appropriately addressed using the legal strategy outlined earlier.

Wanda Romero, the student in case example 16, must be regarded as the primary "client" of the university, and not of the individual professor, Dolores Hickey. This situation is evident from the fact that Wanda has contracted with the university to receive educational services, and the university has agreed to provide them through its many educators and staff members. Much like the association between any client and a human service agency, Wanda and her university are the primary participants in the professional relationship.

Identifying the parties to the professional relationship in this dilemma helps to explain why it is impossible to impose a duty of confidentiality on Dolores that restricts her sharing of academic and personal information with other members of the university administration. Such a burden would make it impossible to grade, render Dolores unaccountable for her teaching performance and her students' outcomes, and otherwise leave the university incapable of performing its educational mission. For this reason, it is the university that is primarily responsible for the maintenance of confidentiality with respect to student records, personal information, and other aspects of campus life.

If university professors are not bound to a confidential relationship with students, what, then, is the extent of their professional responsibility to them? This is not simply an academic question. It is especially important in explaining the duties of professors who teach courses in social work, counseling, and psychology in university programs. These individuals in a sense function simultaneously as behavioral health professionals and educators. In recent years, university regents, accrediting organizations, legislators, and licensing boards have all struggled with the question of academic accountability as part of a broader effort to seek practical ways to make professors more directly answerable for their performance to professional students and the public.

At least theoretically, university professors who teach behavioral health courses have a duty to practice reasonably competently. In reality, assessing conformance with this standard has proved to be most problematic. Courts addressing the issue have described the relationship between teachers and their students to be a special one, largely dependent on subjective factors unique to individual educational environments. Put another way, some bad teachers have good students who learn everything they are supposed to, and some good teachers have bad students who fail. Thus, although tempted to, most courts have refused to enforce any claim for "educational malpractice" or, indeed, to otherwise define the professional responsibilities of teachers.

What does the foregoing discussion reveal about confidentiality? Most importantly, it underscores the role of privacy as a defining element of any professional relationship. When confidentiality does not or cannot exist, the professional relationship between provider and client is compromised. In the university, as in all large agency settings, the development of discrete professional relationships—aided as they are by the development of a bond of trust between individual provider and client—is sacrificed in the name of promoting the efficient delivery of services by the institution. The larger the organization, the less likely are individual employees in a position to maintain client confidences. In the most extensive bureaucracies, the ultimate result may be the fundamental alienation of clients from the unique human providers who deliver each particular service. This problem is most exacerbated in areas where racial and ethnic differences separate clients from their providers. This being the case, steps should be taken by large behavioral health and human service agencies to encourage individual employees voluntarily to honor the privacy of their clients to the extent consistent with the reasonable functioning of the agency.

Case Example 24: Dr. Linda

A certified counselor licensed by the New Mexico Counseling and Therapy Practice Board, Dr. Linda Pacheco has varied experience in marriage and family counseling. A zealous advocate of the exploration of new media in the practice of psychotherapy, Dr. Linda, as she is known in the community, also wishes to meet the needs of Spanish-speaking New Mexicans in rural areas of the state who lack access to culturally relevant counseling strategies. For these reasons, Dr. Linda has accepted an offer to host a Spanish-language radio call-in show in Las Vegas, New Mexico, to be called *El Programa de Dr. Linda.* During the show, Dr. Linda intends to answer listeners' questions concerning family problems, relationships, dating, and other issues that her audience may raise.

Per the request of the station manager, the show's announcer will offer the following disclaimer in English and Spanish at the beginning and end of each two-hour program: "While Dr. Linda welcomes her listeners' questions, they should be reminded that her answers are for general information purposes only, and that her answers are not a substitute for a thorough evaluation by a licensed therapist." Listeners are reminded by Dr. Linda's switchboard operator not to give their real names on the air, so that "privacy may be ensured."

This case example is indicative of the increasing tendency by behavioral health professionals, notably counselors, to use mass media for the dissemination of advisory information to the public. Dr. Linda's legal disclaimer notwithstanding, use of mass media is often fully intended as a substitute for more formal, in-person professional assistance. So prevalent has counseling through electronic media become that counselors who seek to engage in it are required by the NBCC Code (Section B12) to "present clients with local sources of care before establishing a continued short or long-term relationship." Nothing in the NBCC Code, however, otherwise restricts the use of long-distance counseling.

Of particular interest in this scenario is the potential confidentiality problem created by the Dr. Linda radio program. Using legal analysis, several points become immediately apparent: Most importantly, Dr. Linda and her call-in guests voluntarily assume a professional relationship, with the show participants assuming the role of primary clients. This is plainly true despite the disclaimer offered periodically during the program. Given the reasonable expectations of callers, the NBCC Code's authorization of long-distance counseling through electronic means, and the services freely offered by the host, it is indefensible to remove from Dr. Linda the duty to maintain confidentiality unless knowingly waived by each client.

Considering the professional relationship created between Dr. Linda and each of her call-in guests, her duty to maintain confidentiality must be honored through the exercise of reasonable competence. Arguably, the show's format fails to ensure this standard. In a rural community, where people know one another more readily than in urban areas, any descriptive information is likely to give listeners a fairly good sense of many callers' identities. Moreover, in view of the community and cultural traditions that guide practice, *plática* ("small talk") and informal conversation during the clinical relationship are likely to amplify each violation of privacy when broadcast over the airwaves.

How can Dr. Linda minimize the violation of confidentiality that her show's format threatens? She can do so most easily by changing her format drastically to avoid its more exploitative elements. No reasonable clinical purpose justifies the exposure of a professional dialogue on the air. When the main purpose of this device is entertainment, the risk to each client far outweighs the benefits offered either to callers or the listening community as a whole. Providing general information to the public based on Dr. Linda's recapitulations of her private conversations with consenting clients offers more suitable protection of client confidentiality and more usable knowledge for public consumption.

Case Example 25: Gabriel's Problem

Gabriel Tafoya, 12, refuses to attend school. Midway through the fall semester of his middle school in Raton, New Mexico, he has complained that he has no friends, is bullied by other children, and hates his teachers. The school guidance counselor has contacted Gabriel's parents regarding his chronic absences. "It's a mental health issue," suggests the guidance counselor, "but it's also a disciplinary problem that has to be dealt with before it gets worse."

Upset by Gabriel's behavior, and spurred on by their conference with the guidance counselor, the Tafoyas make an appointment to have Gabriel evaluated at their community mental health center. Cecilia Roanhorse, a clinical social worker at the center, has scheduled an initial meeting with the entire family, during which time she intends to assess the need for an intervention.

This case example presents a typical case scenario involving the management of adolescent mental health issues. The deceptively simple clinical situation nevertheless raises important questions about appropriate confidentiality oversight, as well as the public policy guiding it. The initial decisions Cecilia makes about client privacy will affect her future interactions with the Tafoya family and Gabriel's success in treatment.

Based on the presenting issue, Gabriel is Cecilia's primary client, at least at the inception of services, which include the initial interview and assessment. In New Mexico, as in other states, Gabriel at the age of 12 has the right to grant informed consent for mental health services. Consequently, his right to confidentiality exists at the moment Cecilia agrees to provide services.

Consistent with his authority to grant informed consent, Gabriel enjoys the right to confidentiality. This point compels a private interview with Gabriel that identifies all mental health issues related to his presenting problem. This dialogue must include the therapist's reasonably competent—including age appropriate—psychosocial assessment. At such time as

Gabriel's informed consent is obtained, and his permission is gained to include the Tafoyas in a therapeutic group, it is appropriate for Cecilia to engage the entire family in an appropriate intervention.

The foregoing analysis may unnerve any therapist familiar with the experience of having parents drag a reticent child to the "shrink's office" for the purpose of a mental health consultation during which the parents at once become the enthusiastic providers of information concerning the child's condition and behavior at school. However, the strict maintenance of Gabriel's right to confidentiality is consistent with the clinical objective of isolating individual factors, such as home environment and family relationships, that may help to define a diagnosis. These considerations may include, most notably, child abuse or neglect.

Cecilia's professional training may have emphasized a family systems approach to clinical issues. Indeed, some research suggests that this is an appropriate stance for work with Hispanic, and particularly Mexican American families (Bean, Perry, & Bedell, 2001). Nevertheless, if Cecilia's assumptive predisposition to this treatment approach causes her prematurely to treat the whole family as a singular primary client, and ignores Gabriel's right to be a voluntary participant in his treatment, then she undermines not only Gabriel's right to privacy but also his receptivity to success in therapy. Assessing Gabriel's level of acculturation, which may be different from that of his parents and a major contributing cause of his problem, should be an important part of his initial, private assessment. The results of this individual dialogue may very well affect future interviews with the parents and ultimately direct the nature of the intervention chosen (Bean, Perry, & Bedell, 2001).

8

Incorporating Law, Ethics, Context, and Pragmatism in Decision Making

Understanding the scope of each of the essential legal principles governing the behavioral health professions is a necessary first step in the consideration of practice dilemmas. It is not, however, the final step. The behavioral health decision maker must be prepared to understand how these principles interrelate with each other and are interpreted within a particular community. For these purposes, learning to assess the applicability of law in individual practice situations provides an invaluable tool in the resolution of dilemmas. Additionally, understanding the manner in which legal principles are interpreted by local policies, as well as by ethical standards and regional and cultural practices, is the best way to ensure that professional decisions correspond with the expectations imposed on behavioral health providers in a specific region. Moreover, these steps advance the communitarian purpose of promoting both the client's best interests and the shared social goals of the decision maker's community.

Completing a Legal Inventory

In responding to any practice dilemma, the decision maker needs to consider the potential application of each legal principle outlined in the framework. These include

- The duty to practice reasonably competently
- The duty to seek informed consent
- The duty to identify the primary client
- The duty to treat clients and co-workers with due process and equal protection
- The duty to maintain confidentiality

In assessing whether particular principles apply in any dilemma, the decision maker is urged to follow the order maintained in the framework. The legal principles are presented in sequence from general to specific, and each successive rule builds generally upon preceding ones. Consequently, the decision maker should evaluate any important practice decision by assessing the applicability of each of the aforementioned principles individually, in the order presented. This inventory approach ensures efficiency in the framework's use.

As an example of the legal inventory's application in resolving a practice dilemma, consider the following scenario: The director of patient services at a public mental health treatment program receives a call from a board member of one of the clinic's supportive foundations. The call concerns the board member's brother, who is suffering from major depression. The program has an extensive waiting list, and the director suspects that he may enhance the program's ability to receive additional funding by boosting the board member's brother to the top of the list. He can do so by subtly manipulating the criteria upon which urgent care admissions are based. In his own mind, the director is prepared to rationalize that the ends justify the means; specifically, the potential for increased funding will ultimately serve the greater good of the program's catchment area. He withholds his decision, however, pending the completion of a legal inventory.

This rather obvious scenario offers an opportunity to demonstrate the usefulness of the legal inventory. Applying the framework's first two principles, the duty to practice reasonably competently and the duty to seek informed consent, only the most general assistance is obtained, and it does not relate specifically to the situation at hand. Proceeding further, more immediate guidance is received from the duty to identify the primary client and the duty to treat clients and co-workers with due process and equal protection. Either of these is useful in arriving at an ultimate decision: The conflict of interest created by aiding the board member's cause undermines the quality of care provided to other patients and arguably denies due process and also possibly equal protection to potential patients.

Completing a legal inventory is aided by reference to ordinary sources of law and policy to which behavioral health professionals commonly have access. Most obvious among these is agency or personal counsel, whom the decision maker is urged to consult first as a reference for explanation of regional legal standards governing professional practice.

The act of seeking legal consultation is often thwarted by the intimidation that this type of deliberation may cause the hesitant decision maker. To the behavioral health professional who might never think of using the law in everyday decision making, consulting an attorney often does not become an option until a practice problem becomes so overwhelming or out of control as to mandate legal assistance. The result all too frequently is that the professional presents an over-generalized description of a case scenario to an attorney, and then defers to that person for an "opinion." This is an ineffective method of seeking legal advice and usually results in a complete abdication of responsibility for decision making in favor of the attorney. Moreover, it defies the principle that decision making founded upon legal reasoning is within the reach of every behavioral health professional.

An alternative approach to using legal counsel allows the provider to maintain a preeminent role in decision making. In this system, consultation with a lawyer occurs earlier in the decision making process, and is aided by the provider's specification of the subject area in which guidance is sought. Thus, the decision maker should be prepared to ask for guidance with respect to each of the framework's legal principles. Examples of appropriate questions to ask an attorney include the following:

- In the present scenario, under this state's laws, what are my responsibilities with regard to reasonably competent practice?
- How much information must I share in order to satisfy informed consent?
- Does my agency's admission process comply with due process and equal protection standards?
- What are the limits of confidentiality?
- Who is my primary client in this scenario?

By obtaining an answer to these specific questions from the lawyer and bringing prior understanding of these principles to the legal consultation, the decision maker and attorney can arrive at a resolution in a collaborative and fully informed manner. Moreover, using the attorney interview to address specific questions elevates the role of the behavioral health professional from deferential advice seeker to primary issue adjudicator.

The foregoing discussion assumes the luxury of ready access to legal counsel. The harsh reality of contemporary behavioral health practice—particularly in rural areas—is that formal legal assistance may be neither readily available nor affordable. Lack of such access should not dissuade the decision maker from incorporating the framework in daily professional choices. Indeed, the framework presumes that legal counsel may not be immediately available to respond to practice questions pertaining to professional responsibilities. Instead, the framework's usefulness in resolving practice dilemmas depends upon the decision maker's creative ability to recognize and apply legal principles in everyday situations. These skills are best developed through an understanding of important public policy driving the law, as well as by practice in applying the framework.

Regardless of the availability of legal support services, the decision maker's success in using the framework is aided immeasurably by a general familiarity with regional interpretations of basic legal principles by courts, legislatures, and even county and municipal governmental bodies. This familiarity is best obtained through an awareness of the protections afforded by one's state constitution, local legislation, and regional appellate courts.

Acquiring the ability to perform basic research is a skill to be expected of contemporary behavioral health professionals. Although a review of legal research techniques is beyond the scope of this book, several essential elements need to be established here:

First, court decisions interpreting basic legal principles may be located in books—commonly referred to as *digests*—that compile judicial decisions in individual cases and organize them by subject matter. The most famous of these digests in the U.S. are those compiled by the West Publishing Company, which over the course of years has developed an expansive *key number system* that organizes the decisions in particular court cases, and then assigns them key numbers based upon each legal topic area. Because West publishes individual digests for the state and federal court systems, and also uses the same uniform numbering system in each, it is possible to trace the interpretation of a particular legal principle by numerous state and federal courts. For assistance in using digests as well as the key number system, the reader is referred to the many treatises available for behavioral health professionals that present a general review of basic legal research strategies.

Second, the wide availability through the Internet of state and federal legislation and administrative policies has given the most geographically isolated behavioral health professional immediate access to the regional standards that govern professional practice. Because this material is ordinarily presented in the form of a database searchable by keyword, the availability of basic legislative and administrative information pertaining to the behavioral health professions has become markedly enhanced in the past several years. For help in accessing this material, the reader is again referred to the myriad of books currently available that offer guidance in Internet research techniques.

In addition to a basic familiarity with local legislation, administrative policies, and court decisions, application of the framework is aided by the decision maker's conscious awareness of agency policies and procedures that guide practice decisions in the professional's own practice environment. Thus, agency policies defining the services offered to clients, and governing their intake and assessment, may be of invaluable assistance in the consideration of standards defining competent practice and informed consent. Moreover, they may assist the professional to understand who the agency's primary client is.

The legal inventory is also aided by the agency based decision maker's thorough familiarity with personnel rules and hiring contracts that define the terms and conditions of employment. Such documents typically contain important guidance concerning the professional's contractual obligations to an agency, including job performance expectations. These standards may in turn help to clarify the parameters of competent practice expected from the professional. Moreover, they may impose obligations above and beyond basic duties defined by law. For example, rules governing the maintenance of client confidentiality may define specific procedures to be applied in the handling of client records and databases, the maintenance of privacy with respect to agency policies and practices, and the continued honoring of such secrets after the professional's cessation of employment.

Finalizing the legal inventory is assisted by the decision maker's consideration of law beyond the elemental principles addressed in the framework. For example, all practice decisions benefit from the professional's general familiarity with regional criminal and civil law; indeed, such familiarity should be considered an important aspect of reasonably competent practice. The decision maker should therefore be prepared to assess whether any practice choice is consistent with relevant federal, state, or tribal law. This awareness of certain legal principles does not suggest familiarity with the law comparable to that of a licensed attorney. Rather, it implies knowledge sufficient to give the professional an awareness that a problem has legal implications requiring further consultation with an attorney. Plainly, if an agency or client seeks to involve the professional in activities that may be criminal or subject multiple parties to civil liability, this possibility is an important consideration in arriving at a practice decision.

The foregoing strategy can be summarized in a series of steps that require the decision maker to complete a legal inventory by reviewing each of the following:

- The application of the framework's legal principles, from general to specific, i.e., Principles 1 through 5 (see appendix, pp. 247–253)
- Regional legislative and judicial interpretations of each of the basic principles
- The impact of other relevant federal, state, or tribal laws and administrative rules and regulations

- Any internal agency policies and procedures that define client services or the professional's job responsibilities or contract obligations

As an example of how these steps support completion of a legal inventory, consider the following situation: A social worker employed by the income support division of a state welfare bureau has learned during an interview with a client that the client's ownership interest in a real estate parcel renders him ineligible for continuing public assistance. The client has received this assistance for several months, including payments under the Temporary Aid to Needy Families (TANF) program, a welfare reform initiative inaugurated under the Personal Responsibility and Work Opportunity Reconciliation Act of 1996 (PRWORA), and food stamps. The client remains impoverished and malnourished, yet the failure to reveal the existence of the real estate during the first three months of his receipt of benefits likely will result in liability for the overpayment of benefits. The social worker must consider a practice decision that concerns the appropriate use of the information revealed by the client.

Following the legal inventory's steps, the social worker might reasonably conclude that the duties to practice reasonably competently and to identify the primary client generally support a commitment to serve the client's best interests, but that they do not offer more specific guidance concerning the client's plight. The duty to maintain confidentiality clearly does not mandate absolute protection of the client's secret because sharing of information with other agency personnel is required in order that the agency meet its obligation to provide appropriate services to the public.

Proceeding further through the inventory's steps, the social worker would likely conclude that both law and agency policies and regulations require identification and reporting of factors that render a client ineligible for benefits. Given this reality, the social worker is obliged to follow the law. The social worker is also bound, however, to assist the client to take steps that might help in the reestablishment of eligibility and the securing of emergency aid pending resolution of the problem. Stated differently, the duty to provide reasonably competent services does not end simply because additional obligations limit the range of services the professional can render.

Using Ethics in Making Professional Decisions

Much has been stated previously regarding the difficulties posed by the use of ethical codes in specific professional situations. When the decision maker relies upon a profession-specific ethical code as an initial step in the resolution of a practice problem, it is often quickly noted that the broad, aspirational, and occasionally conflicting ideals presented raise more questions than they answer. The idealistic, goal-oriented tone adopted by some professional codes often leaves the decision maker with insufficient practical guidance for everyday practice situations. Often the most usable and enforceable standards included in ethical codes, such as those governing competent practice, informed consent, and conflicts of interest, merely restate duties that already exist under the law.

In view of the foregoing discussion, what role should ethical codes play in the resolution of practice decisions? As noted earlier, ethical codes offer interpretive practice standards—unique to each of the behavioral health professions—that can help the decision maker to interpret basic legal principles, most notably the duty to practice reasonably competently. With this in mind, ethical codes are best reviewed only as a second step supplementing the legal inventory described earlier. Additionally, it is important to remember that the law should represent the paramount consideration in any practice decision, and that conflicting or ambiguous ethical standards should be considered and applied in a light that gives support to each of the legal principles outlined in the framework.

The framework's emphasis on the legal inventory should not be read to imply that ethical principles are either irrelevant or unnecessary in making practice choices. Rather, as a strategic point of efficient decision making, they are best considered only *after* the legal inventory is completed. In some practice situations, the decision maker may be satisfied that the legal inventory has yielded no helpful guidance. In this event, the decision maker is encouraged to undertake a thorough review of ethical standards that offer assistance in the resolution of a dilemma.

Another practical reason to perform a thorough review of ethical standards is that they may jog the decision maker's reasoning process in a manner that prompts a reconsideration of the law. Thus, for example, reviewing a variety of ethical principles may inspire the decision maker to identify competent practice issues, informed consent problems, or primary client concerns that were not immediately apparent upon the initial consideration of the problem. For this reason, the maximum benefit is obtained from the framework if the decision maker first performs the legal inventory, then reviews relevant ethical standards, and finally returns to the legal inventory once more.

The decision making framework as outlined in the appendix presents a summary of ethical standards from the NASW, NBCC, and APA that outline professional expectations imposed on social workers, counselors, and psychologists. The reader will note that there is much overlap in the subject areas covered, suggesting that the formal goals of the behavioral health professions are similar. Because the framework offers only an outline of each code's salient points, the decision maker is urged to consult the full text of a relevant code when considering any practice choice.

As an example of how ethical standards can supplement the legal inventory, consider the following practice situation: A community mental health agency in northern New Mexico, serving a largely Hispanic and Native American client base, decides to embark on a public outreach campaign to address the underusage of services by minority persons. It elects to do so through a community open house and festival featuring live music, health exhibits, and public speakers. The agency's director, a clinical psychologist, has received an offer from a regional alcohol distributor to donate a substantial portion of the funding for the festival. The director must consider the implications of accepting funding in light of the potential good it may do for the community.

The director's decision must begin with a legal inventory. In this scenario, the director on initial review receives no clear guidance from the framework's basic legal principles. Turning to relevant APA Code standards, the director is impressed by Ethical Standard 1.17, which outlines standards governing multiple relationships, i.e., conflicts of interest, and by Ethical Standards 3.01 to 3.06, which govern advertising and exhort psychologists to refrain from false and deceptive statements. Additionally, the director is influenced by Ethical Standard 1.08, governing human differences, which urges psychologists to engage in culturally relevant practice techniques.

Summarizing the applicable ethical standards, the director concludes that it would advance the interests of potential clients, including the community at large, if funding from the distributor is accepted. As the director reasons, taking the money would not be inherently different from the government's funding of smoking prevention programs and DUI victims' funds through "vice taxes" on cigarettes, alcohol, and traffic violations. The director also, however, interprets ethical standards to mandate that acceptance of funding be conditioned on the stipulation that advertising or other public acknowledgment of the distributor's involvement be restricted. The director's aim in taking this position is to minimize the possibility that public alcohol consumption be promoted, that the agency's objectivity might be interfered with by the acceptance of funding, and that the agency could be understood to endorse the distributor's business practices.

Having completed an ethical review, the director returns to consider the legal inventory. The ethical standards already examined prompt the director to revisit in a new light the duties to practice reasonably competently, to seek informed consent, and to identify the primary client; they may indeed have application in this scenario after all. As the director now sees it, competent practice should include prudent administrative and fiscal management, a point that might argue in favor of the solicitation and acceptance of the funding. At the same time, however, protecting the needs of the agency's primary clients mandates the agency's avoidance of financial entanglements that compromise the independent delivery of good mental health services. Additionally, the requirements of informed consent suggest that, if the funding is accepted, details concerning it and other gifts should be made available to potential clients.

As another example of the use of ethical standards in supplementing a legal inventory, consider the following scenario: A social worker employed by an adult day care service is assigned the task of visiting, interviewing, and assessing the agency's new client, an elderly woman who has been reported by her family to be neglecting herself physically and not eating regularly, although she is mentally alert in every other respect. Fearing for her safety, members of her family report that they would "like her in a nursing home in the neighborhood," but will consider the agency's services as a first option. One of the social worker's tasks is to provide a report to the agency administrator on the woman's suitability for the agency's services. If the social worker's assessment indicates that the woman requires round-the-clock supervision, long-term institutional nursing home care will be recommended to the family.

Applying the framework, the social worker's legal inventory at once suggests the applicability of the duties to practice reasonably competently, to seek informed consent, and to identify the primary client. These responsibilities indicate that the social worker should conduct an interview and assessment of the woman independent from the family's influence. However, these duties also require that the social worker perform the client evaluation immune from subtle agency pressure that might inspire a presupposed need for the agency's services. Further, the social worker must explain to the woman in plain language the risks and benefits of any proposed intervention, including those presented by assisted living and long-term nursing care, respectively.

Moving on to the NASW Code of Ethics, the social worker notes the applicability of Ethical Standard 1.02, which supports the social worker's duty to promote client self-determination. The social worker interprets this standard to suggest that the legal responsibilities to competently assess and provide appropriate services to the woman further mandate reasonable efforts to maintain her independent living arrangement.

Incorporating Context in Decision Making

Cultural and regional characteristics play a role in the definition of legal standards governing the behavioral health professions. As noted previously, reasonably competent practice is in part defined by reference to the expectations imposed on providers in the localities where they work. Similarly, the cultural and language traditions of clients can have a significant impact on the interpretation of legal responsibilities governing informed consent and confidentiality.

Apart from their role in assisting the decision maker to interpret legal principles, cultural and regional factors stand alone as considerations that may aid in the resolution of practice dilemmas where law and ethics fail to offer sufficient guidance. As an example, the earlier scenario involving an agency director's consideration of a grant from an alcohol distributor may have a somewhat different resolution if the decision maker takes into account the long-standing alcoholism and substance abuse problems that exist within the minority communities of northern New Mexico. Considering the proliferation in New Mexico communities of *dual diagnoses,* i.e., joint diagnoses of alcoholism or substance abuse and mental illness within one patient, the symbolic gesture of accepting money from an alcohol distributor may compromise the agency's ability to solicit funding from other regional sources. More than that, if the agency's acceptance of the gift becomes widely known, it may provoke distrust of the agency's agenda within its catchment area and therefore discourage the client use it is attempting to promote.

The acceptance of funding from the alcohol industry has been an issue hotly debated in recent years by concerned members of various Indian nations, which have often declined such funding based upon the considerations noted above. Thus, despite the stark need for the financing of major public health initiatives, Indian nations have sometimes estimated the negative long-term consequences of promoting alcohol consumption to overshadow the short-term good that might result from the funding. This discussion must be understood in light of the devastating social effects of chronic alcoholism within the Indian country of New Mexico and the Southwest. In addition to the chronic health issues associated with alcoholism, it continues to be linked to violent crime, child abuse, and family decay, among other problems (Kunitz & Levy, 2000). Consequently, the legitimation—however indirect or implied—of alcohol consumption within a reservation might well violate the collective social ethic of a Native American community.

Raising Pragmatic Concerns in Decision Making

Recognizing cultural and regional context in decision making has a practical side. Enhancing diversity through the culturally competent design and implementation of behavioral health and human services is the best way to ensure that they will be used by all members of a community. Moreover, understanding the culturally based expectations that clients place upon their behavioral health providers enhances every professional relationship to the extent that service costs are lowered. Even an Indian nation considering the acceptance of funding from an alcohol distributor is likely to find over time that the long-term costs of taking this money might be severe; the indirect encouragement of drinking, together with a tribal government's diminished public credibility, might have a profound economic cost.

The common experience of all behavioral health professionals is likely to demonstrate that, despite the overall effectiveness of legal, ethical, and cultural considerations in the resolution of practice dilemmas, the solutions to some problems are best arrived at by reference to the exigencies of life within the community in which the problem is experienced. The practical consequences of any choice therefore must be a part of any decisional approach in which legal and ethical principles do not provide an immediate, overriding answer. When law and ethics do suggest a general outcome, pragmatic concerns help to shape what that outcome should be.

The concept that pragmatic concerns should be a part of a decision making framework is not so obvious a point as it would seem at first glance. Indeed, the behavioral health professions—particularly within their ethical codes—often exhort licensees to attain lofty goals, including social justice, the advancement of the general welfare of society, and the improvement of global living conditions (see, e.g., NASW Code, Ethical Standard 6.01), without providing a mechanism for doing so that satisfies the constraints of the average professional. To the typical agency based social worker, counselor, or psychologist, these limitations most often include budgetary restrictions. Despite the exhortations of ethical codes, the average professional meeting daily obligations cannot persistently be asked to do what is simply not possible, either for budgetary, administrative, personnel, or other practical reasons.

In view of the foregoing, how and when should pragmatic considerations be introduced in decision making? Put simply, they should be a final step in the decision making process that requires each professional to consider the practical consequences of any decision, whether they are immediate budgetary repercussions or long-term, communitywide effects unique to one region. Consistent with the framework, it is not appropriate to consider these pragmatic concerns first, because the primacy of the law—to the extent that it presumptively advances the best interests of individual clients and their communities—should always be respected and advanced by every decision maker. Moreover, a premature reliance on pragmatic factors may lead the decision maker to ignore the long-term consequences of a decision, and to shy away from problems, including significant social dilemmas, whose resolution may not be simple. Instead, along with a thorough review of the cultural and regional context of any decision, practical considerations should be applied in the evaluation of any problem to which the legal inventory and ethical review provide no clear-cut solution. Even in situations in which the decision maker has identified the applicability of relevant legal principles, a further review of the practical consequences of applying them may reinforce a decision or inspire a reconsideration of the law, both of which occurred in the examples cited earlier.

The fact that pragmatic concerns may reinforce legal principles demonstrates the point that the law itself is often a reflection of practicality in everyday life. Indeed, legislation and judicial decisions are often based upon a functional analysis of the immediate consequences of problematic behavior. Even the landmark decision in the *Tarasoff* case in part rested upon the California Supreme Court's mundane consideration that liability for a murder should reasonably be imposed upon the defendants because they had insurance available to pay for its consequences (*Tarasoff v. Regents of Univ. of Cal.,* 1976, p. 435). In view of this reality, incorporating a review of pragmatic considerations serves to complete the cycle of decision making that begins with the legal inventory.

As an example of the consideration of pragmatism in the resolution of a practice dilemma, examine the following scenario: A partially disabled student at a regional community college has a muscular disorder that causes his arms to fatigue after prolonged writing. He has requested assistance from the government vocation and rehabilitation office, but the application has been denied. He now seeks through the university counselor in charge of disability services a new laptop computer upon which he can complete papers, type class notes, and take examinations. The disability counselor must make a recommendation to the dean of students about the student's case, but is also aware of a funding shortfall that has curtailed the college's budget.

If guided by the framework, the counselor's decision will include a legal inventory that recognizes the importance of basic legislative principles protecting the access of disabled persons to an education. The counselor should specifically recognize the applicability of ADA. Knowing that the law requires the college to take feasible steps to equalize the student's access—the "reasonable accommodation" rule—the counselor must now translate this principle into specific action.

Considering the framework's pragmatism step, the counselor assesses the college's reasonable response to the student's disability in light of budgetary issues. The counselor concludes that the student's problem can appropriately be addressed in a more affordable manner than by providing an expensive laptop for the student's exclusive use. Specifically, the college can provide the student with assistance in the form of student note takers, and can grant him special access to computer lab facilities in the library. This more modest response conserves valuable resources for the immediate use of needier students with more profound disabilities.

The measured response of the counselor is virtually mandated by the legal principles first reviewed. This example therefore serves as a good illustration of the manner in which pragmatism may ultimately drive the legal resolution of a dilemma.

Compare the present scenario with case example 14, "The School Social Worker," which concerned the Ramirez family and their educationally disabled child. In that situation, the guidance counselor prematurely applied pragmatic concerns in apparent violation of applicable law. Specifically, the counselor was prepared to propose an individual education plan that removed the child from her primary classroom, in breach of the rule mandating mainstreaming for the educationally disabled.

Another way to analyze the school social worker dilemma is to recognize the long-term practicality of mainstreaming. Even if the guidance counselor failed initially to recognize his responsibilities under the law, he still might have reached the conclusion that the removal of the child from her social environment might cause substantially greater immediate harm to the child, as well as higher potential financial costs to the school, than the reasonable alternative—providing available services to her in her regular classroom. Despite the counselor's instinctive reluctance to break his school district's budget, he might well have found through careful planning and economic analysis that the overall administrative costs resulting from segregated special education might ultimately prove more devastating than bringing these services to the child's own natural environment.

As a final example of the use of pragmatism to address practice dilemmas, consider the following scenario: A community based agency in a rural town in northern New Mexico targets the needs of minority "latchkey" children and their families. Funded by public grants as well as by research subsidies from a local college, the agency offers several discrete services to clients. Among these are a series of after-school activities for elementary school children, a counseling program for children and their families, and a fathering support group. The agency is administered by an executive director, who has a doctorate in social work, a clinical director, who is a psychiatrist, and several staff counselors. The executive director has recently learned that funding from one of the grants has been slashed significantly, forcing important decisions about service cutbacks.

Applying the framework, the executive director realizes that the duty to provide reasonably competent services must not be compromised by the funding problem. However, the cutbacks create a budget shortfall requiring the practical consideration of program changes. If the executive director recommends modifications *within* individual programs, such as elimination of one-on-one therapy sessions, a critical component of the agency's counseling services, the basic integrity of the clinical services offered to clients may be significantly affected. Similarly, if the executive director eliminates staff positions within the after-school program, the agency's ability to provide adequate supervision to children may be endangered.

A review of practical considerations suggests that the executive director's best choices lie in the entire removal or redefinition of one or more of the individual programs that the agency offers. Thus, elimination of the fathering group and a folding over of fathering-related issues into the counseling program may be the most effective choice and also eliminate some repetition of services. More than anything, pragmatism requires that the executive director strive to reduce administrative costs in a way that avoids hindering the agency's essential clinical purposes.

Integrating Law, Ethics, Context, and Pragmatism in Professional Decisions: Case Examples

The framework for making professional decisions combines a legal inventory with a review of interpretive factors; these include professional ethical standards, cultural and regional context, and individual pragmatic concerns that may influence unique practice situations. The utility of this system is that it integrates objective and subjective factors in a unified process that advances communitarian ideals yet also recognizes the individuality of clients, behavioral health professionals, and the practice situations that bind them. It therefore promotes the goal that, in every practice decision, behavioral health professionals should strive to advance the values shared within each community while respecting the principle that all clients are distinct.

The subsequent case examples offer the reader an opportunity to "put it all together." They present scenarios whose resolutions depend on the consideration of all of the framework's steps. For that reason, they each serve as a paradigm for decision making in the behavioral health professions.

Case Example 26: Suspected Neglect in Ledoux

Estrella Montoya is a 43-year-old single mother living in the rural northeastern New Mexico community of Ledoux. Estrella has recently suffered a badly broken leg. After treatment at a regional health clinic, an infection has set in. Following a brief hospital stay, Estrella has been released to her home with a discharge plan calling for a series of 10 nurse visits. Estrella is confined to bed rest and required to take a regimen of antibiotics.

Lambert Urbano is the visiting nurse assigned to the Montoya family's case. During Lambert's initial home visit, he surveys the rustic cabin in which Estrella lives with her 10-year-old daughter, Esperanza. Lambert notices that the Montoyas have no running water, but instead draw their supply from a nearby well. Having no plumbing facilities, they rely rather on an outhouse and an old tub that they fill with heated water to bathe in. Several of the cabin's windows are broken, with glass shards surrounding the outside areas. Hastily prepared cardboard covers are taped to the inside of two windows, protecting the cabin from the elements. The family has a wood stove on which Estrella cooks and which provides heat during the winter months.

Lambert, a recent transplant from Chicago, is not used to the living conditions he witnesses. Observing Esperanza, Lambert notes that she is very thin, wears a dress she probably has worn for some time, and that her arms and legs are dirty.

During his examination of Estrella, her leg shows no signs of healing. To make matters worse, Lambert receives hesitant and conflicting reports from Estrella regarding her bed rest and attention to the discharge plan. In particular, Lambert suspects that Estrella might not be taking her prescribed medications. When asked about this, Estrella responds that she "tries to."

Lambert has concerns about the family's living conditions and more specifically believes that the environment might be sufficiently unhealthy for Esperanza as to constitute child neglect. Moreover, he has fears about Estrella'a ability and/or willingness to care for herself. In view of these concerns, Lambert elects to consult with his agency supervisor, Clara Tobarn, a licensed social worker and Ledoux native, regarding the possibility of making a referral to the Children, Youth, and Families Department, a step that would then require a formal investigation by the regional child protective services division office.

In beginning their legal inventory, Lambert and Clara will probably at once recognize and apply the duties to practice reasonably competently and to identify the primary client. In the present scenario, the professional relationship established by Lambert with Estrella exists for the sole purpose of providing home health care and associated services. It is not, therefore, Lambert's duty to diagnose or treat any condition that does not fall within the scope of this professional relationship. The duty to practice reasonably competently, however, also entails the responsibility to recognize and report suspected child abuse and neglect to appropriate authorities. Additionally, it requires the protection of vulnerable adults who may be self-neglectful to the degree that they pose a reasonable threat of harm to themselves.

Legal duties that are specific to Clara include the responsibility to give reasonably competent supervision to Lambert. In the exercise of that duty, Clara must draw upon her understanding of community expectations in rural New Mexico regarding the daily lifestyles of local people.

Understanding the legal duties applicable to both, Clara and Lambert initially agree that in this case they are required to report suspected child neglect or adult self-neglect in the event that there is a reasonable suspicion either harm is occurring. This cautious standard is intended as a precaution to ensure that marginal cases are investigated. Consequently, as a relative newcomer unaccustomed to the lifestyles of some New Mexicans, Lambert's initial assessment is that the reasonable suspicion standard is satisfied with respect to both Estrella and Esperanza, and that the agency should err on the side of caution. At the least, Lambert believes making the report will provide the family needed support services.

In consultation with Clara, Lambert shares his opinion but finds that Clara regards the situation to be more ambiguous. If Clara brings an understanding of community traditions to her assessment of the Montoya family, she is likely to conclude that the family's living arrangements are not unusual for Mora County, which has in the past ranked the poorest in New Mexico and among the poorest in the U.S. (Bureau of the Census Staff,

2001). In consultation with her agency counsel, Clara may well conclude that poverty in itself must never give rise to the presumption of child abuse or neglect.

As to the possibility of Estrella's self-neglect, Clara's interpretation of the conduct Lambert has described should also be based on a consideration of community norms. Specifically, Clara might note that Estrella's apparent reticence in describing her self-care is as likely the result of fear and suspicion as of subterfuge. Moreover, in a community in which herbal *remedios* are a common medical treatment, and antibiotics are not deemed the only acceptable response to infection, Lambert's immediate assumption that Estrella's noncompliance represents self-neglect is an unhelpful hypothesis.

Summarizing the foregoing considerations, a regionally and culturally based interpretation of applicable law argues against an abrupt referral for suspected neglect in this case. Consistent with reasonably competent practice, further assessment—with the assurance of cultural consistency—should follow in order to clarify some of the medical issues that have identified themselves with respect to Estrella's self-care. This assessment should include attention to the duty to seek informed consent, which in this scenario requires an open and appropriate discussion of health issues specifically related to the progress of Estrella's leg. Although Estrella's living arrangements may distress Lambert, they are not necessarily within the scope of his assessment, at least to the extent that they do not affect the healing of Estrella's leg. Moreover, Lambert cannot allow his initial impression of the family to dictate his future course of services. His attention to his primary role as a medical provider with limited, agency-defined duties advances his patient's best interests in this instance.

A review of pragmatic considerations supports the legal and cultural assessment. Specifically, it underscores the consequences of a premature referral for an investigation of neglect. The imposition of an outside intervention on a family that is marginal economically but functional in other respects may upset the family's equilibrium and drive it into social isolation, perhaps hastening the very health problems that the agency wishes to prevent. Indeed, while good intentions here may support the early reporting of suspected neglect, thoughtful consideration of the consequences does not.

Case Example 27: The Telethon

In response to flash flood conditions in Albuquerque that have claimed the lives of several families, a private community development agency, Albuquerque Cares, has embarked on a fundraising initiative. As part of this enterprise, the agency has opened a bank account under the name "The Flood

Fund" and has attempted through several agency-sponsored social events to raise public awareness about the plight of survivors of the disaster.

In the past, the activities of Albuquerque Cares have addressed a variety of basic human needs within the community and have been eclectic in their design. The agency has organized food banks for the hungry, a homeless shelter, services for the victims of family violence, and a recycling program for children's clothing, among other notable programs. Although its staff members have dedicated themselves enthusiastically to organizational efforts on behalf of the people who need their help, intensive fundraising organized around a limited theme is beyond the scope of the agency's experience. Indeed, the agency has supported itself largely through the donated services of committed volunteers, together with modest individual contributions and small grants from several private foundations.

In undertaking their fundraising drive for persons affected by the flood, agency staff have decided to "get it right." They have engaged the assistance of a regional telemarketing organization experienced with organized charitable collection activities. With the donated support of a local television station, the agency has planned a three-hour telethon whose proceeds will be earmarked for the agency's relief efforts, and possibly for other agency purposes. Consistent with charitable telemarketing practices, a small percentage of the funds pledged will go to administrative costs and telemarketing fees.

Disagreement among the agency's board members has occurred as to exactly how much of the proceeds should be applied specifically to the flood fund. Several members believe that it is wrong to collect money for one specific purpose, and that doing so will divert necessary attention away from all of the important work of the agency. The aftermath of the flood, they believe, should not distract potential contributors from other persistent community problems, including hunger, homelessness, and domestic violence. Indeed, other charitable organizations have already reported a decrease in gift-giving as a presumed result of the attention that has been focused on the flood and its consequences.

The framework provides a tool for analysis of the agency's dilemma. If board members conduct a thorough legal inventory, they will at once note the applicability of the duties to practice reasonably competently, to seek informed consent, and to identify the agency's primary clients.

In the present scenario, reasonably competent practice provides the general standard by which the agency must conduct its fundraising. This includes management of the fiduciary responsibility connected with solicitation of funds from the public. The agency board has taken an appropriate first step in fulfilling this obligation by affiliating with an experienced fundraising organization that can compensate for the board's lack of expertise in this area. Fundraising is a discrete responsibility totally different from the agency's duty to design, organize, and implement service programs funded by the money collected. Nevertheless, the agency bears as much responsibility for the competent completion of this task as it does for its other projects.

From whom must informed consent be sought in this situation? The answer depends on the board members' proper creation of a professional relationship with one or more primary clients. The most critical professional relationship in this scenario is the one the agency board seeks to create with flood survivors. After all, money to be collected ostensibly is to be directed to their benefit, as well as toward the development of family services. This point suggests that the agency cannot act without the voluntary support of the families and the seeking of informed consent from them. The agency's informed consent–related duty includes its responsibility to reveal fully its proposed fundraising strategy and to obtain clear permission from the families to collect funds and to design and provide services on their behalf. Without first identifying the families' immediate needs regarding support services, the collection of funds is ill-advised.

If flood survivors are the agency's primary clients, what association exists between the agency and the donating public? Although not strictly in the nature of a professional relationship, as that term has been used previously, it is nonetheless a fiduciary association, akin to the contractual bond that exists between a service provider and a third-party payor or insurance company. Viewed in this light, the agency has a responsibility to use fair solicitation techniques that include openness and clarity in identifying the purposes to which donated funds are to be applied.

In completing the legal inventory, board members should evaluate the impact of federal and state policies governing trade practices and fund solicitation. This assessment is likely to support the result mandated by informed consent and competent practice standards: Money solicited for flood survivors must be earmarked expressly for those persons and programs that directly support them.

A supplemental review of ethical, regional, and cultural factors enriches the legal inventory in this case. It reveals that persons touched by human tragedy are sometimes motivated to help alleviate its effects regardless of the cost. It is therefore not unusual in such circumstances to find individuals of modest means pledging donations out of proportion to their family income. This is true especially in tightly knit communities whose kinship ties extend beyond the immediate family nucleus. For that reason, such people are particularly vulnerable to any fundraiser wishing to manipulate a newsworthy event for temporary gain. In less populated areas, people rely particularly upon the media to obtain news and public information, and also to choose charities they wish to support. These considerations make it clear that the fundraisers in the present example have a special responsibility to their community to be honest and fair in their efforts.

Finally, pragmatic considerations compel the conclusion that solicitations pursued for a particular purpose must be dedicated to that purpose. Although it is true that tragic public events can exacerbate social problems of long standing, this tenuous association cannot justify the violation of immediate professional duties owed to primary clients in need of services—in this case, flood survivors. In practical terms, violation of these duties compromises the agency's public credibility, and may hamper its ability to respond to the variety of social causes with which the agency is ordinarily involved. In short, the funding deficit that agency board members most fear may be the inevitable result of their own conduct.

This final case example, inspired as it is by recent national events and the practices of a major charitable organization, is intended to alert the professional decision maker to the utility of a law based framework in the resolution of practice dilemmas both small and large. The scenario stands as a model for the maintenance of a community focus in all daily practice decisions. With respect to each important choice made by every behavioral health professional, this approach surely is the most effective way to champion both the client's best interests and the community's shared values.

Appendix

Decision Making Framework

Legal Principles to Apply in Any Practice Dilemma

Principle 1: The Duty to Practice Reasonably Competently

When to Consider the Duty. The duty should be considered in all practice situations.

Elements of the Duty. What defines reasonably competent practice varies depending on the profession and the jurisdiction. Generally, however, a professional owes a legal duty to the client to practice reasonably competently according to the nature and scope of one's professional training. This duty extends to the client and also members of the public who can reasonably be expected to suffer if the professional fails to honor this duty (see, e.g., *Tarasoff v. Regents of Univ. of Cal.*). It also includes the duty to protect vulnerable individuals, primarily children and frail elderly, at risk for physical or emotional abuse, neglect, or exploitation. This duty may include warning appropriate authorities about the existence of the suspected abuse or neglect.

Reasonably competent practice includes the following:

- Conforming to the standards expected of professionals within a discipline, including social work, counseling, psychology, or other behavioral health profession
- Conforming to the standards expected of professionals within a particular specialty area, such as psychotherapy, counseling, child welfare investigations, research, teaching, and community organizing
- Recognizing the extent and limits of one's training and understanding the scope of any physical or mental limitations affecting the capacity to practice
- Understanding the need to seek consultation or refer a client to another professional when appropriate
- Culturally and regionally competent practice
- The duty to make appropriate documentation and to maintain adequate records concerning services

Reasonably competent administration and supervision include the following:

- The duty to administer programs and services and to supervise employees appropriately, as well as to provide consultation to supervisees whose level of training and terms of employment should reasonably be expected to require it

Finding Local Information About the Duty. The duty is governed by individual licensing standards in each behavioral health profession, and also by state law, including court-made and legislative standards.

Principle 2: The Duty to Seek Informed Consent

When to Consider the Duty. The duty should be considered especially in the following situations:

- When working with children, mentally ill, frail elderly, and other vulnerable clients
- When clients have been directly and indirectly solicited by means of professional seminars and advertising
- Whenever there are cross-cultural or language differences between the professional and the client
- When conducting research

Elements of the Duty. It is incumbent upon professionals to obtain informed consent from their clients prior to the commencement of services. In a legal sense, informed consent refers not so much to the document that the client signs agreeing to these services, but rather to the quality and completeness of the dialogue engaged in by the provider and client that forms the basis of their agreement for professional services. This dialogue must address the following points:

The client must have an *understanding* of the benefits and risks of various services, together with the *capacity* to understand this information. Capacity means both *legal capacity* and *mental capacity*. Informed consent also requires that the client consent to services *voluntarily*.

The law may modify the legal capacity to consent by either augmenting it or diminishing it; thus, underage minors in some states have the legal capacity to consent to limited mental health treatment and the receipt of contraceptive information. Courts that mandate the receipt of behavioral health services by a client can be thought of as assuming on the client's behalf the right to consent to services.

Finding Local Information About the Duty. The duty is governed by state law, including court-made and legislative standards.

Principle 3: The Duty to Identify the Primary Client

When to Consider the Duty. The duty should be considered especially in the following situations:

- Whenever one is employed as a public agency professional
- When asked as a public agency professional to provide multiple behavioral or human services to individuals and families
- When working with children, frail elderly, mentally disabled, and other vulnerable persons
- When a client has an insurance company or other third-party reimburser responsible for the client's bills or otherwise interested in the client's progress
- When conducting research
- When a court has ordered a client to receive services
- When a client has been referred for services by an attorney or other professional
- When retained to offer an expert opinion concerning a client's condition and/or the services a client has received from another professional

Application to Public Sector Behavioral Health Professionals. Public agencies, including child welfare bureaus, state hospitals, and mental health bureaus, probation service departments, and educational systems, among others, have legal responsibilities defined by state and federal laws. Their public responsibilities often include the protection of certain classes of vulnerable citizens, and create specific professional-client relationships between the agency and the vulnerable group.

Behavioral health professionals employed by public agencies agree to accept the agency's legal responsibilities as their own. As examples, in the case of a social worker employed by a child protective service agency, a psychologist, clinical social worker, or counselor employed by a government mental health facility, a public school counselor, or a probation service worker, the professional's *primary* clients are the vulnerable members of the public whom the provider agency is required to protect, such as abused or neglected children and the elderly. This duty ordinarily supersedes any other professional obligation.

Application to Behavioral Health Professionals in Private Practice. A behavioral health professional in private practice must evaluate *who* the primary client is and what legal obligations are owed to that client according to state, federal, or tribal law. This issue must be considered carefully when the behavioral health professional is providing services *primarily* to one person, but the interests of family members or others may be peripherally involved and may threaten to interfere with the duty owed to the primary client.

A professional must also avoid conflicts of interest with the primary client. Conflicts of interest may include social or business relationships with the primary client or a close relation of the primary client's, professional responsibilities imposed by the provider's position that control or limit the nature of services provided to the primary client, and the professional's proprietary or research interest in services that are offered to the primary client.

Finding Local Information About the Duty. The duty is governed by state, federal, and tribal law, including court-made and legislative standards.

Principle 4: The Duty to Treat Clients and Co-workers With Due Process and Equal Protection

When to Consider the Duty. The duty should be considered especially in the following situations:

- When making decisions as a public agency administrator or employee that may affect clients' rights to benefits or services
- When considering disciplinary action against a public employee
- When making decisions as a private behavioral health or human service agency administrator or employee that may affect clients' rights to services
- When considering transfer of or disciplinary action against the student or resident of a public or private educational or rehabilitative institution
- When considering the hiring of a public or private agency employee

Elements of the Duty: Procedural Due Process. When the federal government or a state, county, or municipality, through its public agencies and employees, threatens to interfere with a client's or employee's right to *life*, *liberty,* or *property*, the client or employee has a right to *procedural due process*. Procedural due process means *fairness*, and generally requires that the affected client or employee must have *notice* of the government's intent to interfere with an interest and an *opportunity to be heard* (i.e., a hearing or trial).

Examples of property and liberty rights that require notice and a hearing or trial include the following situations:

- A state employee or federal employee faces disciplinary proceedings
- A state welfare client has benefits suspended
- A veterans' administration mental hospital recommends transfer of a patient
- A public school student is suspended or expelled
- A child welfare authority seeks to change the custody of a child
- A person is arrested and charged with a crime punishable by imprisonment

Elements of the Duty: Substantive Due Process. Some rights are so important that they are considered *fundamental*. These include all of the privileges guaranteed by the Bill of Rights (such as freedom of speech, religion, assembly, press, and the protection from unlawful searches and seizures) and the right to individual and family privacy (consisting of, among other things, the right to make medical decisions, the right to marry, the right to raise a family, and the freedom from bodily restraint). The government and its agents and employees must never interfere with these fundamental rights unless they can demonstrate a *compelling interest*. A compelling interest ordinarily means an interest related to the government's responsibility to maintain the health and safety of the public or to perform some important government function.

Examples of the relationship between fundamental rights and compelling government interests include the following:

- A state psychologist usually cannot seek commitment of a patient without demonstrating the patient's violence
- A public school counselor cannot be required to live in the town where the counselor is employed
- A state welfare authority can seek custody of a child it believes is threatened by abuse or neglect
- A city can require protest marchers to register in advance of the demonstration

Elements of the Duty: Equal Protection. Equal protection requires that diverse clients and employees must not be *classified* on the basis of *suspect* categories, including race, religion, ethnicity, and national origin. Some classifications, including family income and socioeconomic status, are not considered to be suspect.

Examples of suspect and nonsuspect classifications include the following:

- A state child welfare authority may not deny licensure to foster parents on the basis of their race
- A state welfare authority may deny welfare benefits to a family whose income rises above the maximum qualifying amount

Elements of the Duty: Civil Rights Legislation. Various laws, including the Civil Rights Act of 1964 and other federal and state legislation extend some of the constitutional obligations and protections imposed by the Fourteenth Amendment to public *and* private agencies and their clients.

Finding Local Information About the Duty. The duty is governed mainly by the U.S. Constitution (Fifth and Fourteenth Amendments), including interpretive state and federal court decisions and legislation. Additional rules and regulations regarding due process and equal protection are often defined by state and federal agencies, and in some instances extend to private parties providing services under government contract.

Principle 5: The Duty to Maintain Confidentiality

When to Consider the Duty. The duty should be considered especially in the following situations:

- At the time informed consent is sought from clients
- Prior to all practice decisions that may interfere with clients' privacy
- Prior to all practice decisions that may test the limits of confidentiality
- When seeking informed consent from all clients
- When working with clients who have insurance companies or other third-party reimbursers responsible for bills or otherwise professionally interested in client progress
- When providing services to a primary client that may also affect the interests of family members or others peripherally involved
- When providing services to children, mentally disabled, or frail elderly for whom a parent, guardian, or other third party has consented to services

Elements of the Duty. The duty to maintain confidentiality generally requires behavioral health professionals, and especially psychotherapists (social workers, counselors, and psychologists) to keep their clients' statements confidential unless

- The statements concern the intent to commit a violent, criminal, or other harmful and preventable act against an identified person
- The statements invoke the professional's legal duty to report child abuse or neglect
- Clients have waived the right in writing
- Clients have brought malpractice charges or disciplinary complaints

Generally, the right to confidentiality is expressed in terms of a privilege belonging to the client and a duty imposed on the professional. It impacts the extent to which professionals may communicate with courts, police, insurance companies, and other parties concerning the services provided to and the information revealed by the client.

The public policy behind confidentiality is to encourage those in need of behavioral health and human services to seek them out. Conversely, the public policy behind the limitations on the duty of confidentiality is that professionals who are in a position to help prevent a foreseeable harmful act should have the legal responsibility to take reasonable action to prevent it from occurring.

The client's right to confidentiality assumes the client's capacity to grant informed consent (i.e., the legal and mental capacity to engage in a professional relationship with the provider). For that reason, the duties to seek informed consent and to maintain confidentiality are interdependent.

Finding Local Information About the Duty. The duty is governed by state, federal, and tribal law, including court-made and legislative standards. The limits of confidentiality are defined by the law of the jurisdiction one practices in. Fifty states have legislation governing confidentiality as it applies to social workers, counselors, psychologists, other licensed psychotherapists, medical doctors, clergy, attorneys, and additional behavioral health and human service professionals. This legislation generally appears either in professional licensing acts or in evidentiary codes.

Principle 6: Completing a Legal Inventory

When to Complete a Legal Inventory. A legal inventory should be completed after the behavioral health professional considers the potential application of each of the preceding legal principles. It suggests that the professional be versed in the state and local court and legislative interpretations of each of these principles, including understanding the protections offered by state constitutions and other regional legislation that may address a problem. Access to legal advice, including agency or personal counsel, concerning all potential legal aspects of a practice decision is especially helpful for this purpose. In completing an inventory, the professional should be prepared to ask several key questions concerning the legal impact of a practice decision. These include the following:

- Will the professional's decision be consistent with all relevant federal, state, and/or tribal law and administrative rules and regulations?
- If the professional is employed by an agency, what are the legal obligations of the professional to the agency and of the agency to the professional?
- Which if any agency rules, regulations, or policies govern the situation or the agency's delivery of client services?
- Which if any agency rules, regulations, or policies define the professional's job responsibilities or employment contract obligations?
- Is an employee or client seeking to involve the professional in potentially unlawful behavior?
- Which if any state constitutional provisions create fundamental rights? (See Principle 4, the duty to treat clients with due process and equal protection, pp. 250–252.)

Codes of Ethics

Using Codes of Ethics to Supplement the Legal Inventory

Following completion of the legal inventory, the behavioral health professional should examine applicable standards from a relevant ethical code. This review may enhance the legal inventory by helping to explain or interpret individual legal duties, particularly with respect to profession-specific practice guidelines. It may also prompt a consideration of additional legal principles that govern a practice situation. For these purposes, a summary of ethical standards from the social work, counseling, and psychology professions follows.

Table 2: Summary of NASW Code's Ethical Standards

NASW Code Standard	Summary of Standard
	Social workers should
1.01 Commitment to Clients	Promote client well-being
	Obey legal obligations that supersede loyalty to clients
1.02 Client Self-determination	Promote client independence
1.03 Informed Consent	Seek informed consent
	Use clear and understandable language with clients
1.06 Conflicts of Interest	Avoid social and business contacts that risk harm to or exploitation of clients
1.07 Confidentiality	Maintain confidentiality except for compelling professional reasons
	Use technology—including electronic mail and fax machines—properly to safeguard confidentiality
1.08 Access to Records	Provide clients with reasonable access to records
1.09 Sexual Relationships	Refrain completely from sexual relationships with current clients
	Refrain from sexual relationships with clients' relatives and friends when there is a risk of exploitation or harm
2.07 Sexual Relationships With Colleagues	Avoid sexual relationships with colleagues when there is potential for a conflict of interest
	Refrain from sexual relationships with supervisees, students, and others over whom professional authority is exercised
3.01 Colleague Relationships Supervision/Consultation	Provide competent supervision
	Avoid conflicts of interest that risk harm to or exploitation of supervisees
3.02 Education and Training	Practice competently
3.07 Administration	Be competent and fair administrators
3.09 Duties to Employers	Honor commitments to employers
4.02 Discrimination	Refrain from all forms of discrimination
4.07 Solicitations	Refrain from advertising services to vulnerable persons
6.01 Duty to Society	Promote the general welfare of society
	Promote social justice
	Promote development of people, communities, and environments;
6.04 Social and Political Action	Engage in social and political action that ensures equal access to resources
	Work to prevent exploitation of individuals and groups

Table 3: Summary of NBCC Code's Ethical Standards

NBCC Code Section	Summary of Standard
	Certified counselors should
A1, A6, A7	Practice competently Refrain from diagnosing, assessing, or treating clients unless prior training or supervision has been obtained Be guided in their work by prior research
A2	Honor commitments to clients and agency employers
A8, A9, B9	Avoid dual relationships that may harm clients or impair professional judgment Personal, social, organizational, financial, or political activities that might lead to a misuse of influence
A10	Refrain from sexual relationships with present clients entirely and with past clients for a minimum of two years after the counseling relationship has been terminated
A12	Be aware of the impact of stereotyping and discrimination on their clients Safeguard the personal dignity of the client
A13	Obey moral and legal standards Promote public confidence in the counseling profession Be accountable at all times for their behavior
A15	Withdraw from practice in the event of unethical conduct or mental disability
B1	Promote client welfare as a primary interest Protect the integrity of the client
B8	Seek informed consent
B4, B6, B14, B16	Maintain confidentiality except where there is a clear and imminent danger to the client or others Ensure that electronic data are secure Use electronic systems and data appropriately Ensure clients are emotionally compatible with computer applications
B5	Recognize the client's property interest in information contained in the counselor's records
B9	Refrain from dual relationships that might impair objectivity and judgment
B12	Avoid electronic means of counseling unless clients are told first of local sources of care Abide by NBCC Standards for Web Counseling
F1	Use accurate advertising

Table 4: Summary of APA Code's Ethical Principles and Standards

APA Code Principle/Standard	Summary of Principle/Standard
	Psychologists should
Principle A: Competence	Maintain high standards of competence
Principle B: Integrity	Promote integrity in the science, teaching, and practice of psychology
Principle C: Professional/ Scientific Responsibility	Uphold professional standards of conduct
Principle D: Respect for Rights/Dignity	Promote client autonomy
Principle E: Concern for Others' Welfare	Weigh the rights of their patients and clients, students, supervisees, and human and animal research subjects
Principle F: Social Responsibility	Promote human welfare and work to alleviate suffering
1.02 Conflicts Between Law and Ethics	Resolve law-ethics conflicts responsibly
1.04 Boundaries of Competence	Practice competently according to training
1.07 Describing Services	Avoid jargon in speaking/writing
1.08 Human Differences	Use culturally competent practice
1.14 Avoiding Harm	Avoid harming clients, students, and colleagues
1.17 Multiple Relationships	Avoid conflicts that risk harm to the client or impaired objectivity or judgment
	Recognize that avoiding social conflicts may not be possible in small towns
2.01 Evaluation/Diagnosis	Conduct competent client evaluations, diagnoses, and interventions
2.02 Assessments	Design and use competent client assessments
3.01-06 Advertising	Avoid false, deceptive statements in advertising
	Refrain from "uninvited" in-person solicitation of business from actual or potential clients
4.02 Informed Consent	Seek informed consent from clients
4.06 Formal Sexual Partners	Refrain from accepting past sexual partners as clients
4.07 Sexual Relationships with Clients	Refrain from sexual relationships with present clients entirely and with past clients for a minimum of two years
5.02-5.05 Confidentiality	Maintain confidentiality except where necessary to protect the client or others from harm
	Follow laws governing confidentiality
	Maintain client information databases properly
	Minimize intrusions on client privacy
5.10 Ownership of Records	Follow laws governing access to client records and other data
6.08 Research	Conduct research competently and lawfully

Incorporating Cultural and Regional Context

Using Cultural and Regional Context to Supplement the Legal Inventory

Cultural and regional issues should be considered both during and after the legal inventory and ethical review. They may aid considerably in the interpretation of legal and ethical principles or help to resolve an issue where no clear legal or ethical answer emerges. With this in mind, the behavioral health professional should

- Apply community standards to interpret legal and ethical duties
- Apply personal ideological or moral standards

Using Pragmatism to Supplement the Legal Inventory

Practical considerations may aid in the interpretation of legal and ethical standards. They should be applied only after the legal inventory and ethical review have been completed. Pragmatic concerns include the following:

- The practical consequences of any decision, including but not limited to budgetary issues and unforseen costs to an agency, its administration, personnel, and clients
- Whether any internal agency policies and procedures are already in existence to govern the situation
- Past methods of handling a particular problem

References

Books, Journals, and Other Scholarly Sources

Alan Guttmacher Institute. (2002, January 1). Minors' access to contraceptive services. *State Policies in Brief.* Retrieved February 3, 2002, from http://www.agi-usa.org/pubs/spib.html.

Albee, G. W. (1999). Prevention, not treatment, is the only hope. *Counseling Psychology Quarterly, 12,* 133–146.

American Psychiatric Association. (1994). *Diagnostic and statistical manual of mental disorders* (4th ed.). Washington, DC: Author.

Applewhite, S. L. (1995). Curanderismo: Demystifying the health beliefs and practices of elderly Mexican Americans. *Health & Social Work, 20,* 247–253.

Bakker, A. B., Schaufeli, W. B., Sixma, H. J., & Bosveld, W. (2001). Burnout contagion among general practitioners. *Journal of Social and Clinical Psychology, 20,* 82–98.

Bean, R. A., Perry, B. J., & Bedell, T. M. (2001). Developing culturally competent marriage and family therapists: Guidelines for working with Hispanic families. *Journal of Marriage and Family Therapy, 27,* 43–54.

Berkman, C. S., Turner, S. G., Cooper, M., Polnerow, D., & Schwartz, M. (2000). Sexual contact with clients: Assessment of social workers' attitudes and educational preparation. *Social Work, 45,* 223–235.

Brucker, P. S., & Perry, B. J. (1998). American Indians: Presenting concerns and considerations for family therapists. *American Journal of Family Therapy, 26*, 307–319.

Bureau of the Census Staff. (2001). *Statistical abstract of the United States: The national data book 2000* (120th ed.). Springfield, VA: United States Department of Commerce, National Technical Information Service.

Calkins, C. A., & Murray, M. (1999). The effectiveness of court appointed special advocates to assist in permanency planning. *Child & Adolescent Social Work Journal, 16,* 37–45.

Colmant, S. A., & Merta, R. J. (1999). Using the sweat lodge ceremony as group therapy for Navajo youth. *Journal for Specialists in Group Work, 24,* 55–73.

Conry, E. J., & Beck-Dudley, C. L. (1996). Meta-jurisprudence: A paradigm for legal studies. *American Business Law Journal, 33,* 691–754.

Corcoran, J. (2001). Multi-systemic influences on the family functioning of teens attending pregnancy programs. *Child & Adolescent Social Work Journal, 18,* 37–49.

Daniels, B. (1996, July 24). Social worker pleads not guilty in foster case. *Albuquerque Journal,* p. C1.

Daniels, B. (1997, January 1). Outgoing D.A. agrees to drop charges. *Albuquerque Journal,* p. A1.

Davidson, P. R., & Parker, K. C. (2001). Eye movement desensitization and reprocessing (EMDR): A meta-analysis. *Journal of Consulting and Clinical Psychology, 69,* 305–316.

Editorial: Prescription for failure. (2000, July 30). *Los Angeles Times,* p. M4.

Edwards, E. D., & Edwards, M. (1998). Community development with American Indians and Alaska Natives. In F. G. Rivera & J. L. Erlich (Eds.), *Community Organizing in a Diverse Society* (3rd ed., pp. 25–42). Needham Heights, MA: Allyn & Bacon.

Etzioni, A. (1998). *The new golden rule: Community & morality in a democratic society.* New York: Basic Books.

Ewoh, A. I. (1999). An inquiry into the role of public employees and managers in privatization. *Review of Public Personnel Administration, 19,* 8–27.

Gibelman, M., & Demone, H. W. (1998). *The privatization of human services: Policy and practice issues* (Vol. 1). New York: Springer.

Goicoechea-Balbona, A. (1997). Culturally specific health care model for ensuring health care use by rural, ethnically diverse families affected by HIV/AIDS. *Health & Social Work, 22,* 172–180.

Graef, M. I., & Hill, E. L. (2000). Costing child protective services staff turnover. *Child Welfare 79,* 517–533.

Haley, A. N., & Watson, D. C. (2000). In-school literary extension: Beyond in-school suspension. *Journal of Adolescent & Adult Literacy, 43,* 654–661.

Harris, M. L. (1998, September). *Curanderismo and the* DSM-IV*: Diagnostic and treatment implications for the Mexican American client* (Occasional Paper No. 45). East Lansing, MI: Michigan State University, The Julian Samora Research Institute.

Hellwage, J. (2000). Law of informed consent poised for revolution, experts say. *Trial, 36,* 128–130.

Hewlett, S. (1996). Consent to clinical research—adequately voluntary or substantially influenced? *Journal of Medical Ethics, 22,* 232–237. Adapted and reprinted with the permission of the BMJ Publishing Group.

Joas, H. (1993). *Pragmatism and social theory.* Chicago: University of Chicago Press.

Keegan, L. (1996). Use of alternative therapies among Mexican Americans in the Texas Rio Grande valley. *Journal of Holistic Nursing, 14,* 277–294.

Kunitz, S. J., & Levy, J. E. (2000). *Drinking, conduct disorder, & social change: The Navajo Experience.* New York: Oxford University Press.

Lehrman, N. S., & Sharay, V. H. (1997). Ethical problems in psychiatric research. *Journal of Mental Health Administration, 24,* 227–250.

Littell, J. H., & Tajima, E. A. (2000). A multi-level model of client participation in intensive family preservation services. *Social Service Review, 74,* 404–435.

McMichael, A. J., & Beaglehole, R. (2000). The changing global context of public health. *The Lancet, 356,* 495–499.

Mercer, J. (2001). Attachment therapy using deliberate restraint: An object lesson on the identification of unvalidated treatments. *Journal of Child and Adolescent Psychiatric Nursing, 14,* 105–114.

Murphy, L. (2001). Beneficence, law, and liberty: The case of required rescue. *Georgetown Law Journal, 89,* 605–665.

Nicholson, K. (2001, June 19). 'Rebirth therapists' get 16 years. *Denver Post,* p. A1.

Peebles, I. E. (1999). Therapeutic jurisprudence and the sentencing of sexual offenders in Canada. *International Journal of Offender Therapy and Comparative Criminology, 43,* 275–290.

Pilisuk, M., McAllister, J., & Rothman, J. (1996). Coming together for action: The challenge of contemporary grassroots community organizing. *Journal of Social Issues, 52,* 15–37.

Quigley, W. (2001, August 11). Health-care ads due for an exam. *Albuquerque Journal,* p. A1.

Regehr, C., & Antle, B. (1997). Coercive influences: Informed consent in court-mandated social work practice. *Social Work, 42,* 300–306.

Rittner, B., & Dozier, C. D. (2000). Effects of court-ordered substance abuse treatment in child protective services cases. *Social Work, 45,* 131–140.

Rosenberg, M. A., & Browne, M. J. (2001). The impact of the inpatient prospective payment system and diagnosis-related groups: A survey of the literature. *North American Actuarial Journal 5,* 84–94.

Rouse, K. (2001, April 22). Rebirthing verdict may curb restraint therapy. *Denver Post,* p. A3.

Rousey, A., & Longie, E. (2001). The tribal college as family support system. *American Behavioral Scientist, 44,* 1492–1504.

Russell, S. (1996, September 13). Hospital released patient with knife in belly—i'll pick the deck when i'm out back [*sic*]. *San Francisco Chronicle,* p. A1.

Schaufeli, W., & Enzmann, D. (1998). *The burnout companion to study and practice: A critical analysis.* London: Taylor and Francis.

Schorr, A. L. (2000). The bleak prospect for public child welfare. *Social Service Review, 74,* 124–136.

Shalin, D. N. (1986). Pragmatism and social interactionism. *American Sociological Review, 51,* 9–29.

Shaw, W. H. (1998). *Contemporary Ethics: Taking account of utilitarianism* (Contemporary Philosophy Series). Malden, MA: Blackwell Publishers.

Sheets, J. (1996). Designing an effective in-school suspension program to change student behavior. *National Association of Secondary School Principals Bulletin, 80,* 86–90.

Sparrow, M. K. (1998). *License to steal: Why fraud plagues America's healthcare system.* Boulder, CO: Westview Press.

Stefl, M. E. (1999). Editorial. *Frontiers of Health Services Management, 16,* 1–2.

Tam, H. (1998). *Communitarianism: A new agenda for politics & citizenship.* New York: New York University Press.

Tamanaha, B. Z. (1999). *Realistic socio-legal theory: Pragmatism and a social theory of law* (Oxford Socio-Legal Studies). New York: Oxford University Press.

Taylor, M. (2001). A costly strategy. *Modern Healthcare, 31,* 34–35.

Terrell, S. (2001, July 13). Judge denies inmate more access to religious items, rituals. *Santa Fe New Mexican,* p. B5.

Thrower, A. W., & Martinez, J. M. (2000). Reconciling anthropocentrism and biocentrism through adaptive management: The case of the waste isolation pilot plant and public risk perception. *Journal of Environment & Development, 9,* 68–97.

Topper, K. (2000). In defense of dignity: Pragmatism, hermeneutics, and the social sciences. *Political Theory, 28,* 509–539.

Turner, D. C. (1996). The role of culture in chronic illness. *American Behavioral Scientist, 39,* 717–728.

U.S. Department of Health and Human Services, Office of the Surgeon General. (2001). *Mental Health: Culture, race and ethnicity* (SAMHSA Report). Washington, DC: Author.

Villa, R. F. (2001). *Program evaluation and community assessment: Project Recovery of northern New Mexico* (Cerro Grande Fire Disaster, FEMA-1329-DR-NM). Las Vegas, NM: NM Highlands University.

Watson, B. C. (1999). Liberal communitarianism as political theory. *Perspectives on Political Science, 28,* 211–217.

Wattenberg, E., Kelley, M., & Kim, H. (2001). When the rehabilitation fails: A study of parental rights termination. *Child Welfare, 80,* 405–431.

Yankura, J., & Dryden, W. (1997). *Using REBT with common psychological problems: A therapist's casebook.* New York: Springer.

Court Decisions

Achterhof v. Selvaggio, 886 F.2d 826 (6th Cir. 1989).

Adarand Constructors, Inc. v. Pena, 515 U.S. 200, 115 S. Ct. 2097, 132 L. Ed. 2d 158 (1995).

Alabama Coalition for Equity, Inc. v. Hunt, Nos. CV-90-883R, CV 91-0117-R (Ala. April 27, 1993) (consolidated civil actions).

Alejo v. City of Alhambra, 75 Cal. 4th 1180, 89 Cal. Rptr. 2d 768 (1999).

Almonte v. New York Med. College, 851 F. Supp. 34 (D. Conn. 1994).

Altman v. Bedford Cent. Sch. Dist., 45 F. Supp. 2d 368 (S.D.N.Y. 1999), *rev'd in part*, 245 F.3d 49 (2d Cir. 2001).

Anderson v. United States, 55 F.3d 1379 (9th Cir. 1995).

Ashe v. Radiation Oncology Assocs., 9 S.W.3d 119 (Tenn. 1999).

Associated Indus. v. Commonwealth, 912 S.W.2d 947 (Ky. 1995).

Aufrichtig v. Lowell, 85 N.Y.2d 540, 650 N.E.2d 40 (1995).

Ball v. Massanari, 254 F.3d 817 (9th Cir. 2001).

Bates v. State Bar, 429 U.S. 1059, 97 S. Ct. 782, 50 L. Ed. 2d 775 (1977).

Bee v. Greaves, 744 F.2d 1387 (10th Cir. 1984).

Besh v. Bradley, 47 F.2d 1167 (6th Cir. 1995).

Bielaska v. Orley, Nos. 215286, 215287 (Mich. Ct. App. Feb. 9, 2001).

Blum v. Yaretsky, 47 U.S. 991, 102 S. Ct. 2777, 73 L. Ed. 2d 534 (1982).

Board of Regents v. Roth, 408 U.S. 564, 92 S. Ct. 2701, 33 L. Ed. 2d 548 (1972).

Board of Trustees of Univ. of Ala. v. Garrett, 531 U.S. 356, 121 S. Ct. 955, 148 L. Ed. 2d 866 (2001).

Bogan v. Scott-Harris, 523 U.S. 44, 118 S. Ct. 966, 140 L. Ed. 2d 79 (1998).

Bolling v. Sharpe, 347 U.S. 497, 74 S. Ct. 693, 98 L. Ed. 884 (1954).

Bottoms v. Bottoms, 457 S.E.2d 102 (Va. 1995) (quoting Roe v. Roe, 324 S.E.2d 691, 694 (1985)).

Branch v. Turner, 27 F.3d 1334 (8th Cir. 1994).

Breck v. Michigan, 203 F.3d 392 (6th Cir. 2000).

Briscoe v. Prince George's County Health Dep't, 323 Md. 439, 593 A.2d 1109 (1991).

Brokaw v. Mercer County, 235 F.3d 1000 (7th Cir. 2000).

Brown v. Board of Education, 347 U.S. 483, 74 S. Ct. 686, 98 L. Ed. 873 (1954).

Buckey v. County of Los Angeles, 968 F.2d 791 (9th Cir. 1992).

Chavez v. Lemaster, No. D-101-CR-9900896 (N.M. Dist. Ct. Santa Fe County Oct. 2, 2001) (consolidated cases).

Chew v. Meyer, 72 Md. App. 132, 527 A.2d 828 (Ct. Spec. App. 1987).

City of Cleburne v. Cleburne Living Center, 473 U.S. 432, 105 S. Ct. 3249, 87 L. Ed. 2d 313 (1985).

Claremont Sch. Dist. v. Governor, 142 N.H. 462, 703 A.2d 1353 (1997).

Commonwealth v. Bruno, 432 Mass. 489, 735 N.E.2d 1222 (2000).

Conner v. Donnelly, 42 F.3d 220 (4th Cir. 1994).

County of Sacramento v. Lewis, 523 U.S. 833, 118 S. Ct. 1708, 140 L. Ed. 2d 1043 (1998).

Cox v. Miller, No. 01-3751 (S.D.N.Y. Jul. 31, 2001) (habeas corpus petition).

Cox v. New Hampshire, 312 U.S. 569, 61 S. Ct. 762, 85 L. Ed. 1049 (1941).

Crawford-El v. Britton, 93 F.3d 813, 829 (D.C. Cir. 1996) (Silberman, J., concurring), *vacated on other grounds*, 523 U.S. 574, 118 S. Ct. 1584, 140 L. Ed. 2d 759 (1998).

Crumpton v. Gates, 947 F.2d 1418 (9th Cir. 1991).

Cynthia B. v. New Rochelle Hosp., 60 N.Y.2d 452, 470 N.Y.S.2d 122 (1983).

Danskine v. Miami Dade Fire Dep't, 253 F.3d 1288 (11th Cir. 2001).

Davis v. Monroe County Bd. of Educ., 526 U.S. 629, 119 S. Ct. 1661, 143 L. Ed. 2d 839 (1999).

Deatherage v. Examining Bd. of Psychology, 134 Wash. 2d. 131, 948 P.2d 828 (1997).

Denver Area Educ. Telecommunications Consortium, Inc. v. Federal Communications Comm'n, 518 U.S. 727, 782, 116 S. Ct. 2374, 2404–2405, 135 L. Ed. 2d 888, 927 (1996) (Kennedy, J., concurring and dissenting) (finding that "state action lies in the enactment of a statute altering legal relations between persons").

Doe v. Claiborne County, 103 F.3d 495 (6th Cir. 1996).

Doe v. Finch, 133 Wash. 2d 96, 942 P.2d 359 (1997).

Doe v. Gates, 981 F.2d 1316 (D.C. Cir. 1993).

Dunn v. Catholic Home Bureau for Dependent Children, 537 N.Y.S.2d 742, 142 Misc. 2d 316 (Sup. Ct. N.Y. County 1989).

Duran v. Apodaca, No. Civ-77-721-C (D.N.M. July 14, 1980).

Eckhardt v. Charter Hosp., 124 N.M. 549, 953 P.2d 722 (Ct. App. 1997).

Elliott v. North Carolina Psychology Bd., 126 N.C. App. 453, 485 S.E.2d 882 (Ct. App. 1997), *rev'd in part,* 348 N.C. 230, 498 S.E.2d 616 (1998).

Engineering Contractors Ass'n v. Metropolitan Dade County, 122 F.3d 895 (11th Cir. 1997).

Equality Foundation v. City of Cincinnati, 128 F.3d 289 (6th Cir. 1997).

Ernst v. Child and Youth Servs., 108 F.3d 486 (3d Cir. 1997).

F. G. v. MacDonell, 696 A.2d 697, 150 N.J. 550 (1997).

Figueiredo-Torres v. Nickel, 321 Md. 642, 584 A.2d 69 (1991).

Flagner v. Wilkinson, 241 F.3d 475 (6th Cir. 2001).

Gibbs v. Ernst, 538 Pa. 193, 647 A.2d 882 (1994).

Goldberg v. Kelly, 397 U.S. 254, 90 S. Ct. 1011, 25 L. Ed. 2d 287 (1970).

Good News Club v. Milford Cent. Sch., 533 U.S. 98, 121 S. Ct. 2093, 150 L. Ed. 2d 151 (2001).

Goss v. Lopez, 419 U.S. 565, 95 S. Ct. 729, 42 L. Ed. 2d 725 (1975).

Greenville Women's Clinic v. Bryant, 222 F.3d 157 (4th Cir. 2000).

Grey v. Allstate Ins. Co., No. 81 (Md. Apr. 9, 2001).

Griffin v. City of Opa-Locka, 261 F.3d 1295 (11th Cir. 2001).

Griswold v. Connecticut, 381 U.S. 479, 85 S. Ct. 1678, 14 L. Ed. 2d 510 (1965).

Gruenke v. Seip, 225 F.3d 290 (3d Cir. 2000).

Grutter v. Bollinger, No. 01-1447 (6th Cir. May 14, 2002).

Hafner v. Beck, 185 Ariz. 389, 916 P.2d 1105 (Ct. App. 1995).

Hammons v. Norfolk S. Corp., 156 F.3d 701 (6th Cir. 1998).

Harper v. Virginia Bd. of Elections, 383 U.S. 663, 86 S. Ct. 1079, 16 L. Ed. 2d 169 (1966).

Haynie v. Bass, 902 F.2d 33 (6th Cir. 1990).

Hazelwood Sch. Dist. v. Kuhlmeier, 484 U.S. 260, 108 S. Ct. 562, 98 L. Ed. 2d 592 (1988).

Hazen Paper Co. v. Biggins, 507 U.S. 604, 113 S. Ct. 1701, 123 L. Ed. 2d 338 (1993).

Heinmiller v. Department of Health, 127 Wash. 2d 595, 903 P.2d 433 (1995).

Hertog v. City of Seattle, 138 Wash. 2d 265, 979 P.2d 400 (1999).

Holloway v. Brush, 220 F.3d 767 (6th Cir. 2000).

Hopwood v. Texas, 78 F.3d (5th Cir. 1996).

Horak v. Biris, 130 Ill. App. 3d 140, 474 N.E.2d 13 (App. Ct. 1985).

Huether v. District Court, 300 Mont. 212, 216, 4 P.3d 1193, 1197 (2000) (Trieweiler, J., dissenting or concurring [*sic*]).

In re Application of Casillo, 580 N.Y.S.2d 992, 151 Misc. 2d 420 (Sup. Ct. Suffolk County 1992).

In re Columbia/HCA Healthcare Corp. Litig., Civ. A. No. 01-MS-50 (RCL) (D.D.C. Aug. 7, 2001) (order approving a settlement agreement between the United States, Columbia/HCA, and other defendants in numerous consolidated cases and requiring HCA to pay the government civil damages in the amount of $731,367,246.33 plus interest).

In re Columbia Valley Reg'l Med. Ctr., No. 13-00-726-CV (Tex. App. Mar. 8, 2001).

In re D. W., M. B., and D. B., No. 2D00-3845 (Fla. Dist. Ct. App. May 23, 2001).

In re Gault, 387 U.S. 1, 87 S. Ct. 1428, 18 L. Ed. 2d 527 (1967).

In re Investigation of Underwager, No. C0-97-55 (Minn. Ct. App. July 8, 1997).

In re J. A. & L. A., 601 A.2d 69 (D.C. 1991).

In re Kendall J. and Darris P., 235 Wis. 2d 277, 616 N.W.2d 525 (2000).

In re McKnight, 406 Mass. 787, 550 N.E.2d 856 (1990).

In re Mental Illness of Thomas, 108 Ohio App. 3d 697, 671 N.E.2d 616 (Ct. App. 1996).

In re Rebekah R., 27 Cal. App. 4th 1638, 33 Cal. Rptr. 2d 265 (Ct. App. 1994).

In re R. G., 283 Ill. App. 3d 183, 669 N.E.2d 1225 (App. Ct. 1996).

In re R. M. J., 455 U.S. 191, 102 S. Ct. 929, 71 L. Ed. 2d 64 (1982).

In re T. R., J. M., C. R., & C. R., 557 Pa. 99, 731 A.2d 1276 (1999).

Jackson v. Fort Stanton Hosp. & Training Sch., 757 F. Supp. 1243 (D.N.M. 1990), *rev'd in part*, 964 F.2d 980 (10th Cir. 1992).

Jackson v. State, 287 Mont. 473, 956 P.2d 35 (1998).

Jaffee v. Redmond, 518 U.S. 1, 116 S. Ct. 1923, 135 L. Ed. 2d 337 (1996).

Jensen v. Lane County, 222 F.3d 570 (9th Cir. 2000).

Jones v. Lurie, 32 S.W.3d 737 (Tex. App. 2000).

Joseph A. v. New Mexico Dep't of Human Servs., 575 F. Supp. 346 (D.N.M. 1983).

Kansas v. Hendricks, 521 U.S. 346, 117 S. Ct. 2072, 138 L. Ed. 2d 501 (1997).

Kaplan v. United States, 133 F.3d 469 (7th Cir. 1998).

Karen L. v. Dep't of Health and Human Svcs., 953 P.2d 871 (Alaska 1998).

Karlin v. IVF America, Inc., 93 N.Y.2d 282, 712 N.E.2d 662, 690 N.Y.S.2d 495 (1999).

Kazmier v. Widmann, 225 F.3d 519 (5th Cir. 2000).

Kelm v. Kelm, 749 N.E.2d 299 (Ohio 2001).

Kimel v. Florida Bd. of Regents, 528 U.S. 62, 120 S. Ct. 631, 145 L. Ed. 2d 522 (2000).

K. J. v. Pennsylvania Dep't of Pub. Welfare, 767 A.2d 609 (Pa. 2001).

Kovacs v. Freeman, 957 S.W.2d 251 (Ky. 1997).

Kus v. Sherman Hosp., 268 Ill. App. 3d 771, 644 N.E.2d 1214 (App. Ct. 1995).

Lanigan v. Village of E. Hazel Crest, 110 F.3d 467 (7th Cir. 1997).

Lansing v. City of Memphis, 202 F.3d 821 (6th Cir. 2000).

Laskowitz v. Ciba Vision Corp., 632 N.Y.S.2d 845, 215 A.D.2d 25 (App. Div. 1995) (dictum).

Lassiter v. Department of Soc. Servs., 452 U.S. 18, 101 S. Ct. 2153, 68 L. Ed. 2d 640 (1981).

Lavia v. Pennsylvania, 224 F.3d 190 (3d Cir. 2000).

Lehr v. Roberston, 463 U.S. 248, 103 S. Ct. 2985, 77 L. Ed. 2d 614 (1983).

Lewis v. Thompson, 252 F.3d 567 (2d Cir. 2001).

Lofton v. Kearney, No. 99-10058-CIV-KING (S.D. Fla. Aug. 30, 2001).

Mabe v. San Bernardino County Dep't of Soc. Servs., 237 F.3d 1101 (9th Cir. 2001).

Maio v. Aetna, Inc., 221 F.3d 472 (3d Cir. 2000).

Maldonado v. Josey, 975 F.2d 727 (10th Cir. 1992).

Martin v. Commissioner, 232 F.2d 901 (10th Cir. 2000).

Martino v. Family Serv. Agency, 112 Ill. App. 3d 593, 445 N.E.2d 6 (App. Ct. 1982).

McCormick v. England, 328 S.C. 627, 494 S.E.2d 431 (Ct. App. 1997).

McKinney v. Maynard, 952 F.2d 350 (10th Cir. 1991).

Meyer v. Nebraska, 262 U.S. 390, 43 S. Ct. 625, 67 L. Ed. 1042 (1923).

Miller v. Ratner, 114 Md. App. 18, 688 A.2d 976 (Ct. Sp. App. 1997).

Mills v. New Mexico Bd. of Psychologist Examiners, 123 N.M. 421, 941 P.2d 502 (1997).

Mississippi Bd. of Psychological Examiners v. Hosford, 508 So. 2d 1049 (Miss. 1987).

M. L. B. v. S. L. J., 519 U.S. 102, 117 S. Ct. 555, 136 L. Ed. 2d 473 (1996).

Modi v. West Virginia Bd. of Med., 195 W. Va. 230, 244, 465 S.E.2d 230, 244 (1995) (Workman, J., concurring).

Mohr v. Commonwealth, 421 Mass. 147, 653 N.E.2d 1104 (1995).

Moore v. City of E. Cleveland, 431 U.S. 494, 97 S. Ct. 1932, 52 L. Ed. 2d 531 (1977).

Moore v. Regents of Univ. of Cal., 51 Cal. 3d 120, 793 P.2d 479, 271 Cal. Rptr. 146 (1990).

Naidu v. Laird, 539 A.2d 1064 (Del. 1988).

Narragansett Indian Tribe v. National Indian Gaming Comm'n, 158 F.3d 1335 (D.C. Cir. 1998).

New York State Nat'l Org. for Women v. Pataki, 261 F.3d 156 (2d Cir. 2001).

Nieves v. University of Puerto Rico, 7 F.3d 270 (1st Cir. 1993).

Northeast Ga. Radiological Assocs. v. Tidwell, 670 F.2d 507 (5th Cir. 1982).

Oberti v. Board of Educ., 995 F.2d 1204 (3d Cir. 1993).

Olagues v. Russoniello, 797 F.2d 1511 (9th Cir. 1986).

Open Door Baptist Church v. Clark County, 140 Wash. 2d 143, 995 P.2d 33 (2000).

Ortez v. Washington County, 88 F.3d 804 (9th Cir. 1996).

Overton v. Board of Examiners in Psychology, No. 01-A-01-9603-CH-00098 (Tenn. Ct. App. Nov. 14, 1996).

Paul v. Davis, 424 U.S. 693, 96 S. Ct. 1155, 47 L. Ed. 2d 405 (1976).

People v. Simms, 119 Ill. 2d 348, 736 N.E.2d 1092 (2000).

Perreira v. State, 768 P.2d 1198 (Colo. 1989).

Petrillo v. Syntex Labs., Inc., 102 Ill. 172, 148 Ill. App. 3d 581, 499 N.E.2d 952 (App. Ct. 1986).

Phillip Leon M. v. Greenbrier County Bd. of Educ., 199 W. Va. 400, 484 N.E.2d 909 (1996).

Pierce v. Caday, 244 Va. 285, 422 N.E.2d 371 (1992).

Planned Parenthood v. Farmer, 165 N.J. 609, 762 A.2d 620 (2000).

Pollack v. Marshall, 845 F.2d 656 (6th Cir. 1988).

Proenza Sanfiel v. Department of Health, 749 So. 2d 525 (Fla. Dist. Ct. App. 1999).

Pyle v. School Comm., 423 Mass. 283, 667 N.E.2d 869 (1996).

Rasmussen v. Fleming, 154 Ariz. 207, 741 P.2d 674 (1987).

Rauser v. Horn, 241 F.3d 330 (3d Cir. 2001).

Reed v. Reed, 404 U.S. 71, 92 S. Ct. 251, 30 L. Ed. 2d 225 (1971).

Reiff v. Northeast Fla. State Hosp., 710 So. 2d 1030 (Fla. Dist. Ct. App. 1998).

Reynolds v. Giuliani, No. 98cv08877 (S.D.N.Y. Jan. 19, 1999).

Rich v. Woodford, 210 F.3d 961, 965 (9th Cir. 2000) (Kozinski and Wardlaw, JJ., dissenting).

Richardson v. McKnight, 521 U.S. 399, 117 S. Ct. 2100, 138 L. Ed. 2d 540 (1997).

Richenberg v. Perry, 97 F.3d 256 (8th Cir. 1996).

Riggins v. Nevada, 504 U.S. 127, 112 S. Ct. 1810, 118 L. Ed. 2d 479 (1992).

Rodriguez-Silva v. Immigration and Naturalization Serv., 242 F.3d 243 (5th Cir. 2001).

Roe v. Catholic Charities, 167 Ill. 713, 225 Ill. App. 3d 519, 588 N.E.2d 354 (App. Ct. 1992).

Roe v. Wade, 410 U.S. 113, 93 S. Ct. 705, 35 L. Ed. 2d 147 (1973).

Rosales-Garcia v. Holland, 238 F.3d 704 (6th Cir. 2001).

Sain v. Cedar Rapids Community Sch. Dist., No. 155/98-2273 (Iowa Apr. 25, 2001) (en banc).

Saur v. Probes, 476 N.W.2d 496, 190 Mich. App. 636 (Ct. App. 1991).

Schneckloth v. Bustamonte, 412 U.S. 218, 93 S. Ct. 2041, 36 L. Ed. 2d 854 (1973).

Seal v. Morgan, 229 F.3d 567 (6th Cir. 2000).

Sexton Law Firm v. Milligan, 329 Ark. 285, 948 S.W.2d 388 (1997).

Seymour v. Elections Enforcement Comm'n, 258 Conn. 78, 762 A.2d 880 (2000).

Sheff v. O'Neill, 238 Conn. 1, 678 A.2d 1267 (1996).

Shrum v. Kluck, 249 F.3d 773 (8th Cir. 2001).

Simescu v. Emmet County Dep't of Human Servs., 942 F.2d 372 (6th Cir. 1991).

Simmons v. United States, 805 F.2d 1363 (9th Cir. 1986).

Smith-Bozarth v. Coalition Against Rape and Abuse, Inc., 329 N.J. Super. 238, 747 A.2d 322 (Super. Ct. App. Div. 2000).

Smothers v. Gresham Transfer, Inc., 332 Or. 83, 23 P.3d 333 (2001).

Snell v. Tunnell, 920 F.2d 673 (10th Cir. 1990).

Stanley v. Swinson, 47 F.3d 1176 (9th Cir. 1995).

Stanton v. City of W. Sacramento, 226 Cal. App. 3d 1438, 277 Cal. Rptr. 478 (Ct. App. 1991).

State v. Aetna U.S. Healthcare, Inc., No. GV-000584 (Tex. Dist. Ct. Travis County April 11, 2000).

State v. Kelly, 256 Conn. 23, 770 A.2d 908 (2001).

State v. Lattimer, 624 N.W.2d 284 (Minn. Ct. App. 2001).

State v. Louis, 614 N.Y.S.2d 888; 161 Misc. 2d 667 (Sup. Ct. N.Y. County 1994).

State v. Oakley, No. 99-3328-CR (Wis. July 10, 2001).

State v. Watkins, Nos. 00 CR 1255, 1257 (Colo. Dist. Ct. Jefferson County filed May 17, 2000) (multiple consolidated cases).

State *ex rel.* Taylor v. Johnson, 125 N.M. 343, 961 P.2d 768 (1998).

Stebbings v. University of Chicago, 244 Ill. 825, 312 Ill. App. 3d 360, 726 N.E.2d 1136 (App. Ct. 2000).

Steele v. Hamilton County Community Mental Health Bd., 90 Ohio St. 3d 176, 736 N.E.2d 10 (2000).

T. D. v. New York State Office of Mental Health, 626 N.Y.S.2d 1015 (Sup. Ct. N.Y. County 1995), *aff'd and modified in part*, 228 A.D.2d 95, 650 N.Y.S.2d 173 (App. Div. 1996).

Tarasoff v. Regents of Univ. of Cal., 17 Cal. 3d 425, 551 P.2d 334, 131 Cal. Rptr. 14 (1976).

Tenenbaum v. Williams, 193 F.3d 581 (2d Cir. 1999).

Thapar v. Zezulka, 994 S.W.2d 635 (Tex. 1999).

Thomasson v. Perry, 80 F.3d 915 (4th Cir. 1996).

Trujillo v. Taos Mun. Sch., 91 F.3d 160 (10th Cir. 1996).

United Food & Commercial Worker Union v. Southwest Ohio Reg'l Transit Auth., 163 F.3d 341 (6th Cir. 1998).

United States v. Antelope, 430 U.S. 641, 97 S. Ct. 1395, 51 L. Ed. 2d 701 (1977).

United States v. Deninno, 103 F.3d 82 (10th Cir. 1996).

United States v. Glass, 133 F.3d 1356 (10th Cir. 1998).

United States v. Hayes, 227 F.3d 578 (6th Cir. 2000).

United States v. Morrison, 529 U.S. 598, 120 S. Ct. 1740, 146 L. Ed. 2d 658 (2000).

United States v. Virginia, 518 U.S. 515, 116 S. Ct. 2264, 135 L. Ed. 2d 735 (1996).

Valcin v. Public Health Trust, 473 So. 2d 1297 (Fla. Dist. Ct. App. 1984), *modified sub nom.*, Public Health Trust v. Valcin, 507 So. 2d 596 (1987).

Vanderhurst v. Colorado Mountain College Dist., 208 F.3d 908 (10th Cir. 2000).

Victor v. Nebraska, 511 U.S. 1, 114 S. Ct. 1239, 127 L. Ed. 2d 583 (1994) (quoting Commonwealth v. Webster, 59 Mass. 295, 320 (1850)).

W. B. v. Matula, 67 F.3d 484 (3d Cir. 1995).

Wear v. Walker, 800 S.W.2d 99 (Mo. Ct. App. 1990).

Weaver v. Dep't of Soc. and Health Servs., No. 25366-6-II (Wash. Ct. App. Aug. 10, 2001).

Weber v. Cranston Sch. Comm., 212 F.3d 41 (1st Cir. 2001).

Weitz v. Lovelace Health Sys., Inc., 214 F.3d 1175 (10th Cir 2000).

West v. Atkins, 487 U.S. 42, 108 S. Ct. 2250, 101 L. Ed. 2d 40 (1988).

White v. North Carolina Bd. of Examiners of Practicing Psychologists, 97 N.C. App. 144, 388 S.E.2d 148 (Ct. App. 1990).

Williams v. Coleman, 194 Mich. App. 606, 488 N.W.2d 464 (Ct. App. 1992).

Winegar v. Des Moines Indep. Community Sch. Dist., 20 F.3d 895 (8th Cir. 1994).

Wolff v. McDonnell, 418 U.S. 539, 94 S. Ct. 2963, 41 L. Ed. 2d 935 (1974).

Wolotsky v. Huhn, 960 F.2d 1331 (6th Cir. 1992).

Wyatt v. Fetner, 92 F.3d 1074 (11th Cir. 1996).

Yniguez v. Arizonans for Official English, 69 F.3d 920, 940 n. 24 (9th Cir. 1994), *vacated sub nom.*, Arizonans for Official English v. Arizona, 520 U.S. 43 (1997).

Zagaros v. Erickson, 558 N.W.2d 516 (Minn. Ct. App. 1997) (dictum).

Zinermon v. Burch, 494 U.S. 113, 110 S. Ct. 975, 108 L. Ed. 2d 100 (1990).

Ethical Codes

American Bar Association Model Rules of Professional Conduct (1983 & Supp. 2001).

American Psychological Association Ethical Principles of Psychologists and Code of Conduct (1992). Copyright © 1992, American Psychological Association. Adapted with permission.

National Association of Social Workers Code of Ethics (1996 & Supp. 1999). Copyright © 1992, National Association of Social Workers, Inc.

National Board for Certified Counselors, Inc. Code of Ethics (1982 & Supp. 1997).

Legislation and Administrative Rules

Abuse and Neglect Act, 6 N.M. Stat. Ann. §32A-4-1 *et seq.* (1978 & Supp. 1999).

Adoption and Safe Families Act of 1997, 42 U.S.C. §§673b, 679b, & 678 (Supp. 2000).

Adoption Assistance and Child Welfare Act of 1980, 42 U.S.C. §670 *et seq.* (Supp. 2000).

Age Discrimination in Employment Act of 1967, 29 U.S.C. §621 *et seq.* (Supp. 2000).

Americans with Disabilities Act of 1990, 42 U.S.C. §12101 *et seq.* (Supp. 2000).

Cerro Grande Fire Assistance Act, Pub. L. No. 106-246, 114 Stat. 584 (2000).

Children's Mental Health and Developmental Disabilities Act, 6 N.M. Stat. Ann. §32A-6-1 *et seq.* (1978 & Supp. 1995).

Civil Rights Act of 1871, 42 U.S.C. §1983 (Supp. 2000).

Civil Rights Act of 1964, 42 U.S.C. §2000 *et seq.* (Supp. 2000).

Civil Rights Act of 1991, Pub. L. No. 102-166, 105 Stat. 1071 (1991).

Clinical Social Workers, 3B Cal. Bus. & Professions Code §4996 *et seq.* (West 1990 & Supp. 2002).

Consent for Health Services, 14A Ala. Code §22-8-1 *et seq.* (1975).

Counseling and Therapy Practice Act, 11 N.M. Stat. Ann. §61-9A-1 *et seq.* (1978 & Supp. 1999).

Emancipation of Minors Act, 6 N.M. Stat. Ann. §32A-21-1 *et seq.* (1978 & Supp. 1995).

Harassment and Stalking Act, 6 N.M. Stat. Ann. §30-3A-1 *et seq.* (1978 & Supp. 1997).

Human Immunodeficiency Virus Test Act, 5 N.M. Stat. Ann. §24-2B-1 *et seq.* (1978 & Supp. 2000).

Indian Child Welfare Act of 1978, 25 U.S.C. §1901 *et seq.* (Supp. 2001).

Indian Civil Rights Act of 1968, 25 U.S.C. §1301 *et seq.* (Supp. 2001).

Indian Gaming Regulatory Act, 25 U.S.C. §2701 *et seq.* (1988 & Supp. 2001).

Individuals With Disabilities Education Act, 20 U.S.C. §1400 *et seq.* (1975 & Supp. 2001) (formerly known as the Education for All Handicapped Children Act).

Legal Capacity of Minors, 8A S.C. Code Ann. §20-7-250 *et seq.* (1985).

National Defense Authorization Act for Fiscal Year 1994, 10 U.S.C. §654(b) (Supp. 2001).

Model State Public Health Privacy Act (Georgetown University Law Center, Model State Public Health Privacy Project, 1999).

Native American Counseling Act, 6 N.M. Stat. Ann. §30-10-4 (1978 & Supp. 1993).

N.M. Const. art. VII, §3.

N.M. Const. art. XII, §§1, 10.

New Mexico Drug, Device and Cosmetic Act, 5 N.M. Stat. Ann. §26-1-2 (1978 & Supp. 2002) (as amended by H.B. 170, 45th Leg., 2d Gen. Sess., 2002 N.M. Laws Ch. 100) (effective date July 1, 2002).

Omnibus Budget Reconciliation Act of 1993, Pub. L. No. 103-66, 107 Stat. 379 (1993).

Personal Responsibility and Work Opportunity Reconciliation Act of 1996, Pub. L. 104-193, Title I, §103(a)(1), 110 Stat. 2112 (1996).

Personal Rights of Residential Clients, 7 N.M. Stat. Ann. §43-1-6 (1978 & Supp. 1989).

Professional Psychologist Act, 11 N.M. Stat. Ann. §61-9-1 *et seq.* (1978 & Supp. 1999).

Public Health Service Act, 42 U.S.C. §290dd-2 (1992 & Supp. 2000).

Restatement of Bill of Rights for Mental Health Patients, 42 U.S.C. §10841 (1991 & Supp. 2000).

Sexual Offenses, 6 N.M. Stat. Ann. §30-9-1 *et seq.* (1978 & Supp. 2001).

Social Work Practice Act, 11 N.M. Stat. Ann. §61-31-1 *et seq.* (1978 & Supp. 1999).

Uniform Health-Care Decisions Act (1993) (proposed act drafted by the National Conference of Commissioners on Uniform State Law).

Uniform Health-Care Decisions Act, 5 N.M. Stat. Ann. §24-7A-1 *et seq.* (1978 & Supp. 1997) (New Mexico's version of the Uniform State Law Commissioners' 1993 proposed act).

Uniform Health-Care Information Act (1985).

Uniform Probate Code, 7 N.M. Stat. Ann. §45-5-303 (1978 & Supp. 1998) (procedure for court appointment of a guardian of an incapacitated person).

U.S. Const. amend. XIV.

U.S. Const. amends. I–X.

U.S. Const. art I, §8, cl. 3.

U.S. Department of Health and Human Services Rules Governing the Protection of Human Subjects, 45 C.F.R. §46 *et seq.* (1991 & Supp. 1994).

U.S. Department of Health and Human Services Standards for Privacy of Individually Identifiable Health Information, 65 Fed. Reg. 250 (2000) (to be codified at 45 C.F.R. §§160, 164).

Violence Against Women Act of 1994, Pub. L. No. 103-322, 108 Stat. 1796, 1902–1955 (1994).

White Cane Law, 5 N.M. Stat. Ann. §28-7-1 *et seq.* (1978).

Index